Strategic Financial Management

Strategic Financial Management: A Managerial Approach

EDITED BY

MUHAMMAD ALI

Taylor's University, Malaysia

LEONG CHOI-MENG

Swinburne University of Technology, Malaysia

CHIN-HONG PUAH

Universiti Malaysia Sarawak, Malaysia

SYED ALI RAZA

Iqra University, Pakistan

AND

PREMAGOWRIE SIVANANDAN

Taylor's University, Malaysia

United Kingdom – North America – Japan – India – Malaysia – China

Emerald Publishing Limited
Emerald Publishing, Floor 5, Northspring, 21-23 Wellington Street, Leeds LS1 4DL

First edition 2024

Reprints and permissions service
Contact: www.copyright.com

British Library Cataloguing in Publication Data
A catalogue record for this book is available from the British Library

ISBN: 978-1-83608-107-4 (Print)
ISBN: 978-1-83608-106-7 (Online)
ISBN: 978-1-83608-108-1 (Epub)

INVESTOR IN PEOPLE

'To our cherished families, whose boundless love, unwavering support and enduring encouragement have not only shaped our journey but have also inspired the pages of this book. With heartfelt gratitude and profound admiration, we dedicate these words as a token of our appreciation for the pillars of strength that you are'.

Contents

List of Contributors

Muhammad Ali	Taylor's University, Malaysia
Tehzeeb Sakina Amir	Bahria University, Pakistan
Muhammad Asim	University of Karachi, Pakistan
Zhang Can	UCSI University, Malaysia
Israr Ahmed Jatoi	KASB Institute of Technology, Pakistan
Kashif Mehmood	KASB Institute of Technology, Pakistan
Hassan Muaaz	UCSI University, Malaysia
Kashif Riaz	Shaheed Zulfiqar Ali Bhutto University of Law, Pakistan
Rabia Sabri	Institute of Business Management, Pakistan
Premagowrie Sivanandan	Taylor's University, Malaysia
Muhammad Faisal Sultan	KASB Institute of Technology, Pakistan
Wu Weijian	Jingdezhen University, China
Wei Xi	UCSI University, Malaysia
Zhang Xiaoqi	UCSI University, Malaysia
Muhammad Raghib Zafar	KASB Institute of Technology, Pakistan
Sun Zhuyin	UCSI University, Malaysia
Liu Zihang	UCSI University, Malaysia

Preface

Muhammad Ali, Leong Choi-Meng, Syed Ali Raza, Chin-Hong Puah,
Premagowrie Sivanandan

Greetings to every individual embarking on the perceptive voyage outlined in *'Strategic Financial Management: A Managerial Approach'*. This research book proves to be a useful companion, providing a careful road map through the complex landscape of modern finance. Financial managers face difficulties in the dynamic business environment of today, and this book provides genuine thoughts and tactics that thoughtfully solve those challenges. Financial managers find themselves at the nexus of tradition and innovation in a period characterised by rapid transformations. More than just a guide, this research book seeks to be a reliable partner for anyone negotiating the challenges of making financial decisions in a setting that necessitates flexibility and critical thinking. The environmental, social and governance (ESG) elements and sustainability have become increasingly important, causing a significant change in the financial landscape. This book explores the relationship between value generation, effective corporate governance and sustainability reporting from a managerial standpoint. Its objective is to provide managers with the knowledge and skills necessary to reconcile profit-driven financial objectives with morally and responsibly conducted businesses. Managers need to re-evaluate international finance plans considering the ways that globalisation has changed the business landscape.

This book rises to the occasion, giving managers navigating the global financial arena insightful perspectives on the opportunities and challenges presented by globalisation. This book examines techniques for controlling financial risks in the face of technical breakthroughs in the digital age, where opportunities and threats abound, particularly in financial risk management. The goal is to provide managers with the tools they need to prosper in the digital age, not just get by. As they are the backbone of economies, small- and medium-sized enterprises (SMEs) require a special approach to financial regulation. A special chapter that offers theoretical frameworks and useful consequences for managers, entrepreneurs and policymakers tackles the unique problems that SMEs encounter. The capacity to gather, process and evaluate information is an essential managerial skill in a world where 'data is king'. This book examines data analytics and management in the finance industry, providing insights into using data to make well-informed decisions – a critical ability in today's data-driven business climate.

The dynamic nature of regulatory environments presents a challenge to compliance. The chapter on regulatory changes and compliance challenges explores how changing regulations affect financial management and provides guidance on how to deal with the difficulties associated with compliance. Building trust and transparency requires effective stakeholder connections and financial communication. A special chapter looks at ways to build positive connections with stakeholders. The final section of our journey across these pages looks at making financial decisions in erratic and unpredictable markets. Managers must have ways to make wise judgements that endure market swings in a volatile and unpredictable environment. This book invites you to go out on a voyage of exploration, where each chapter reveals a fresh aspect of financials and money management. Whether you are an experienced manager or a novice, the pertinent and insightful information presented in this research book intends to equip you with the skills and understanding required to successfully negotiate the complex curves of today's financial environment.

When you open 'Strategic Financial Management: A Managerial Approach', picture yourself as an avid and involved reader who is actively exploring tips and tactics that can help you to strengthen your current financial success as well as provide useful information to climb out of current financial difficulties. Either way, this research book is here to make strategic financial management more understandable and relatable for you.

Acknowledgements

We extend our sincere gratitude to the gifted writers who shaped the story of this book with their commitment, knowledge and teamwork. They are the real designers of this project, and each chapter has benefited from their contributions, which have given it more depth and richness.

We would also like to thank our families for being our steadfast source of support and for giving us the time and space we needed to learn about the intricacies of contemporary finance.

We express our gratitude to the hard-working staff of the Emerald publishing team. The dedicated staff of Emerald publishing has played an essential role in transforming concepts into the concrete information that is contained on these pages. We received wonderful support from team Emerald throughout the publishing process.

Finally, we would like to thank all of you, the readers. We are inspired by your dedication to overcoming the obstacles of contemporary finance and your quest for knowledge. We all contributed to this book, and we genuinely hope it will be a useful tool for you as you pursue your managerial goals.

Chapter 1

Sustainability Reporting, Value Creation and Effective Corporate Governance: A Managerial Perspective

Premagowrie Sivanandan

Taylor's University, Malaysia

Abstract

Sustainability reporting has gained momentum in recent years, especially with the enhanced attention paid by market participants and regulators to environmental, social and governance (ESG) practices. This chapter discusses the interconnected link between sustainability reporting and ESG and helps readers comprehend how businesses evaluate and communicate their social performance (i.e.ESG) and financial performance (i.e. economic) to businesses' key stakeholders. This chapter also reviews the inclusion of corporate governance into the presumably simple yet certainly complex sustainability reporting–ESG–corporate governance mix that provides businesses with the opportunities to do good in the pursuit of financial success and sustainable growth. Additionally, sustainability reporting that reports authentic ESG practices in the presence of effective corporate governance also helps to enhance a company's public image, attract investors, reduce risks and contribute to environmental and societal well-being. The successful integration of sustainability reporting and ESG with traditional financial reports, thus, is in the hands of managers who are expected to lead in the best interest of the company's shareholders and other stakeholders. Effective corporate governance, therefore, is seen as crucial for this convergence to create value, promote economic growth and address environmental and social concerns for long-term growth and sustainability.

Keywords: Sustainability; sustainability reporting; ESG; environmental; social; governance; economic; corporate governance

Strategic Financial Management, 1–12

Copyright © 2024 Premagowrie Sivanandan

Published under exclusive licence by Emerald Publishing Limited

doi:10.1108/978-1-83608-106-720241001

1. Introduction

The concept of sustainability's most widely used definition is 'Development that meets the needs of the present without compromising the ability of future generations to meet their own needs' (Brundtland, 1987, p. 41). Brundtland (1987) further describes that sustainability encompasses the concept of 'needs' and the idea of 'limitations'. The concept of 'needs' prioritizes the necessities of the world's impoverishment for which top emphasis should be accorded. On the other hand, the idea of 'limitations' refers to the notion that the status of technology and social structure places constraints on the environment's capacity to meet current and future needs of the world's population. On the other hand, Székely and Knirsch (2005) describe sustainability as economic growth, shareholder value, prestige, corporate reputation, customer relationships, and the quality of products and services that are sustainable and constantly expanding. This definition of sustainability also entails implementing and upholding moral corporate conduct, generating long-term employment opportunities, adding value for all parties involved in the company and meeting the needs of the underprivileged. The notion of sustainability, which has become one of the driving forces that spur companies to attain financial growth and success, must thus be measurable for managers, regulators and other stakeholders to assess how sustainability is achieved and the extent of success of the companies' sustainable practices. This brings us to sustainability reporting, also known as triple-bottom-line reporting, corporate social responsibility (CSR) reporting, ESG reporting, non-financial reporting and sustainable development reporting (Siew, 2015).

Sustainability has become such an integral part of business, both locally and globally, that regulators, companies and governments have taken numerous proactive steps and meaningful actions to adopt sustainability reporting in their national and international agenda. This is primarily due to the constant pressure for improved sustainability or ESG practices from a variety of stakeholders, including institutional investors, lenders, customers, non-governmental organizations and regulators, as well as disclosures from businesses (*Bursa Malaysia Sustainability Reporting Guide*, 2022). Ensuring that businesses operate responsibly, ethically and sustainably while also enhancing the communities in which they operate is the aim of corporate sustainability. Corporate sustainability may ensure successful and socially responsible business operations by addressing a range of issues, including reducing greenhouse gas (GHG) emissions, improving labour standards, safeguarding the environment and furthering human rights (HSBC, 2023). Malaysia, for example, through its Ministry of Investment, Trade and Industry (MITI) is taking a significant step towards sustainability and its goal of reaching net-zero emissions by 2050 with the introduction of the *Industry Environmental, Social and Governance (iESG) Framework* (Tan, 2023). The iESG framework could potentially be a key factor in assisting Malaysia in meeting its sustainability targets within a seven-year timeframe and gaining access to the US$12 trillion global ESG market (Tan, 2023). From the global perspective, the *Global Reporting Initiative (GRI)* released the revised *GRI Standards 2023*, which provide companies with a reference point and guide to prepare integrated ESG reports or standalone sustainability/non-financial reports. Nevertheless, challenges arise in the form of economic upheavals, natural disasters such as floods and earthquakes and political instability, which threaten to deter companies from executing their sustainable initiatives and reporting with sustainable practices fairly and equitably.

Companies, therefore, must negotiate a challenging terrain in the constantly evolving field of corporate governance, one that is characterized by environmental obstacles, stakeholder demands and economic uncertainties, to maneuver the complex yet rewarding practice of sustainability reporting. In a time of increased environmental consciousness and changing public expectations, the combination of sustainable reporting with sound corporate governance has become essential for companies all over the world. Sustainable practices, thus, are investments for the future that can support core business objectives rather than merely duties or campaigns of public relations (NST Business, 2023). Ernst and Young (2023) elucidate that achieving sustainability is essential to the fight against climate change, achieving the 17 *United Nations Sustainable Development Goals (UNSDGs)* (also known as 'Agenda 2030') and building a more equitable society. The nexus between corporate governance and sustainable reporting in the modern business context offers managers and business leaders a dynamic environment to attain financial success 'with a heart'.

In today's economic environment, managers are essential in guiding companies towards the attainment of sustainability and long-term profitability while maintaining strong corporate governance standards. This is supported by ACCA (2023), which states that a company's reputation, positive innovation and eventually profitability are largely determined by how the company handles its non-financial challenges, e.g. environmental and social challenges. The benefits of integrating sustainability into business are numerous, and this should motivate managers of Malaysian businesses, publicly listed companies and small and medium enterprises (SMEs) alike to expand their sustainability initiatives to enjoy advantages such as improving risk management, fostering creativity, stimulating the entry of new customers, boosting output, reducing expenses, building brand value and reputation, and maintaining an operating licence. However, despite the growing trend and emphasis on the importance of sustainability, an alarming 45% of Malaysian corporates and SMEs admit to not allocating a budget for their sustainability initiatives (*Malaysia Businesses Sustainability Pulse Report 2022*), which brings us to question the role of managers in ensuring sustainable reporting for their companies. According to *FTSE Russell*, the overall ESG score for Malaysian companies in 2022 was 2.5 out of 5, and this represents a 33.7% increase in the overall ESG score of Malaysian companies since 2018 (The Edge Malaysia, 2023). Even though there is a notable improvement in how publicly listed companies in Malaysia are implementing and reporting their sustainability initiatives, the overall ESG score of 50% shows that there is still considerable room for improvement in terms of how the companies manage their ESG facets of the business.

The 'E' in ESG stands for 'Environmental', which refers to the influence of an organization on ecosystems, air, water, lands and other living and non-living natural systems, such as the use of water and energy, emissions released into the atmosphere and loss of biodiversity. The 'S' in ESG is 'Social', which makes references to the effects that an organization has on the social structures in which it functions including the organization's ties to the community, its workers and its clients. The 'G' in ESG, on the other hand, is defined as 'Governance', which refers to the governance aspects of decision-making in an organization, ranging from policymaking to the allocation of rights and obligations among various corporate stakeholders (*GRI G4 Sustainability Reporting Guidelines*), such as the C-suite (i.e. the CEO, COO, CFO and CIO), managers, employees, customers, shareholders and the board of directors. However, conflicting perceptions about ESG pose a challenge on the road towards achieving sustainability due to factions that perceive ESG or sustainable practices to be a form of 'greenwashing' with zero impact by companies that try to paint a positive picture to 'hide' their environmentally damaging business activities. These factions such as environmental activists and civil society organizations observe that companies' managers are not entirely honest about the companies' ESG efforts, and some companies tend to overstate their sustainability efforts with a hidden agenda (Tan, 2023). Hence, the role of managers in nurturing sustainability reporting through effective corporate governance becomes more prominent due to the need to ascertain whether the companies are actually 'walking the talk' and are engaging in sustainable practices for the good of the environment and society. The managerial viewpoint on how governance procedures and strategic decision-making support sustainable reporting is, hence, discussed in this chapter. This chapter also explores the mutually beneficial relationship between sustainable reporting and corporate governance and how important a role they play in forming ethical and resilient businesses in the future.

2. Literature Review

2.1 Sustainability Reporting and ESG: The Road Towards Value Creation

Sustainability and ESG are two concepts that are correlated with each other yet display distinct characteristics. The evaluation of a company's effects on the environment, society and governance is conducted using a set of criteria known as ESG. According to Evanson (2023), the adoption of ESG principles can lead to long-term value creation and a better future for the planet, people and businesses (i.e. profit). The three pillars of ESG are provided in the indicative list in Table 1.1 below:

Table 1.1. ESG Pillars With Indicative Constituents.

E (Environment)	S (Social)	G (Governance)
Climate change	Human rights	Board independence
Carbon emission	Labour standards	Board diversity
Pollution	Poverty	Transparency
Resource erosion	Equal health opportunities	Shareholders' participation
Biodiversity	Equal Education	Employee wellness
Green coverage	Social security	Equal opportunity

Source: A Review of ESG Performance as a Measure of Stakeholders' Theory, Kumar (2023).

Sustainability, on the other hand, emphasizes the capacity to persist in the long run using the interaction between a business' environmental, social and economic aspects (HSBC, 2023). The goal of environmental sustainability is to minimize GHG emissions, cut back on waste and pollution and conserve natural resources to reduce or eliminate adverse effects on the environment. The social component prioritizes human rights, community involvement, health and safety, and fair and safe labour practices to advance social fairness, diversity and inclusion. Finally, the economic side of sustainability is concerned with preserving long-term profitability, generating economic value and assuring prudent resource allocation. ESG, thus, can be considered a subset of sustainability that embraces the economic facets of a business. The primary distinction between sustainability and ESG is that the latter is a wide concept that includes a variety of ethical business practices, whereas ESG is a particular approach used to assess a company's environmental, social and economic performance. ESG indicators are, thus, employed to assess how well a company is performing in specific domains, such as executive remuneration, diversity and inclusion and carbon emissions (HSBC, 2023).

A company's report regarding the ESG impacts of its operations is known as a sustainability report or ESG report. The sustainability report makes it viable for the business to communicate its possibilities and risks more openly to its shareholders and other stakeholders and acts as a communication tool to persuade cynics and doubtful parties that the company's actions are sincere (PwC, 2023). As sustainability is a broad, multifaceted and rarely measurable concept, ESG provides a precise quantitative measure of a company's sustainability and corporate social performance, making it possible to better understand how sustainability practices affect the measurable results of a business's financial and operational performance (Clark & Viehs, 2014) through sustainability reporting. McBride Sustainability (2023) states that sustainability reporting can benefit companies and society by lowering risks, boosting stakeholder participation and increasing transparency. Zumente and Bistrova (2021) affirm that managers of businesses with greater knowledge of sustainability ensure that shareholders' value is created through enhanced financial performance, better management and lower risk indicators. Furthermore, qualitative non-financial characteristics like reputation, stakeholders' trust, employee satisfaction and engagement have also been found to have an even greater impact on long-term value (Zumente & Bistrova, 2021). Through the participation of external stakeholders and regulators in the process, sustainability reporting enables companies to publish transparent, current and verifiable information on ESG performance (World Business Council for Sustainable Development, 2018). The importance of sustainability reporting in corporate Malaysia has steered *Bursa Malaysia* to disclose in September 2022 that publicly listed companies in Malaysia would be required to report on sustainability more comprehensively with the gradual implementation of the reporting rules with the first financial year end in 2023. This strategy provides enlightening insights that *Bursa Malaysia* has tightened its disclosure requirements to encourage Malaysian public listed companies to embrace and share sustainable practices that might boost organizational resilience and competitiveness in luring additional capital to assist the shift to net zero (Ernst & Young, 2022) and subsequently leading to long-term value creation.

Value creation has become inclusive, and creating long-term shareholder value is no longer exclusive to only shareholders. Even though the phrase 'shareholder value' was originally coined primarily to represent an emphasis on short-term returns, it is now increasingly used to highlight the necessity for managers of companies to act sustainably and ethically to secure the companies' place in the economy in the long run (Bistrova & Lace, 2012). Value creation, thus, has evolved to include satisfying the needs of other stakeholders as well such as managers, suppliers, customers and employees. In the same vein, Henisz et al. (2019) find that a sound ESG proposition opens the door to enhanced value creation that encompasses exceptional financial growth through better access to resources, reduction in costs due to lower energy consumption, legal and regulatory intervention through government support and subsidies and increased production capacity due to boost in employee morale. Friske et al. (2023) further attest that when businesses learn how to better communicate sustainability objectives to stakeholders and investors learn how to correctly evaluate financial reports and sustainability reports, sustainability reporting, which is initially a costly signal, ultimately enhances company value. To phrase it simply, sustainability reporting through ESG measures focuses on how companies can create value for all their stakeholders including the expected financial returns for their shareholders. Thus, managerial commitment and altruistic behaviour are important to drive efficient and effective planning and decision-making for value creation through the institutionalization of sustainability reporting. However, it is also vital to note that not all sustainable practices are conducted to do good, and managers may engage in sustainable activities to hide the company's misdeeds and portray an 'angelic' front to shareholders and other stakeholders. This is supported by Zimon et al. (2022) who affirm that managers are driven to act morally and socially to try to cover up the company's errors and improve its standing in the eyes of shareholders and other stakeholders.

2.2 Sustainability Reporting and Corporate Governance: Making It Work

Sustainability reporting incorporates ESGconsiderations in addition to financial gains. Sustainability reporting, thus, transcends beyond financial indicators as sustainable reporting represents a company's overall financial performance and social performance taking ESG factors into account. As more Malaysian businesses realize the link between sustainability reporting, long-term financial viability and ESG performance, the incorporation of sustainable practices into business models is gaining traction. In this context, corporate governance completes the sustainability reporting–value creation–ESG mosaic by serving as a facilitator to guarantee that business strategies are in line with sustainable ideals.

Corporate governance refers to the mechanisms and internal controls that are put in place in a company to ensure that the company is managed in an ethical and accountable manner to attain maximisation of shareholders' wealth.

Corporate governance creates a three-fold structure for transparency, ethics and accountability within a company. According to Boiral and Henri (2017), corporate governance considers every interest that has an impact on the competence, morality and viability of an organization. It is imperative for businesses that aim to succeed in the long run to mandatorily embrace sustainable practices in corporate governance. Managers are, thus, urged to think about the wider effects of their strategic decisions and choices on the environment, society and governance rather than only concentrating on financial success. In other words, sustainability reporting transcends beyond the bottom line. According to L'Huillier (2014), under the auspices of agency theory, the connotative definition of 'corporate governance' relates to enforcement strategies used to oversee the actions and decisions of managers who are 'agents' selected by the company's 'principal', i.e. the shareholders. The need to oversee the actions and decisions made by managers stems from the notion that managers are motivated to manage their companies' earnings to boost performance-linked remuneration that is linked to firm equity value especially when specific performance targets are required to be achieved or maintained before the managers can enjoy the fruits of their labour (Sivanandan & Abdul Wahab, 2020). This in turn can impair the quality of earnings reported in the financial statements when managers' actions and decisions are driven by opportunism and greed rather than altruism for the benefit of the company's shareholders and other stakeholders, which in turn can affect the quality of sustainability reporting. It is, therefore, the responsibility of managers to preserve moral principles, guarantee openness and promote an accountable culture within their companies in the pursuit of wealth and financial gains.

Effective corporate governance entails the implementation of sound corporate governance mechanisms, such as board diversity, audit committee, institutional ownership and executive and non-executive remuneration, to ensure the company is managed fairly and ethically. Extant literature (for example, Beji et al., 2021; Masud et al., 2018; Mudiyanselage, 2018; Ong & Djajadikerta, 2018) shows that there is a positive relationship between sustainability reporting and corporate governance, which exhibits that good corporate governance drives sustainability reporting, which in turn results in value creation for companies. For example, Githaiga and Kosgei (2023) discover a positive and significant correlation between sustainability reporting and board independence, gender diversity and financial expertise because board characteristics are essential to quality financial reporting, voluntary disclosure and reduction in information asymmetries. Similarly, Perrault and McHugh (2015) and Cormier and Magnan (2015) explain that the board of directors is compelled to earn, preserve and fix a company's legitimacy by promoting transparency and advocating disclosure of the company's social and environmental performance through sustainability reporting. This is underpinned by the legitimacy theory (Dowling & Pfeffer, 1975), which proposes that companies engage in the disclosure of their CSR information to present a virtuous and socially responsible image to legitimize their corporate and social behaviour to the companies' multiple stakeholders. This is supported by Ntim and Soobaroyen (2013) who assert that a diverse board can advance a company's legitimacy by reaching out to a larger range of stakeholders and fostering stronger bonds between the company and its constituents.

Sustainability reporting, which is an integral element of financial reporting, acts as a stakeholder engagement tool that helps to validate a company's corporate ethical behaviour to its shareholders and other stakeholders. In line with this, Buallay et al. (2020) find that the level of ESG disclosure via sustainability reporting increases when the presence of females on the board of directors increases. Additionally, Ahmad et al. (2018) claim that directors with a background in finance and training in social accounting are more aware of the significance of social and environmental issues, and are therefore, more likely to support the company's sustainability reporting efforts due to the high priority they place on society and the environment. Similarly, Ong and Djajadikerta (2017) find that the proportion of independent directors, multiple directorships and the presence of females on the board of directors is significantly and positively correlated with sustainability reporting and disclosures. Olayinka et al. (2022), on the other hand, report that audit expertise, frequency of audit committee meetings and audit committee size are significantly and positively related to sustainability reporting in Nigerian public listed companies. This is because the audit committee of a company oversees financial reporting procedures, chooses the company's independent auditor and receives both internal and external audit results from the internal and external auditors.

Institutional ownership refers to the ownership of shares in firms that are held by financial and non-financial institutions. Institutional investors act as the agents of corporate governance in their capacity as large shareholders who are deemed to possess the ability and power to mitigate the agency problem that arises between a firm's managers and its shareholders through monitoring of managers' behaviour, actions and decision-making process. The *Malaysian Code for Institutional Investors 2014* regards institutional investors as major players in the global economy due to the significant influence that institutional investors exert over the firms they invest in (i.e. 'investees') arising from their large shareholdings in the firms (Minority Shareholders Watch Group, 2014). It is, thus, expected that institutional investors play a key role in driving sustainability reporting in their investee firms through sound corporate governance. Alomran and Alsahali (2023) find that long-term institutional investors significantly affect the reliability of companies' sustainability reports through external assurance. This is due to the long-term institutional investors' oversight role and a keen interest in long-term financial performance as opposed to short-termism which usually attracts short-term institutional investors. Strampelli and Balp (2023) in the same vein assert that institutional investors are the primary users of sustainability reporting because measuring the impact of sustainability practices implemented by investee companies is becoming more and more important to evaluate how ESG elements affect firm profitability and risk, and consequently, the overall returns on their investment portfolios.

3. Conclusion

Corporate sustainability strategies must include sustainability reporting since it helps businesses to assess, track and report to stakeholders on their economic, governance, social and environmental performance. Companies that use sustainability reporting can improve their standing with the public, draw in investors, lower risks and add value for the environment and society. The fact that investors and other stakeholders are pressuring businesses to reveal more about their sustainability and ESG plans lends credence to the growing significance of sustainability reports. Companies in Malaysia, particularly publicly listed companies, must prepare the necessary next steps considering the impending implementation of the enhanced sustainability disclosures by *Bursa Malaysia*. These steps include conducting a materiality assessment, choosing appropriate sustainability indicators, compiling pertinent data on sustainability issues and indicators, setting meaningful and quantifiable targets and boosting the credibility of sustainability information that has been disclosed (Ernst & Young, 2022). It is with effective corporate governance that sustainability reporting can continue to create value and lead companies towards economic growth, preservation of the environment and being champions of social causes, ultimately resulting in long-term sustainability for the current and future generations. As the Native American proverb says, 'We do not inherit the Earth from our ancestors. We borrow it from our children'.

3.1 Policy Recommendations to Managers

The interwoven relationship between sustainability reporting, value creation and corporate governance leads to the high probability that sustainability reports may soon converge with 'traditional' financial and business reports. It is, therefore, a necessity that sound corporate governance mechanisms are implemented within the companies to promote effective corporate governance, quality sustainability reporting and positive value creation. As financial and non-financial information become more connected, this convergence could cause significant changes to the financial reporting structure and might potentially lead to the shift towards shorter, maybe more frequent and more focused reporting. PwC (2011) proposes four action steps that managers of companies can undertake to implement sustainability reporting comprising 'differentiate', 'innovate', 'be inspired' and 'fix'. Managers are, thus, compelled to choose sustainability reporting with a competitive edge, challenge the current traditional financial reporting with integration, structure and content, take note of contemporary and current reporting best practices and keep updated with current industry trends through benchmarking and paying added attention to competitors' actions. Al-Shaer et al. (2022) further add that corporate managers must involve different stakeholders in the sustainability reporting process and should fortify their internal and external governance structures to improve the comprehensiveness and credibility of sustainability reports. In the same vein, Sancak (2023) finds that sustainability transformation entails implementing planned organizational change models resulting in the governance (G) factor in ESG playing the most vital role in driving sustainability. It is, thus, imperative that managers come to the acute realization that sustainability reporting and ESG are here to stay, and the business value creation, going concerned and sustainability lie in promoting effective corporate governance mechanisms within the company.

References

ACCA. (2023). *Things you need to know: Sustainability reporting.* https://www.accaglobal.com/gb/en/student/sa/professional-skills/masterclass-sustainability-reporting.html. Accessed on December 17, 2023.

Ahmad, N. B. J., Rashid, A., & Gow, J. (2018). Corporate board gender diversity and corporate social responsibility reporting in Malaysia. *Gender, Technology and Development, 22*(2), 87–108.

Al-Shaer, H., Albitar, K., & Hussainey, K. (2022). Creating sustainability reports that matter: An investigation of factors behind the narratives. *Journal of Applied Accounting Research, 23*(3), 738–763. https://doi.org/10.1108/JAAR-05-2021-0136

Alomran, A. A., & Alsahali, K. F. (2023). The role of long-term institutional ownership in sustainability report assurance: Global evidence. *Sustainability, 15*(4), 1–17. https://doi.org/10.3390/su15043492

Beji, R., Yousfi, O., Loukil, N., & Omri, A. (2021). Board diversity and corporate social responsibility: Empirical evidence from France. *Journal of Business Ethics, 173*(1), 133–155.

Bistrova, J., & Lace, N. (2012). Defining key factors to sustain maximum shareholder value. *Journal of Financial Studies & Research,* 1–14.

Boiral, O., & Henri, J. F. (2017). Is sustainability performance comparable? A study of GRI reports of mining organizations. *Business & Society, 56*(2), 283–317.

Brundtland, G. H. (1987). *Report of the world commission on environment and development: Our common future.* https://sustainabledevelopment.un.org/content/documents/5987our-common-future.pdf. Accessed on December 16, 2023.

Buallay, A., Hamdan, R., Barone, E., & Hamdan, A. (2020). Increasing female participation on boards: Effects on sustainability reporting. *International Journal of Finance & Economics, 18*(5), 886–910.

Bursa Malaysia. (2022). *Sustainability reporting guide* (3rd ed.). Sustainability Reporting Guide 2022_FINAL.pdf (bursaacademy.s3.ap-southeast-1.amazonaws.com). Accessed on December 17, 2023.

Clark, G. L. & Viehs, M. (2014). The implications of corporate social responsibility for investors: An overview and evaluation of the existing CSR literature. https://ssrn.com/abstract=2481877. https://doi.org/10.2139/ssrn.2481877

Cormier, D., & Magnan, M. (2015). The economic relevance of environmental disclosure and its impact on corporate legitimacy: An empirical investigation. *Business Strategy and the Environment, 24*(6), 431–450.

Dowling, J., & Pfeffer, J. (1975). Organizational legitimacy: Social values and organizational behavior. *Pacific Sociological Review, 18*(1), 122–136.

Ernst and Young. (2022). *Bursa Malaysia: Enhanced sustainability disclosure requirements*. https://www.ey.com/en_my/take-5-business-alert/bursa-malaysia-enhanced-sustainability-disclosure-requirements#:~:text=Bursa%20Malaysia%3A%20Enhanced%20sustainability%20disclosure%20requirements,-14%20Dec%202022&text=In%20September%202022%2C%20Bursa%20Malaysia,year%20end%20(FYE)%202023. Accessed on December 16, 2023.

Ernst and Young. (2023). *Sustainable Development Goals*. https://www.ey.com/en_in/sustainable-development-goals. Accessed on December 16, 2023.

Evanson, D. (2023). *Reasons to adopt ESG agenda, NST Business Times*. https://www.nst.com.my/business/2023/07/935363/reasons-adopt-esg-agenda. Accessed on December 16, 2023.

Friske, W., Hoelscher, S. A., & Nikolov, A. N. (2023). The impact of voluntary sustainability reporting on firm value: Insights from signaling theory. *Journal of the Academy of Marketing Science*, *51*, 372–392. https://doi.org/10.1007/s11747-022-00879-2

Githaiga, P. N., & Kosgei, J. K. (2023). Board characteristics and sustainability reporting: a case of listed firms in East Africa. *Corporate Governance*, *23*(1), 3–17.

Henisz, W., Koller, T., Nuttall, R. (2019). Five ways that ESG creates value. *McKinsey Quarterly*. http://dln.jaipuria.ac.in:8080/jspui/bitstream/123456789/2319/1/Five-ways-that-ESG-creates-value.pdf

HSBC. (2023). Sustainability vs ESG: What's the difference and why they matter? https://www.businessgo.hsbc.com/en/article/demystifying-sustainability-and-esg. Accessed on December 18, 2023.

Kumar, S. (2023). A review of ESG performance as a measure of stakeholders' theory. *Academy of Marketing Studies Journal*, *27*(S3), 1–7.

L'Huillier, B. M. (2014). What does "corporate governance" actually mean? *Corporate Governance*, *14*(3), 300–319.

Masud, M. A. K., Nurunnabi, M., & Bae, S. M. (2018). The effects of corporate governance on environmental sustainability reporting: Empirical evidence from South Asian countries. *Asian Journal of Sustainability and Social Responsibility*, *3*(1), 1–26.

McBride Sustainability. (2023). *The importance of ESG reporting in corporate sustainability*. https://www.linkedin.com/pulse/importance-esg-reporting-corporate-sustainability-mcbride-2/. Accessed on December 17, 2023.

Minority Shareholders Watch Group. (2014). *Malaysian code for institutional investors*. https://www.iicm.org.my/malaysian-code-for-institutional-investors/. Accessed on December 15, 2023.

Mudiyanselage, N. C. S. R. (2018). Board involvement in corporate sustainability reporting: Evidence from Sri Lanka. *Corporate Governance: The International Journal of Business in Society*, *18*(6), 1042–1056.

NST Business. (2023). *Sustainable practices can benefit fundamental company goals, says Avanade*. https://www.nst.com.my/business/2023/04/902300/sustainable-practices-can-benefit-fundamental-company-goals-says-avanade. Accessed on December 17, 2023.

Ntim, C. G., & Soobaroyen, T. (2013). Corporate governance and performance in socially responsible corporations: New empirical insights from a neo-institutional framework. *Corporate Governance: An International Review*, *21*(5), 468–494.

Olayinka, E., Adegboye, A., & Bamigboye, O. A. (2022). Sustainable development goals (SDG) reporting: An analysis of disclosure. *Sustainability Accounting, Management and Policy Journal, 13*(3), 680–707.

Ong, T., & Djajadikerta, H. G. (2017). Impact of corporate governance on sustainability reporting: Empirical study in the Australian resources industry. In *8th Conference on Financial Markets and Corporate Governance (FMCG)*. https://ssrn.com/abstract=2902495

Ong, T., & Djajadikerta, H. G. (2018). Corporate governance and sustainability reporting in the Australian resources industry: An empirical analysis. *Social Responsibility Journal, 16*(1), 1–14.

Perrault, E., & McHugh, P. (2015). Toward a life cycle theory of board evolution: Considering firm legitimacy. *Journal of Management and Organization, 21*(5), 627–649.

PwC. (2023). ESG reporting and preparation of a Sustainability Report. https://www.pwc.com/sk/en/environmental-social-and-corporate-governance-esg/esg-reporting.html. Accessed on December 18, 2023.

PwC. (2011). Sustainability reporting tips: Simple actions to make your reporting more accessible and effective. https://www.pwc.com/gx/en/audit-services/corporate-reporting/sustainability-reporting/assets/pwc-sustainability-reporting-tips-private-sector.pdf. Accessed on December 19, 2023.

Sancak, I. (2023). Change management in sustainability transformation: A model for business organizations. *Journal of Environmental Management, 330*, 117–165.

Siew, R. Y. J. (2015). A review of corporate sustainability reporting tools (SRTs). *Journal of Environmental Management, 164*, 180–195.

Sivanandan, P., & Abdul Wahab, N. S. (2020). Mediating effects of remuneration on earnings management and firm equity value. *Asian Journal of Accounting and Governance, 14*, 1–16.

Strampelli, G. & Balp, G. (2023). Institutional investors as the primary users of sustainability reporting. Forthcoming in K. Alexander, M. Siri and M. Gargantini (Eds.), *The Cambridge handbook of EU sustainable finance: Regulation, supervision and governance*. Bocconi Legal Studies Research Paper No. 4495602. Cambridge University Press. https://ssrn.com/abstract=4495602. https://doi.org/10.2139/ssrn.4495602

Székely, F., & Knirsch, M. (2005). Responsible leadership and corporate social responsibility: Metrics for sustainable performance. *European Management Journal, 23*(6), 628–647.

Tan, J. (2023). *Driving sustainability and net zero goals in Malaysia*. Kuala Lumpur.

The Edge Malaysia. (2023). *ESG 2023-special issue: Walking the talk*. https://theedgemalaysia.com/microsite/esg2023-special-issue-walking-the-talk. Accessed on December 15, 2023.

World Business Council for Sustainable Development. (2018). *Reporting matters 2018*. https://www.wbcsd.org/resources/reporting-matters-2018/. Accessed on December 14, 2023.

Zimon, G., Arianpoor, A., & Salehi, M. (2022). Sustainability reporting and corporate reputation: The moderating effect of CEO opportunistic behavior. *Sustainability, 14*(3), 1257. https://doi.org/10.3390/su14031257

Zumente, I., & Bistrova, J. (2021). ESG importance for long-term shareholder value creation: Literature vs. Practice. *Journal of Open Innovation: Technology, Market, and Complexity, 7*(2), 127. https://doi.org/10.3390/joitmc7020127

Chapter 2

Sustainability and ESG Integration

Hassan Muaaz[a] *and Muhammad Ali*[b]

[a]UCSI University, Malaysia
[b]Taylor's University, Malaysia

Abstract

In the modern financial landscape, the integration of sustainability and ESG has emerged as an imperative part for managers. Amid growing pressure and demand from multiple stakeholders, managers are confronted with diverse challenges in the integration of sustainability and ESG into the financial system. This chapter scrutinizes the evolving financial system due to sustainability and ESG, elucidating the challenges it presents for managers. Before discussing the challenges, authors delve into related theories namely stakeholder theory and legitimacy theory, followed by a conceptual review and how researchers measure sustainability and ESG. This provides an overview of current research findings and directions to establish a common understanding of the topic discussed. The challenges faced by managers were discussed based on four salient areas. It includes the business case for sustainability, ESG metrics and reporting standards, sustainable investment criteria and stakeholder engagement for sustainability. At the end of this chapter, actionable recommendations were provided to the managers to navigate the challenges faced in the modern financial landscape. Authors recommended high quality audit, disclosure of accurate and consistent information and adoption of a comprehensive ESG matrix that integrates paramount business cases for the company to delineate the challenges faced by them. It further discusses additional techniques and tools that managers can incorporate to manage sustainability and ESG integration effectively.

Keywords: Sustainability; ESG; financial system; stakeholders; financial performance

Strategic Financial Management, 13–33
Copyright © 2024 Hassan Muaaz and Muhammad Ali
Published under exclusive licence by Emerald Publishing Limited
doi:10.1108/978-1-83608-106-720241002

1. Introduction

Environment, social and governance also referred to as ESG are often addressed under sustainability (Sancha et al., 2023). These three dimensions have become an important part of modern finance and for managers. There is growing pressure on managers to achieve better productivity and maximize profitability whilst still facing continuous demand for ESG. Hence, managers face challenges in managing and effectively allocating financial resources to achieve and balance both ESG and financial objectives (Dakhli, 2021). Allocating the financial resources effectively to address sustainability could be an obstacle for managers in the current evolving environment. To achieve superior performance, companies will need to allocate significant financial resources to improve their practices on sustainability and develop effective organizational capacity on ESG. This leads managers a tremendous pressure on addressing these demands.

Previously investing and focussing on environmental or sustainable activities are considered as additional costs that harm the finances of the company (Rahman et al., 2023; Zhou et al., 2022). When companies invest heavily in sustainability (ESG), it is regarded as a reduction of cash flow that diverts the resources from vital business operational activities resulting in a reduction of the overall performance of the company (Duque-Grisales & Aguilera-Caracuel, 2021). Herewith, ensuring financial visibility of ESG investment and allocation of resources is a key issue for managers, and they are responsible for determining whether required investment and resources are justifiable (Aydoğmuş et al., 2022).

Sustainability is defined as 'development that meets the needs of the present without compromising the ability of future generations to meet their own needs' (World Commission on Environment and Development, 1987). Concerning a broader definition of sustainability, corporate sustainability can be referred to as 'meeting the needs of a company's direct and indirect stakeholders without compromising its ability to meet the needs of future stakeholders' (Dyllick & Hockerts, 2002). This concept is gaining momentum among companies and managers after the launch of the 2030 Agenda for Sustainable Development by the United Nations. The role of companies in achieving sustainable goals is as important as actions at the country level (Pizzi et al., 2020). The 2030 Agenda bolsters companies and managers in aligning investment decisions and company strategies following the three dimensions of sustainable development – ESG (Qureshi et al., 2020; United Nations, 2015). The application of the ESG framework can help make it easier to measure and standardize companies' sustainability performance (Ronalter et al., 2023). ESG is defined as 'companies' obligation to improve social welfare and equitable and sustainable long-term wealth for stakeholders' (Mohammad & Wasiuzzaman, 2021). The fundamental purpose is shifting the central focus from shareholders and addressing the interests of all stakeholders equivalently. Table 2.1 provides the concept and sample facets of the three dimensions of ESG.

Table 2.1. Concept and Example of Three Dimensions of ESG.

Dimension	Definition	Sample Facets
Environment	'How company take actions to protect and minimise damage to the environment' (Lee & Suh, 2022)	Energy efficiency Greenhouse Gas Emission Waste, Water & Resource Management
Social	'How a Company treat its employees and the communities that they serve' (Lee & Suh, 2022)	Gender Policies Protection of Human Rights Labour standards Workplace and Product Safety Public Health Income Distribution
Governance	'How a company is led and managed to balance the interest of not only stakeholders such as customers and management executives but also the community' (Sancha et al., 2023)	Independence of the Board Shareholder's Right Manager's Remuneration Control Procedure Anti-competitive practices

Source: Billio et al. (2021), Lee & Suh (2022), and Sancha et al. (2023).

2. Literature Review

2.1 Theories and Conceptual Review

2.1.1 Stakeholder Theory

A stakeholder is defined as 'any group or individual who can affect or is affected by the achievement of the organization's objectives' (Freeman, 1984). Stakeholder theory aims to ascertain a company's relationship with all other bodies involved in its business (Abdi et al., 2022). Stakeholders play an active role in social control (Aouadi & Marsat, 2018). Thus, this theory argues that companies should focus on improving performance in line with all stakeholders' needs, including the environment, society and economy (Rahman et al., 2023). To achieve this, disclosure of ESG information to stakeholders is vital, which also indicates the company's commitment to sustainability (El-Deeb et al., 2023). By including stakeholders' interests in the reporting process, companies will be able to better communicate their objectives and challenges (Zamil et al., 2023).

According to stakeholder theory, ESG and CSR activities imply that companies are taking into account the interest of stakeholders which is considered a source of competitive advantage for the company (Menicucci & Paolucci, 2023). Different stakeholders may have different expectations while core stakeholders expect companies to be more sustainable and embrace ESG (Rahi et al., 2022). From stakeholders' perspective, achieving optimal engagement from stakeholders may enable companies to improve their financial performance (Yoon & Chung, 2018). The framework of stakeholder theory can be relied on to ensure winning conditions for a company while comprehending the ESG aspect in business operations (Mattera & Soto, 2023).

Shareholders are important stakeholders who provide equity and direction for the growth of a company. Hence, their interest and demand are imperative to meet and the manager acts as an agent in this process. Managers should exert to reduce agency conflict because extensive levels of agency conflict will create underutilization of investment and greater agency costs (El-Deeb et al., 2023). Though there may be a conflict of interest and holding that ESG may negatively impact financial performance, ESG practices are believed to be vital for all stakeholders (Menicucci & Paolucci, 2023). To generate superior financial performance, companies need to address the demands and interests of all stakeholders in a fair manner rather than just focussing on maximising the shareholders' profit (Ademi & Klungseth, 2022). For control and risk management of the companies, it is pivotal to balance the interests of shareholders and other stakeholders (Rahi et al., 2022). According to stakeholder theory, companies can be more sustainable when they manage all stakeholders' interests effectively and robustly (Freeman, 1984).

2.1.2 Legitimacy Theory

The fundamental foundation of this theory is society's values, which influence companies' actions and plans (Al Amosh et al., 2023). And when companies disregard this value system, the concept of a 'legitimacy gap' arises (Moloi & Marwala, 2020). To address the gap, companies legitimize their action by engaging in activities such as sustainability and transparent disclosure of non-financial and financial information (Al Amosh & Khatib, 2022). To be seen as legitimized by the stakeholders, the legitimacy theory emphasizes disclosing the ESG performance, which will also enable companies to enhance value and financial performance (Al Amosh et al., 2023). Both legitimacy theory and stakeholder theory highly emphasize ESG disclosure because it assists as a strategic instrument to manage stakeholders and gain legitimacy and endorsement from stakeholders (El-Deeb et al., 2023).

Institutionalization is used interchangeably with legitimacy because structure, practices, organization identity and sense of existence are determined by both institutionalization and legitimacy (Aluchna et al., 2023). Companies that meet the expectations of stakeholders can obtain legitimacy because companies operate in a social context and interact with large groups of stakeholders (Doni et al., 2022).

Companies formulate and implement strategies that address the expectations of stakeholders as a process of legitimizing the business operation. Managers play the role of agents in the process to ensure the company activities and strategies align with stakeholder expectations as they direct to obtain legitimacy. Stakeholder approval and acceptance are vital to achieve legitimacy. Hence, active engagement with internal and external stakeholders is crucial to legitimize the company's contribution to attaining sustainability (Galeone et al., 2023). Moreover, the concept of legitimacy can be used to hold companies accountable for their activities and performance (Patten & Shin, 2019).

2.2 Integrated Framework

In the modern financial system, ESG has become the central focus of many researchers. Due to the frequent financial crises and unforeseen circumstances, this area has been attracting considerable interest from researchers and practitioners (Zhou et al., 2022). However, they found contradictory findings resulting in uncertainty in understanding the mechanism that underpins ESG (Lee & Suh, 2022). Hence, to understand the nexus of ESG on the financial system and develop common insight for managers, it is of paramount significance to explore more on ESG in a financial context. Below the author discusses some of the common factors/constructs that researchers explore in this field.

2.2.1 Outcome

Financial performance is one of the main focused outcome constructs studied by the researchers. Companies' commitment to sustainability and investment in ESG improve financial performance (Abdi et al., 2022; Li et al., 2018). The effect may not be exhibited in a short period, but it will improve financial performance in the long term. The positive effect in the long term can benefit managers in survival in a competitive environment and securing finance for future investment. An increase in corporate socially responsible activities in the presence of best practices improves the company revenue resulting in a positive impact on the financial performance (Okafor et al., 2021). CSR is considered an indication of the presence of good corporate governance practices. The impact of ESG collectively and as individual dimensions have contrasting results on financial performance. For example, ESG collectively improves the financial performance of companies in Levant countries while environmental and social performance except governance performance individually have a positive impact on financial performance (Al Amosh et al., 2023). It is worth pointing out that there are studies that show a negative correlation, in particular an adverse impact on financial performance as a result of ESG activities or performance (Gillan et al., 2021). The plausible justification of a negative relationship could be because of the high cost associated with the ineffective implementation of ESG initiatives, lack of institutional support and less exposure resulting absence of acceptance from stakeholders (Abdi et al., 2022; Duque-Grisales & Aguilera-Caracuel, 2021).

Some researchers use return on assets (ROA) as an indicator of financial performance and report contradicting results. ROA depicts the prosperousness of utilizing the company resources (Aydoğmuş et al., 2022). Duque-Grisales and Aguilera-Caracuel (2021) found that a higher ESG score has a negative impact on ROA as it decreases performance. This result was based on data collected from 104 multinational Latin American companies. On the contrary, the three dimensions of ESG were found to have a positive impact on companies' financial performance (ROA) when the relationship was examined from data obtained from companies listed on the Pakistan Stock Exchange (Rahman et al., 2023) and United State-listed companies (Brogi & Lagasio, 2019).

The market value of the company is also a major construct explored by the researchers. Companies that improve their ESG performance have benefited from an increase in their market value (Zhou et al., 2022). Companies disclose their sustainability activities including environmental, societal and governance activities to gain optimum benefit from those activities. Reporting or disclosing these activities improves the company's value (Qureshi et al., 2020). Disclosing the sustainability activities may gain stakeholders' trust and imply that companies follow the best corporate governance and practices which result in having a positive impact on the value of the company (El-Deeb et al., 2023). The impact of ESG on company value may differ in different industries and each dimension may have different effects. In the airline industry, on the one hand, governance is found to have a positive impact and increase company value; on the other hand, investing in social and environmental dimensions doesn't necessarily improve company value (Abdi et al., 2022). Inversely, analysis based on a combination of companies from different regions indicates that the social and governance dimension has a significant positive impact on company value, while the environment dimension does not show a significant relationship (Aydoğmuş et al., 2022). However, the mentioned study reported that the combination score of ESG improves the company value. The focus on environmental responsibility alone is not sufficient to increase the market value because stakeholders are more concerned with the overall engagement of ESG by the company (Al-Issa et al., 2022).

2.2.2 Moderator

Size: Large companies are more likely to participate and invest in sustainability projects than their smaller counterparts because of the availability of financial resources (Abdi et al., 2022); thus, company size is a significant moderator between ESG and outcome. ESG's impact on larger companies' performance is much greater than that of smaller companies (Minutolo et al., 2019). For small and emerging companies, it may be ineffective to highly invest to address all stakeholder's interests other than business operational activities due to a lack of resources, experience and reputation (D'Amato & Falivena, 2020).

Financial Slack: Financial slack is another construct that moderates the relationship between ESG and financial performance (Duque-Grisales & Aguilera-Caracuel, 2021). It strengthens the relationship as it allows us to focus more and invest in ESG activities. The excess of available resources after meeting the resource demands is referred to as financial slack, which represents the number of net resources that the management can use for its discretion (Picolo et al., 2018). To invest in ESG initiatives to gain the benefit of more visibility and improve financial performance, companies can utilize this financial slack.

International Geographical Diversification: The degree of international geographical diversification has a moderation effect, and if it is high, it improves a company's financial performance by enhancing ESG activities (Duque-Grisales & Aguilera-Caracuel, 2021). International diversification is a growth strategy for a company that expands into different countries and geographical regions beyond the border of its home country (Capar & Kotabe, 2003). International geographical diversification may create contentment among managers for the achievement of international diversification through their research and implementation strategies (Arte & Larimo, 2022). On the other hand, it adds a knowledge burden on managers and hinders their ability to make the right decision at the right time.

Age: Some companies have a long history and decades of experience in the market which may differentiate or have an advantage over new entries or emerging companies. Hence, age was examined as a potential moderator but the results dispute the theoretical understanding. A finding from companies in the airline industry shows that age is not a significant moderator between ESG and outcome (Abdi et al., 2022).

Moreover, several other constructs moderate the nexus of ESG and the outcome. Sustainability strategy of the company and the top management commitment (Rahman et al., 2023) and board representation (Nekhili et al., 2021) audit quality (El-Deeb et al., 2023) are some of such additional constructs that moderate the relationship.

2.2.3 Mediator

The role of mediating effect in the nexus of ESG is to 'demonstrate cause and effect through associations and correlations with a system of non-financial and financial variable that eventually flow into firm-level financial performance variables, explaining the ESG value-enhancing process' (Lee & Suh, 2022). The study of mediating effect in the current literature is scant and not treated much in detail, hence further studies on mediating effect will expand and enhance the literature. The operational capacity of the company and state/privately funded companies were previously examined as a mediator, which shows that operational capacity mediates the relationship between ESG and market value of the company, and companies that are not funded by the state have a full mediating effect (Zhou et al., 2022). Other potential constructs that may mediate the relationship include employee retention, motivation, organizational culture, reputation and branding (Lee & Suh, 2022). Fig. 2.1 shows the integrated framework of this study.

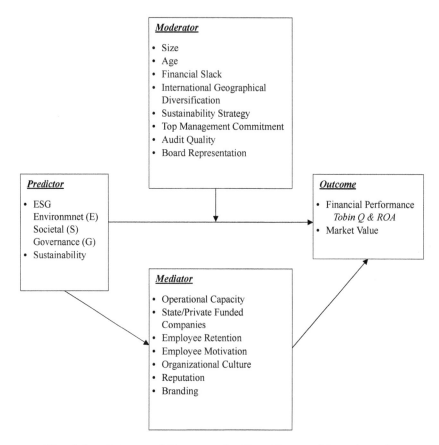

Fig. 2.1.   Integrated Framework. *Note:* Prepared based on the
literature review.

2.3 The Measurement of ESG

To test hypothesis and draw conclusion on research question, the data are mostly collected from secondary sources such as rating agencies (Lee & Suh, 2022). Thomson Reuters Eikon data are one of such databases used by researchers. This database provides sustainability measures and provide combined and separate score of each dimension in ESG (Abdi et al., 2022) (refer to Table 2.2). Their database yield information and metrics grounded on public reports and sustainability activities of the companies. Thomson Reuters Eikon data update on timely manner and considered relevant for ESG studies (Aouadi & Marsat, 2018). These rating agencies provide ESG score to integrate into formulas and statistical equations to conduct the analysis. The added value of CSR performance, derived from several environmental, societal and governance action are attributed to the

Table 2.2. Thomson Reuters Eikon's ESG Categories & Themes.

Dimension	Categories	Themes
Environment	Emission	Emissions Waste Biodiversity Environmental Management Systems
	Innovation	Product Innovation Green Revenues, Research & Development and Capital Expenditure
	Resource Use	Water Energy Sustainable Packaging Environmental Supply Chain
Social	Community	Equally Important to all Industry Groups
	Human Rights	Human Rights
	Product Responsibility	Responsible Marketing Product Quality Monitoring Policy Data Privacy
	Workforce	Diversity and Inclusion Career Development and Training Working Conditions Health and Safety
Governance	CSR Strategy	CSR Strategy ESG Reporting and Transparency
	Management	Structure (Independence, Diversity, Committees) Compensation
	Shareholders	Shareholders Rights Takeover Defences

Source: Al Amosh et al. (2023).

ESG score (Duque-Grisales & Aguilera-Caracuel, 2021). Researchers use different data from different rating agencies based on context of studies and their own discretion. Some of such rating agencies include MSCI ESG KLD STATS used by Brogi & Lagasio (2019), Bloomberg ESC database used by Aydoğmuş et al. (2022), Refinitiv ESG score used by Aydoğmuş et al. (2022) and SynTao Green Finance used by Zhou et al. (2022).

ESG data or score from rating agencies has its own limitations that may impact the finding or the conclusion. The information provided by these agencies may not be systematic and realistic enough to make effective decisions

(Drempetic et al., 2020; Lee & Suh, 2022). Moreover, to allocate investment funds and financial resources, the manager should be more attentive in using ESG scores (Lee & Suh, 2022).

3. Sustainability and ESG Integration: Challenges for Manager

3.1 The Business Case for Sustainability

Due to the detrimental impact on the earth due to environmental deterioration caused by human behaviour, the sustainable business operation has become an obligation (El-Deeb et al., 2023). It is not always straightforward to target sustainability objectives and companies are failing to deliver sustainable strategies (Sancha et al., 2023). There are several benefits of involvement in sustainable activities for a company such as attracting potential investors to raise capital for future investments, building close relationships and enhancing trust with stakeholders (Al Amosh et al., 2023). It is crucial to ensure trust from different groups of stakeholders other than shareholders (Rahi et al., 2022). Companies that emphasiZe cleaner production and support environmental improvement for the benefit of the company and other stakeholders enjoy better profitability (Menicucci & Paolucci, 2023). To improve financial and non-financial performance, managers need to shift their focus and prioritize ESG/sustainability efforts (Ademi & Klungseth, 2022). Therefore, to enhance a company's social performance, managers are entailed to make decisions to use a sustainable corporate governance model which is supported by legitimacy theory (Doni et al., 2022). This insistence challenges managers in the financial decision-making process and complicates the process of financial management. Hence, financial managers have to seek ways to achieve financial viability while concurrently establishing a sustainable business model in the company.

The business case for sustainability is explained as the 'extent and nature of the financial benefits that companies gain from sound environmental practices, social development, and economic progress' (SustainAbility, International Finance Corporation, & Ethos Institute, 2002). Similarly, the World Business Council for Sustainable Development (WBCSD) delineates a business case for corporate sustainability that highly emphasis engaging in eco-efficiency initiatives to generate more value without much negative impact on natural resources (Haywood, 2022). In line with this, managers are compelled to adopt accounting frameworks such as triple bottom line (Elkington, 1998) which create challenges for managers in financial reporting and valuation of the company (Haywood, 2022). Moreover, ensuring the economic and financial viability of every decision and strategy could be a hurdle for managers. They have to take into consideration the long-term consequences of the financial decisions and strategies adapted to the company's business model that may impact the company and stakeholders. The primary tension for managers in this process is maintaining the stability of both ESG and financial performance. Failure to connect the ESG strategies, financial performance and business strategy could result in greater loss to the company and create barriers to surviving in the market.

3.2 ESG Matrix and Reporting Standards

A growing focus on sustainability has led to an increase in sharing and disclosing information about environmental, societal and governance practices by the company (Li et al., 2018). Companies are adopting different sustainability strategies and reporting standards such as the International Organization for Standardization (ISO) related to sustainability, quality management, information security and safe working environments as a result of the immense demand for sustainability (ESG) (Ademi & Klungseth, 2022). Adhering to reporting standards may create transparency in the eyes of investors, which enables managers to exploit it to meet financial and nonfinancial targets (Al Amosh et al., 2023). Managers need to understand that the type of reporting affects the market valuation of the ESG performance of the company (Mervelskemper & Streit, 2017). Financial managers are gatekeepers of financial and non-financial information that has to be reported to stakeholders systematically. Integrating the ESG matrix and sustainability reporting standards gives rise to several challenges for managers.

Compared to previous reporting standards, current managers have to adhere to more complex reporting standards imposed by the legislation and international financial institutions. The practice of sustainability and financial reporting is undergoing an evolution (Bini & Bellucci, 2020) resulting in an increase in complexity for managers. Managers have continuously sought and identified

Table 2.3. Sample Reporting Standards.

Standard	Features
The Sustainability Accounting Standards Board (SASB)	Emphasis on industry-specific standards that analyse risk and opportunities associated with the financial state of the company, operating performance, and risk.
Global Reporting Initiatives	Provide a framework for sustainable reporting standards that meet global best practices and embedded information required by a large body of stakeholders.
Taskforce on Climate-related Financial Disclosure	Assist companies to transform metrics into action by reinforcing and protecting the global financial market from systematic risk and disclosing climate-related risk.
Integrated Reporting Framework	Integration of financial and nonfinancial reporting to improve cohesiveness and quality of reporting standards.

comprehensive reporting standards and guidelines that directly relate to and are relevant to stakeholders in the current financial system. Table 2.3 provides sample reporting standards by different institutions and agencies to disclose sustainability information and integrate it into financial reports. Nevertheless, sustainability reporting is still underdeveloped and what is required to be reported remains unclear (Ramanathan & Isaksson, 2023). This implies that accommodating reporting standards that incorporate sustainability creates more challenges for managers (De Micco et al., 2021). Failure to adopt these standards even though there are hassles may lead managers to be accountable and answerable to shareholders and other stakeholders.

To comply with the modern reporting standard, a systematic and robust data collection and management system is paramount for managers. However, still managers face a dearth of sophisticated technological systems capable of ensuring effective management of sustainability information in the current data management (De Micco et al., 2021). This limits on compiling of reliable, accurate and vigorous financial information concerning sustainability to disclose constructive financial and non-financial reports. Moreover, this limitation exceeds the manager's decision-making process. In the modern financial world, the disclosure of non-financial performance is considered a key part of managerial decision-making (du Toit et al., 2017).

Furthermore, the different stakeholders will have different expectations regarding the reports. Internal reports used within the company and reports that are published have to consider related stakeholders' expectations. Since different stakeholders have heterogeneous expectations, balancing all stakeholders' expectations is a complex process that creates tension among managers (Baret & Helfrich, 2019). Developing a holistic and integrated model to manage stakeholders' expectations in reporting escalates the pressure on managers. To address this, some managers use an ESG matrix that assesses the performance of various important areas for a large group of stakeholders, similar to the financial matrix (Aydoğmuş et al., 2022).

It is worth noting that the challenges discussed above with ESG metrics and reporting standards for managers are mainly rooted in broader challenges in sustainability reporting. To provide broader challenges in sustainable reporting, Ramanathan and Isaksson (2023, p. 1316) highlighted that

> [1] multiple standards and reporting guidelines… leads to no common foundation to baseline, compare reference and benchmark sustainability performance of a company [2] non-mandatory nature of sustainability reporting… leads to no system of enforceable incentives and disincentives for companies and third-party audit providers to work towards a common understanding of sustainability [3] …materiality assessment that impacts sustainability reporting professionals… leads to sustainability reporting accurately accounting only for direct emission from the core business with some degree of accuracy

for emission generated from the energy used and no accounting for upstream and downstream carbon emissions in the value chain.

3.3 Sustainable Investment Criteria

It is paramount for managers to consider ESG and sustainability as an investment instead of considering it as an expense or cost burden (Duque-Grisales & Aguilera-Caracuel, 2021). From a company perspective, any action by the company can be considered an investment (Aydoğmuş et al., 2022). Sustainable investment is used interchangeably as socially responsible investment (SRI) and ethical investment (Sciarelli et al., 2021). Investing and allocating resources for ESG initiatives should be carried out effectively to have a positive impact on financial performance (Abdi et al., 2022). To make better investment decisions, external investors are increasingly considering the sustainability (ESG) performance of the company, and those companies with stronger sustainability performance have higher chances of getting better investors (El-Deeb et al., 2023). Managers should exert effective communication and disclosure of ESG performance to investors to attain solid investors for the company.

The main criteria of sustainable investment are integrating three dimensions of sustainability namely ESG. The ESG rating plays a major role in determining these aspects of sustainability in the investment (Popescu et al., 2021). The ratings provided by the several agencies vary and the information provided by them may not be enough to make effective decisions (Drempetic et al., 2020; Lee & Suh, 2022). Thus, investors and managers solely depending on the rating agencies for sustainable investment decisions may not achieve the true objective of engaging in sustainable investments. Moreover, it is not straightforward for managers to identify green projects since how projects are defined as green is still vague in the current financial system (Liu & Wu, 2023).

A relatively large amount of capital investment is required for sustainable/ green projects or initiatives (Edmans, 2023). To finance sustainable projects, green financial instruments were introduced. Green financial instruments are defined as 'private loan, public bonds (corporate, municipal and sovereign), private equity, public equity, investment funds and other financial instruments that fund environmental and climate-friendly projects such as renewable energy, recycling, and green infrastructure that supports the net-zero carbon economy and mitigate climate changes' (Liu & Wu, 2023). Companies are being stressed by several financial institutions and regulation authorities to adopt green financial policies (Bhandary et al., 2021). This implies that managers have to make appropriate changes in the financial system to incorporate green financial policies to attract investors and comply with demands from stakeholders. The International Monetary Fund categorizes some sustainable financial instruments that can be used to finance projects that will contribute a positive impact on the environment and social aspects (refer to Table 2 4) (Goel et al., 2022). The characteristics of these financial instruments are associated with ESG, and managers can utilize them to

Table 2.4. Sustainable Financing Instrument.

Instrument	Properties
Green Bonds	Specific bonds that are labelled green, with proceeds used for funding new and existing projects with environmental benefits.
Green Money Market Funds	Apply ESG factors to the investment of money market instruments.
Social Bonds	Bonds that raise funds for new and existing projects that create positive social outcomes.
Sustainable Bonds	Bonds with proceeds that are used to finance or refinance a combination of green and social projects.
Sustainability-Linked Bonds	Bonds that use proceeds for pre-defined ESG-related KPIs, targets, and periodic appraisals.
Green Mortgage-Backed Securities (MBS)	Green MBS securitise mortgages that go towards financing green properties.
Green Loans	Loans that have proceeds used to finance or refinance green projects, including other related and supporting expenditures such as R&D.
Sustainability Loans	Loan instruments and/or contingent facilities such as guarantees or letters of credit that incentivise the borrower to meet green or social projects.
Social Loans	Loan instruments that are used to finance eligible social projects.
Sustainability-Linked Loan	Loan instruments that incentivise the borrower to meet predetermined sustainability performance goals.

Source: Goel et al. (2022).

strengthen financial capabilities to invest in sustainable activities. One of the requirements of green/sustainable finance is the publication of information related to the company's sustainable performance to the capital market and related stakeholders (Liu & Wu, 2023). Thus, managers are compelled to identify effective approaches to embed sustainability and financial performance to disclose information related to green financing and capital utilization in the company.

3.4 Stakeholder Engagement for Sustainability

The common understanding of the fundamental principle of company strategy is to maximize shareholder wealth, but this has always been incompatible with the number of other stakeholders' interests (Okafor et al., 2021). Hence, the optimal strategy to achieve a company's financial target in the current context is to maximize the value of all stakeholders (Al Amosh et al., 2023). In shaping corporate culture, stakeholder engagement plays a key role which is subjected to the company's commitment to sustainability (Doni et al., 2022). Published stories that show company concern for different stakeholders' interests and gain attention from them will help companies to reduce and control costs (Freeman, 1984) which may also assist in increasing engagement of stakeholders.

For long-term value creation in the current financial system, stakeholders' engagement is a key component that managers have to take into consideration in policymaking and implementation. An effective approach that can have the right balance of all stakeholders' engagement is imperative due to the competitive pressure in the market (Stocker et al., 2020). It is not ample to consider only consumers as a mechanism to gain a competitive advantage in the consumer market. Demands and pressure from other stakeholders may affect consumer behaviour that directly and indirectly impacts the financial activities of the company. A better relationship with stakeholders is key to gaining competitive advantages (Rahi et al., 2022). Stakeholder engagement should be considered an opportunity to align ESG into financial management and process because stakeholder engagement encourages stakeholders to share their viewpoint on company sustainability and participate in formulating ESG reporting (Ardiana, 2023). However, managers are subject to face challenges in engaging stakeholders such as lack of participation of external stakeholders, less commitment and engagement unwillingness from internal stakeholders and barriers in organization structure and culture (Agyekum et al., 2023; Kaur & Lodhia, 2019). This may hinder the manager's devotion to involve stakeholders in sustainability initiatives.

4. Conclusion and Recommendation

With the development of sustainability and its integration into business, new challenges are likely to emerge. Managers have to be proactive and create effective strategies to tackle the challenges. Managers should understand that they have to confront the challenges while facing obstacles economically, politically, legally and technologically. The external environment is evolving rapidly affecting the companies' strategies, specifically financial strategies. The tension between shareholder interest and stakeholder interest leads to greater tension in managers on balancing all stakeholders' interests and expectations. Addressing these interests and expectations requires effective approaches to managing and allocating financial resources. The mindset of perceiving sustainable initiatives as additional expenses that will alienate investing in vital business operation activities needs to be changed. With the 2030 Agenda for Sustainable Development, managers are aligning their investments and strategies with ESG. Adopting the ESG metrics enables managers to measure sustainable performance.

Stakeholder theory and legitimacy theory assist in understanding sustainability and ESG integration in the current financial landscape. Stakeholder theory emphasizes building good relationships with all stakeholders by recognizing different expectations from stakeholders. According to stakeholder theory, if companies manage all stakeholders' interests effectively and robustly, they will be more sustainable. On the other hand, legitimacy theory focuses on a value system that connects the company and stakeholders. According to this theory, managers play the role of agents in the process to ensure the company activities and strategies align with stakeholders' expectations as it directs to gain legitimacy. Both stakeholder theory and legitimacy theory highly emphasize ESG disclosure to manage stakeholders and obtain legitimacy. Extant literature reviews show that this area has been attracting considerable interest from researchers and practitioners. The findings of past studies are not consistent and need more comprehensive studies in this area. Mainly, financial performance and the market value of the company are examined as outcomes of ESG performance. There is a scant mediating analysis in the field of ESG and finance. The challenges for managers in sustainability and ESG integration in the current financial system were discussed based on four prominent areas namely, the business case for sustainability, ESG metrics and reporting standards, sustainable investment criteria and finally stakeholder engagement for sustainability. Based on the analysis, the following recommendations are proposed for managers to overcome the challenges.

The association between ESG and companies' financial and non-financial performance can be strengthened by having high-quality audits, which also create credibility of financial and non-financial reporting (El-Deeb et al., 2023). Quality audit will assist in developing control mechanisms to reflect stakeholders' interest in company performance and reporting. The disclosure of accurate and consistent information with international standards is important for managers to ensure stakeholder engagement. Thus, proactive strategies to disclose sustainable and ESG information (El-Deeb et al., 2023) along with more policy measures (Aydoğmuş et al., 2022) may create additional benefits. Moreover, managers need to adopt more comprehensive ESG metrics that integrate vital business cases for the company. The current ESG metric is more favourable and supports the interest of executives rather than serving all stakeholder's interests (Liu & Wu, 2023). Hence, the business case matrix by SustainAbility, International Finance Corporation and Ethos Institute (2002) can be utilized to determine viable business cases by associating key sustainable factors (ESG) to a set of business success factors (or benefits) (refer Fig. 2.2). Additional techniques and tools that managers can use include a stakeholder map (De Micco et al., 2021) to identify important stakeholders and their expectations and risk

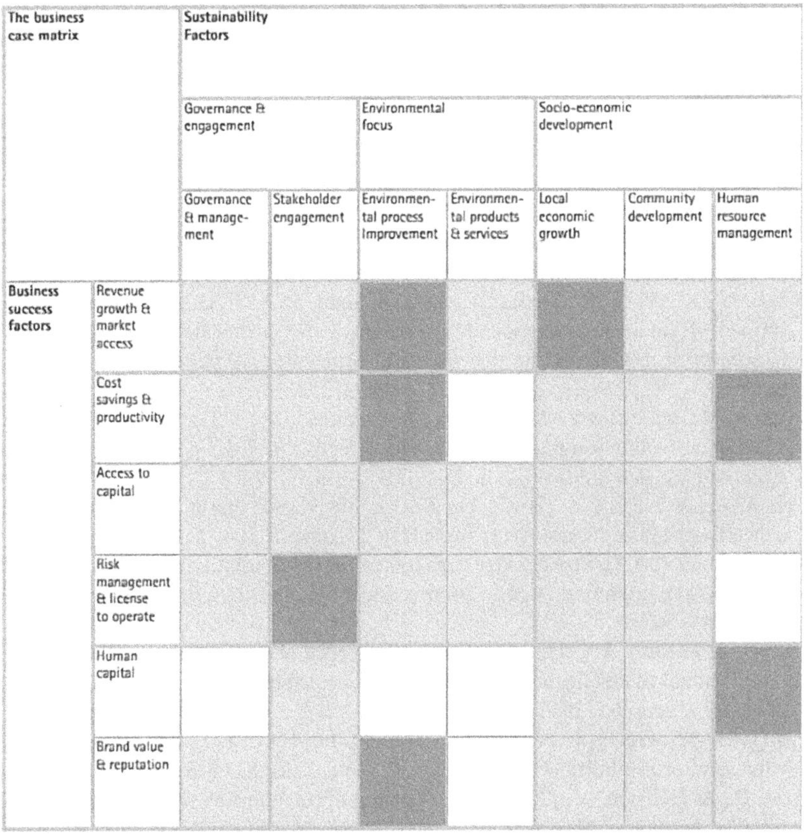

The business case matrix	Sustainability Factors						
	Governance & engagement		Environmental focus		Socio-economic development		
	Governance & management	Stakeholder engagement	Environmental process Improvement	Environmental products & services	Local economic growth	Community development	Human resource management
Business success factors — Revenue growth & market access							
Cost savings & productivity							
Access to capital							
Risk management & license to operate							
Human capital							
Brand value & reputation							

Fig. 2.2.   Business Case Metrics. *Source:* SustainAbility, International Finance Corporation, and Ethos Institute (2002).

management as a tool to manage unprecedented effects on the sustainability of the company (Haywood, 2022).

References

Abdi, Y., Li, X., & Càmara-Turull, X. (2022). Exploring the impact of sustainability (ESG) disclosure on firm value and financial performance (FP) in airline industry: The moderating role of size and age. *Environment, Development and Sustainability*, *24*, 5052–5079.

Ademi, B., & Klungseth, N. J. (2022). Does it pay to deliver superior ESG performance? Evidence from US S&P 500 companies. *Journal of Global Responsibility*, *13*(4), 421–449.

Agyekum, A. K., Fugar, F. D. K., Agyekum, K., Akomea-Frimpong, I., & Pittri, H. (2023). Barriers to stakeholder engagement in sustainable procurement of public works. *Engineering, Construction and Architectural Management, 30*(9), 3840–3857. https://doi.org/10.1108/ECAM-08-2021-0746

Al Amosh, H., & Khatib, S. F. (2022). Ownership structure and environmental, social and governance performance disclosure: The moderating role of the board independence. *Journal of Business and Socio-economic Development, 2*(1), 49–66.

Al Amosh, H., Khatib, S. F., & Ananzeh, H. (2023). Environmental, social and governance impact on financial performance: Evidence from the Levant countries. *Corporate Governance, 23*(3), 493–513.

Al-Issa, N., Khaki, A. R., Jreisat, A., Al-Mohamad, S., Fahl, D., & Limani, E. (2022). Impact of environmental, social, governance, and corporate social responsibility factors on firm's marketing expenses and firm value: A panel study of US companies. *Cogent Business & Management, 9*, 2135214.

Aluchna, M., Roszkowska-Menkes, M., & Kaminski, B. (2023). From talk to action: The effects of the non-financial reporting directive on ESG performance. *Meditari Accountancy Research, 31*(7), 1–25.

Aouadi, A., & Marsat, S. (2018). Do ESG controversies matter for firm value? Evidence from international data. *Journal of Business Ethics, 151*, 1027–1047.

Ardiana, P. A. (2023). Stakeholder engagement in sustainability reporting by Fortune Global 500 companies: A call for embeddedness. *Meditari Accountancy Research, 31*(2), 344–365.

Arte, P., & Larimo, J. (2022). Moderating influence of product diversification on the international diversification-performance relationship: A meta-analysis. *Journal of Business Research, 139*, 1408–1423.

Aydoğmuş, M., Gülay, G., & Ergun, K. (2022). Impact of ESG performance on firm value and profitability. *Borsa Istanbul Review, 22*(2), S119–S127.

Baret, P., & Helfrich, V. (2019). The "trilemma" of non-financial reporting and its pitfalls. *Journal of Management & Governance, 23*, 485–511.

Bhandary, R. R., Gallagher, K. S., & Zhang, F. (2021). Climate finance policy in practice: A review of the evidence. *Climate Policy, 21*(4), 529–545.

Billio, M., Costola, M., Hristova, I., Latino, C., & Pelizzon, L. (2021). Inside the ESG ratings: (Dis)agreement and performance. *Corporate Social Responsibility and Environmental Management, 28*(5), 1426–1445.

Bini, L., & Bellucci, M. (2020). *Integrated sustainability reporting.* Springer Books.

Brogi, M., & Lagasio, V. (2019). Environmental, social, and governance and company profitability: Are financial intermediaries different? *Corporate Social Responsibility and Environmental Management, 26*(3), 576–587.

Capar, N., & Kotabe, M. (2003). The relationship between international diversification and performance in service firms. *Journal of International Business Studies, 34*(4), 345–355.

D'Amato, A., & Falivena, C. (2020). Corporate social responsibility and firm value: Do firm size and age matter? Empirical evidence from European listed companies. *Corporate Social Responsibility and Environmental Management, 27*(2), 909–924.

Dakhli, A. (2021). Does financial performance moderate the relationship between board attributes and corporate social responsibility in French firms? *Journal of Global Responsibility, 12*(4), 373–399.

De Micco, P., Rinaldi, L., Vitale, G., Cupertino, S., & Maraghini, M. P. (2021). The challenges of sustainability reporting and their management: The case of Estra. *Meditari Accountancy Research, 29*(3), 430–448.

Doni, F., Corvino, A., & Martini, S. B. (2022). Corporate governance model, stakeholder engagement and social issues evidence from European oil and gas industry. *Social Responsibility Journal, 18*(3), 636–662.

Drempetic, S., Klein, C., & Zwergel, B. (2020). The influence of firm size on the ESG score: Corporate sustainability ratings under review. *Journal of Business Ethics, 167*, 333–360.

du Toit, E., van Zyl, R., & Schütte, G. (2017). Integrated reporting by South African companies: A case study. *Meditari Accountancy Research, 25*(4), 654–674.

Duque-Grisales, E., & Aguilera-Caracuel, J. (2021). Environmental, social and governance (ESG) scores and financial performance of multilatinas: Moderating effects of geographic international diversification and financial slack. *Journal of Business Ethics, 168*, 315–334.

Dyllick, T., & Hockerts, K. (2002). Beyond the business case for corporate sustainability. *Business Strategy and the Environment, 11*, 130–141.

Edmans, A. (2023). The end of ESG. *Financial Management, 52*(1), 3–17.

El-Deeb, M. S., Ismail, T. H., & El Banna, A. A. (2023). Does audit quality moderate the impact of environmental, social and governance disclosure on firm value? Further evidence from Egypt. *Journal of Humanities and Applied Social Sciences, 5*(4), 293–322.

Elkington, J. (1998). Accounting for the triple bottom line. *Measuring Business Excellence, 2*(3), 18–22.

Freeman, R. E. (1984). *Strategic management: A stakeholder approach.* Pitman.

Galeone, G., Onorato, G., Shini, M., & Dell'Atti, V. (2023). Climate-related financial disclosure in integrated reporting: What is the impact on the business model? The case of Poste Italiane. *Accounting Research Journal, 36*(1), 21–36.

Gillan, S. L., Koch, A., & Starks, L. T. (2021). Firms and social responsibility: A review of ESG and CSR research in corporate finance. *Journal of Corporate Finance, 66*, 101889.

Goel, R., Gautam, D., & Natalucci, F. (2022). *Working paper: Sustainable finance in emerging markets: Evolution, challenges, and policy priorities.* International Monetory Fund.

Haywood, L. K. (2022). Putting risk management into the corporate sustainability context. *Social Responsibility Journal, 18*(8), 1485–1504.

Kaur, A., & Lodhia, S. K. (2019). Key issues and challenges in stakeholder engagement in sustainability reporting: A study of Australian local councils. *Pacific Accounting Review, 31*(1), 2–18.

Lee, M. T., & Suh, I. (2022). Understanding the effects of Environment, Social, and Governance conduct on financial performance: Arguments for a process and integrated modelling approach. *Sustainable Technology and Entrepreneurship, 1*, 100004.

Li, Y., Gong, M., Zhang, X.-Y., & Koh, L. (2018). The impact of environmental, social, and governance disclosure on firm value: The role of CEO power. *The British Accounting Review, 50*(1), 60–75.

Liu, C., & Wu, S. S. (2023). Green finance, sustainability disclosure and economic implications. *Fulbright Review of Economics and Policy, 3*(1), 1–24.

Mattera, M., & Soto, F. (2023). Dodging the bullet: Overcoming the financial impact of Ukraine armed conflict with sustainable business strategies and environmental approaches. *The Journal of Risk Finance*, *24*(1), 122–142.

Menicucci, E., & Paolucci, G. (2023). ESG dimensions and bank performance: An empirical investigation in Italy. *Corporate Governance*, *23*(3), 563–586.

Mervelskemper, L., & Streit, D. (2017). Enhancing market valuation of ESG performance: Is integrated reporting keeping its promise? *Business Strategy and the Environment*, *26*(4), 536–549.

Minutolo, M. C., Kristjanpoller, W. D., & Stakeley, J. (2019). Exploring environmental, social, and governance disclosure effects on the S&P 500 financial performance, *28*(6), 1083–1095.

Mohammad, W. M., & Wasiuzzaman, S. (2021). Environmental, Social and Governance (ESG) disclosure, competitive advantage and performance of firms in Malaysia. *Cleaner Environmental Systems*, *2*, 100015.

Moloi, T., & Marwala, T. (2020). The legitimacy theory and the legitimacy gap. *Artificial Intelligence in Economics and Finance Theories*, 103–113.

Nekhili, M., Boukadhaba, A., & Nagati, H. (2021). The ESG–financial performance relationship: Does the type of employee board representation matter? *Corporate Governance: An International Review*, *29*(2), 134–161.

Okafor, A., Adeleye, B. N., & Adusei, M. (2021). Corporate social responsibility and financial performance: Evidence from U.S tech firms. *Journal of Cleaner Production*, *292*, 126078.

Picolo, J. D., Magro, C. B., Silva, T. P., & Bernardo, L. (2018). The influence of the financial slack on the economical performance of Brazilian and Chilean companies. *Cuadernos de economía*, *41*, 19–30.

Patten, D. M., & Shin, H. (2019). Sustainability Accounting, Management and Policy Journal's contributions to corporate social responsibility disclosure research: A review and assessment. *Sustainability Accounting, Management and Policy Journal*, *10*(1), 26–40.

Pizzi, S., Caputo, A., Corvino, A., & Venturelli, A. (2020). Management research and the UN sustainable development goals (SDGs): A bibliometric investigation and systematic review. *Journal of Cleaner Production*, *276*, 124033.

Popescu, I.-S., Hitaj, C., & Benetto, E. (2021). Measuring the sustainability of investment funds: A critical review of methods and frameworks in sustainable finance. *Journal of Cleaner Production*, *314*, 128016.

Qureshi, M. A., Kirkerud, S., Theresa, K., & Ahsan, T. (2020). The impact of sustainability (environmental, social, and governance) disclosure and board diversity on firm value: The moderating role of industry sensitivity. *Business Strategy and the Environment*, *29*(3), 1199–1214.

Rahi, A. F., Akter, R., & Johansson, J. (2022). Do sustainability practices influence financial performance? Evidence from the Nordic financial industry. *Accounting Research Journal*, *35*(2), 292–314.

Rahman, H. U., Zahid, M., & Al-Faryan, M. S. (2023). ESG and firm performance: The rarely explored moderation of sustainability strategy and top management commitment. *Journal of Cleaner Production*, *404*, 136859.

Ramanathan, S., & Isaksson, R. (2023). Sustainability reporting as a 21st century problem statement: Using a quality lens to understand and analyse the challenges. *The TQM Journal*, *35*(5), 1310–1328.

Ronalter, L. M., Poltronieri, C. F., & Gerolamo, M. C. (2023). ISO management system standards in the light of corporate sustainability: A bibliometric analysis. *The TQM Journal, 35*(9), 256–298.

Sancha, C., Gutierrez-Gutierrez, L., Tamayo-Torres, I., & Thomsen, C. G. (2023). From corporate governance to sustainability outcomes: The key role of operations management. *International Journal of Operations & Production Management, 43*(13), 27–49.

Sciarelli, M., Cosimato, S., Landi, G., & Iandolo, F. (2021). Socially responsible investment strategies for the transition towards sustainable development: The importance of integrating and communicating ESG. *The TQM Journal, 33*(7), 39–56.

Stocker, F., de Arruda, M. P., de Mascena, K. M., & Boaventura, J. M. (2020). Stakeholder engagement in sustainability reporting: A classification model. *Corporate Social Responsibility and Environmental Management, 27*(5), 2071–2080.

SustainAbility, International Finance Corporation, and Ethos Institute. (2002). *Developing Value the business case for sustainability in emerging markets.* SustainAbility Ltd.

United Nations. (2015). *Transforming our world: The 2030 Agenda for sustainable development.* United Nations. http://sustainabledevelopment.un.org/

World Commission on Environment and Development. (1987). *Our common future.* Oxford University Press.

Yoon, B., & Chung, Y. (2018). The effects of corporate social responsibility on firm performance: A stakeholder approach. *Journal of Hospitality and Tourism Management, 37*, 89–96.

Zamil, I. A., Ramakrishnan, S., Jamal, N. M., Hatif, M. A., & Khatib, S. F. (2023). Drivers of corporate voluntary disclosure: A systematic review. *Journal of Financial Reporting & Accounting, 21*(2), 232–267.

Zhou, G., Liu, L., & Luo, S. (2022). Sustainable development, ESG performance and company market value: Mediating effect of financial performance. *Business Strategy and the Environment, 31*(7), 3371–3387.

Chapter 3

Globalization and International Financial Strategies

Wu Weijian

Jingdezhen University, China

Abstract

This research looks at the difficulties managers have in adapting to the modern financial environment in the context of globalization. It looks at several topics related to international financial strategy, such as managing multinational teams, managing market entrance strategies, managing currency risk, adapting managerial style to a global workplace, adhering to international rules and assessing geopolitical risk. The study focuses special attention on the complexity involved in the decision-making process in terms of market entry tactics and currency risk management, drawing on an extensive literature review and real-world examples. It emphasizes the significance of effective communication and leadership styles when managing global teams, as well as the necessity of intercultural competency for managers to function in various cultural contexts. The study also looks at the significance of regulatory compliance for global corporate operations and how geopolitical risk affects investment choices. This report uses critical analysis to pinpoint the opportunities and problems brought about by globalization while offering managers practical advice on how to adapt to the shifting financial landscape.

Keywords: Globalization; market entry strategies; currency risk management; cross-cultural competence; regulatory compliance

1. Introduction

The financial landscape is continuously evolving due to globalization. Globalization means continuous intensification and expansion of economic, social, political, judicial and cultural relations across borders. Globalization is an ongoing process

Strategic Financial Management, 35–47
Copyright © 2024 Wu Weijian
Published under exclusive licence by Emerald Publishing Limited
doi:10.1108/978-1-83608-106-720241003

that shows a reduction in communication and transportation costs, liberalization in the market for goods and services, rise in new information technologies (Christensen & Kowalczyk, 2017). Globalization is changing the ways people work around the world. Further, companies are considering cross-border financial management strategies, which include currency risk management. The expansion in the global market creates challenges for managers in respect of currency risk and other factors like market entry or international regulations. The vast amount of opportunities are present, which also introduces barriers and challenges mainly for the managers when dealing with the international market.

The purpose of the study is to focus on the main theme 'Navigating the Modern Financial Landscape: Challenges for Managers'. The objective of the study is to focus on the topic of globalization and international financial strategies. The sub-topics that are covered in the study are market entry strategies, currency risk management techniques, managerial adaptations to global cultures, compliance with international regulations, managing multinational teams and geopolitical risk assessment. This study is segregated into three sections which consist of a literature review, a managerial perspective and a critical analysis. Further, the study also provides recommendations.

2. Literature Review

2.1 Market Entry Strategies

The past 30 years have brought significant changes in international market practices and research, which is driven by the increase in global competitiveness dynamics and international trade environments. Watson IV et al. (2018) observe that transactional international market entry (IME) approaches mainly focused on risk minimization and profit maximization for delivering products and services to the international market. Relational IME approaches relate to the strategies that tend to establish, develop and maintain mutually beneficial relationships among the exchange partners. Today, technological advances have helped businesses exploit and identify market opportunities in wider geographic locations. Further, Zachary et al. (2014) noted that the entrants need to consider diverse contingencies like resource capability commitment, risk exposure and control over the entry outcomes and processes. Thus, market entry strategies relate to the ways through which an organization enters a new market. From the perspective of the managers, the market entry strategy is important as it has an impact on the overall business, marketing, operations, human resources and finance.

Guercini and Milanesi (2022) observed that when considering foreign market entry, managers and entrepreneurs are required to make significant decisions related to the entry modes like the competitive strategy for a foreign market. This process of decision-making is challenging due to the uncertainty that is involved in the international expansion of the company as the foreign environment is complex and the domestic organization is less aware of the environment. Thus in this context, Hoskisson and Busenitz (2017) pointed out that the most common modes of entry consist of joint ventures, acquisitions and internal new ventures.

The author further notes that the corporate managers conclude that there needs to be adjustments or transforming themselves to keep with the pace of the environmental change and the competition increase.

However, corporate managers have to face challenges because the core competencies do not match or extend to the new development areas and the managerial incentive system. Besides, concerning entering a new market, strategic managers predict the future and consider that there are many complexities, which makes it difficult to know the appropriate response concerning entering a new market. In this context, Buckley and Casson (2009) noted the internationalization theory, which analyses the choices made by the managers, owners and trustees of the company. Theory shows that the choices are rational and highlights that the decision-maker can evaluate a set of options, have a goal through which these options can be ranked and also have the capability of identifying the top-ranked options and selecting the same. Along with the market entry strategy, international expansion also involves currency risk which is highlighted in the next section.

2.2 Currency Risk Management Techniques

Exchange rate risk management is a crucial part of the decision-making process of every organization related to foreign currency exposure. Papaioannou (2006) opines that currency risk hedging strategies have been used by managers to reduce or eliminate the risk related to the exchange rate which can impact operations. The selection of the appropriate hedging strategy is crucial as it consists of complexities in the accurate measurement of the current risk exposure and the decision related to the degree of risk exposure. Most of the multinational companies have risk committees that can manage the exchange rate risk. Issues related to currency risk management are crucial for the firms as they are managed through the underlying assets and liabilities. There are different types of exchange rate risk which consist of transaction risk, translation risk and economic risk.

Wever et al. (2012) stated that concerning large multinationals, it is a complex process for managers to obtain insights related to the exposed risks. Transaction risk relates to the cash flow risk, and it relates to the effect of exchange rate movement on the transactional account in respect of receivables. Changes in the exchange rate in the currency of the denomination can result in a direct transaction exchange rate risk to the organization. Translation risk consists of the balance sheet exchange rate risk. The translation risk of a foreign subsidiary consists of the measurement through the exposure to the net assets to the exchange rate movements. Economic risk mainly relates to the risk to the present value of future operating cash flows of the firm due to the exchange rate moments.

Managers apply different techniques for hedging against currency risk, which mainly relates to the future, forward contracts and options. For instance, tactical hedging is used by organizations for hedging the transaction currency risk which relates to the payable transactions or short-term receivables. On the other hand, strategic hedging has been used for transactions that relate to the long term. In this respect, Wahab et al. (2019) have considered analyzing foreign exchange exposure to Malaysian companies and their engagement with the heading activities. The study has identified that hedging is one of the most effective tools for managing the foreign exchange exposure. The study considered 123 non-financial Malaysian organizations and their decisions related to hedging from 2010 to 2017. The study has used multiple panel logistic regression analysis to evaluate the link between hedging practices and foreign exchange exposure. The results show that the organizations have given attention to foreign exchange exposure as it impacts the decision of the practice of hedging.

2.3 Managerial Adaptations to Global Cultures

The rewards and challenges of the management of cultural boundaries have increased due to the evolution of the global business context. Kai Liao et al. (2021) highlighted that cross-cultural competence is one of the major factors that has emerged and gained attention over a decade. The managers are required to have cross-cultural competence to avoid the failures of the multinational organization. It is observed that when the expatriates lack cross-cultural competence, then it can be difficult to adjust to the new environment, and the goals and objectives can be difficult to achieve. In this respect, cultural adaptability plays a crucial role, which is a process for adding new behaviours and skills, and the ability to utilize the positive behaviours in a new culture. It is observed that 'cultural adaptability' has a major role to play in interpersonal communication and also helps managers grow and survive in a new environment with unfamiliar values, customs and assumptions.

Brewster et al. (2018) have highlighted that as per Hofstede's theory, cultural patterns are dependent upon the value system of the population group and the ways through which it stabilizes. The author highlights the notions that are essential for the understanding of managerial reactions and behaviours. The cultural differences are included in the frame of reference of the managers and the ways through which they think of the specific values that can guide the managerial choices and actions. Thus, cultural values can be considered to be the influences on the ways through which managers make the decisions and perform the activities.

Hofstede theory shows the cultural differences in the ways individuals behave in the power distance situation. Kai Liao et al. (2021) highlighted that as per Hofstede, the cultural value of individuals can be measured through uncertainty avoidance, power distance, masculinity, individualism and long-term orientation. Individuals from different countries can consider their cultural values to be different, which can be because of the diverse ways through which people behave and think. It is observed that interactions and business communications between the host country and expatriates are failing because of cultural differences and the lack of core competencies for handling the differences. Thus, for improving cross-cultural performance and adjustment, it is required that the specific host country's national standards and values be maintained, and they should not be ignored by the expatriates.

2.4 Compliance With International Regulations

Global compliance relates to ensuring compliance with international rules and laws, along with the local rules and laws in the country in which the company operates. Chilton and Linos (2021) stated that there is no global legislation for setting rules, and there is no centralized enforcement body, mainly related to international law, to follow legal commitments. In this respect, Graham and Woods (2006) pointed out that self-regulation is considered by multinational companies for establishing a rule-based constraint on behaviour. The most important is the code of conduct that is provided by the industry associations or individual companies which involves another group of stakeholders and the commitment towards meeting minimum standards of social and environmental conduct. The author pointed out that developed state governments have supported the self-regulatory efforts of the corporate through the Organisation for Economic Co-operation and Development (OECD) guidelines for multinational enterprises that focus on inviting the companies to uphold principles of human rights, environmental conduct and labour rights across global operations.

It is observed that the organizations are encouraged to regulate their conduct according to the board and also agree to international standards where there is no government regulation present. Hence, multinational managers take an important role in the process of implementation of the global public policy. Further, it is reported that with the adoption and development of international standards, the companies will be able to control their conduct with utmost responsibility in comparison to the traditional state-level regulation.

Vigneau et al. (2014) stated that it is interesting to note the ways through which managers examine the standards that are used in day-to-day activities for developing an understanding related to the impact on intra-organizational management practices. The author has highlighted that there is a shift from the hard law which is formal sanctions and rules, towards the soft laws that consist of voluntary self-regulation. Soft law is characterized by the non-legal form of regulation at the global level. Today, multinational corporations have taken a greater place in playing different roles and responsibilities in the global environment. The new regime is helpful in the promotion of greater accountability in the companies as the organizations are voluntarily involved in self-regulation, which helps in the improvement of transparency. However, the author also noted that soft regulation is still under question and has been criticized by many for being less effective in comparison to government regulation mainly in the developed Nations. Besides, the compliance with international regulation is one of the concerns for the managers of the multinational organizations. When a firm considers expanding into the international market then the business is subjected to regulations and rules across countries. One of the major challenges for the managers relates to understanding the complex and vast regulatory landscape.

2.5 Managing Multinational Teams

International teams are one of the most common factors at all levels of the organizational hierarchy. Marketa (2022) states that cultural and national differences are one of the major issues or challenges for the team members as there are differences in the ways of thinking and social categorization, which also leads to the absorption of non-redundant information. On the other hand, the benefits of the international teams relate to making use of the differences in cognition and identity. As there are different identities, it has diverse teams in taping into the social knowledge of multiple cultural groups like the cultural codes and social norms. Another benefit is that international teams are more inclined towards drawing on identity-based differences like the international teams are more innovative and make better decisions. However, there are several challenges as well that the managers face.

One of the most common issues or challenges relates to effective communication for international teams. As there is diversity in the international teams, the team members are required to overcome both the language and the cultural barriers (Marketa, 2022). In the international teams, there is a lack of commonalities in the multinational teams. When there is high diversity in the multinational teams, then it creates challenges for the team members because of the lack of a meaning system and shared identity, for example, collaboration in a project with an individual who is difficult to communicate and tends to struggle in the interpretation of the meaning of the facial expressions. Another challenge relates to the type of tasks and categorizing the type of tasks. Overall, the author indicated the major challenges faced by the multinational teams are related to cross-cultural differences.

Sogancilar and Ors (2018) have also similar views and pointed out that in the case of multinational companies (MNCs), the major issues faced by the organizations relate to the management of cross-cultural differences. The major reason is that the culture influences the manager's attitude, technology transfer, relations in the company and other activities. In this setting, the major issue arises in the working environment, where individuals from diverse cultural backgrounds are starting to work together. The author also noted that there is a need for proper leadership styles, which the managers adopt for managing culturally diverse teams on the issues that the teams are facing, handling the problems consisting of cultural and language differences, miscommunication and misunderstanding. The author pointed out that due to diversity multicultural teams are more prone to facing challenges related to ineffective communication, language barriers and differences in communication styles. These challenges are common in most studies.

2.6 Geopolitical Risk Assessment

Geopolitical risks are the key determinant of the stock market dynamics and investment decisions, which are viewed by the market participants, entrepreneurs and central bank officials. Caldara and Iacoviello (2022) highlighted that the 'Bank of England' has considered the geopolitical risk to be policy uncertainty, which can have a significant negative impact on the economic effects. Recently, the International Monetary Fund, European Central Bank and the World Bank have highlighted the risks due to geopolitical tensions. For instance, out of 1,000 investors, about 75% of the participants reported worries related to the economic impact of different diplomatic and military conflicts. Further, Engle and Campos-Martins (2020) also highlighted related hedging and measuring geopolitical risks. The author noted that the measurement of geopolitical risk can be with the use of financial market prices that are considered to be including all the available information. Besides, the author also noted that geopolitical risk shows weak investment results.

3. Managerial Perspective: Examples and the Case Study

The above section highlights globalization and international financial strategies, which consist of market entry strategies, compliance with international regulations, currency risk management techniques and others. This chapter will highlight the managerial viewpoint, which consists of real-world examples, practical scenarios and case studies to highlight how managers in the financial industry are impacted by the challenges of globalization. In the case of market entry strategies, it is observed that the process of decision-making is challenging because of the uncertainty that is involved in the international expansion of the company as the foreign environment is complex (Guercini & Milanesi, 2022). In this respect, O'Brien (2015) pointed out a case study of market entry strategy failure. The case is 'McDonald's Jamaican Market Entry Failure'. The case highlights that after about 10 years of operations in Jamaica, McDonald's considered closing the stores. The case happened in 2005, where even though the company has been able to maintain its position for 10 years, it has been unable to maintain the long-term sustainability or growth of the business. The major reason observed in the case related to the failure of the challenging decision-making process as the international expansion of the organization has to go through a complex foreign environment. Similarly, in the case of McDonald's, the market entry strategy failed due to the uncertain business environment.

McDonald's is one of the most successful internationally recognized organization in the world, and the failure in Jamaica seems to be odd. It is observed that the lessons learnt through the failure of the company relate to the selection of new markets wisely. McDonald's entered the Jamaica market where Burger King and KFC had already been established and hence McDonald's faced tough competition (O'Brien, 2015). The customers in the country preferred the larger burgers of other brands in comparison to the McDonald's burgers. This shows that the company has failed in bringing new customers and managing the competition. Besides, this has been one of the reasons why McDonald's left Jamaica. Thus, the case study highlights that the decision-making process for managers is challenging due to the uncertainty in the business and the complex foreign environment.

Another major point in the globalization challenges for managers relates to the managerial adaptations to global cultures. The adaptation of the global culture is not only to understand the differences but also to find effective ways to leverage the same for the success of the business. The managers are required to be sensitive to the cultures and make sure that the communication styles and strategies are according to the local preferences. The above section from the literature pointed out that managers are required to have cross-cultural competence to avoid the failures of the multinational organization. Further, the culture values can be considered to be the influences on the ways through which the managers take the decisions and perform the activities. Besides, individuals from different countries can consider their cultural values to be different, which can be because of the diverse ways through which people behave and think.

Similarly, Molinsky and Moriarty (2016) noted that in a foreign culture, one of the most required skills relates to the development of the capability to translate, learn to speak new languages and master key phrases. The article highlights that the main difficulty point of the global adaptation relates to translating the corporate system and procedures in the processes, which means the ways through which the companies do the business in the globalized scenario. For example, one of the examples relates to the Fortune 100 organization, which implemented expat packages according to the number of individuals in the household that means a lower ranking staff who was married and had children could receive a larger housing allowance, in comparison to the higher ranking staffs, who are unmarried and have no children. The primary reason has been the assumptions related to being fair, as per the American culture who has been an individual that moves their family. However, in another aspect, in some of the high power distance markets like Asia mainly Thailand, Taiwan and Hong Kong, the policy can create conflicts among the managers or leaders which can provide confusing signals to the company related to who has more power and higher authority within the company. Thus, the major reason for such distinctive aspects is the cultural differences.

In respect of cultural differences, the literature highlighted that interactions and business communications between the host country and expatriates are failing because of the cultural differences and the lack of core competencies for handling the differences (Kai Liao et al., 2021). Similarly, Molinsky and Moriarty (2016) noted that provided the critical importance of the translation effects, the companies are required to make the leaders aware of the cultural differences. The article highlights that decision-makers of the organization are required to be well-aware of the core competencies and also the cultural differences, which needs focussing on building the cultural competencies and also the knowledge and ability at every level.

4. Critical Analysis

The above managerial perspective section pointed out with examples and case studies that the managers in international business face challenges. One of the major learnings is related to the management of competencies in the international market and also being well aware of uncertain and culturally diverse markets. The global provides opportunities for the introduction of the complexities in cultural adaptation, currency management and regulatory compliance. The managers are required to adapt to the inherent risk so that there can be a flexible strategy.

The literature points out that one of the most common issues or challenges relates to effective communication for international teams. Further, due to the diversity in the international teams, the team members are required to overcome both the language and the cultural barriers. In this respect, Harzing and Feely (2008) noted that cultural differences are one of the significant issues of doing business internationally which is accepted easily. The multinational teams are one of the crucial parts of the company. Jayanthi and Rajandran (2015) noted that the mixture of various people from different social backgrounds shows that the business environment is complex, and adapting the business leads to creating challenges related to sustainability. In this study, it is identified that the diverse multicultural group of people offers both challenges and opportunities to the organization. It is observed that unawareness of the culture, communication issues, perception issues and cultural diversity have an overall impact on the process of decision-making which is challenging for multinational teams.

It can be argued that the needs of the customers can be fulfilled with a heterogeneous team. Although there are several challenges for the managers, there are also opportunities presented. Doukanari et al. (2021) argue that the process of teamwork relates to influencing the learning experience, which is beneficial as teamwork practices provide learning opportunities. In a multicultural team, global members are required to follow similar processes, vision and values, and it needs to be in the same direction. The major opportunities for a multicultural team can be improved creativity. Iberdrola (2023) argues that there are different ideas and points of view of people that are coming from diverse backgrounds and have different education levels. When the experiences of people from different cultural backgrounds are put together, the result is related to a rich variety of ideas and approaches for solving specific issues. Another opportunity for a multicultural team relates to improvement in productivity and reputation.

One of the issues pointed out in the literature is issues of regulatory and legal compliance. Literature highlights that compliance with international regulation is one of the concerns for the managers of multinational organizations. However, an article on LinkedIn 'Accessing International Markets with a Compliance Management Strategy', highlighted that the global economy is offering multiple opportunities for companies that want to access new markets by following the standards and requirements related to regulations of each country. It is well unknown that the requirements and the regulations of the industries are continuously changing, and it is creating compliance challenges. One of the opportunities present in addressing the challenges related to international regulatory is compliance management. Regulatory compliance consists of the regulations, rules and standards that the company needs to satisfy legally for selling goods and services in a specific geographical location or country. Thus, achievement compliance consists of technical compliance, legal compliance and logistical compliance. Effective international compliance management can be beneficial in the early stages of the product design process, documenting everything, remaining alert to the changes, viewing compliance as an investment and finding a partner.

5. Conclusion

The purpose of the study was to focus on the main theme 'Navigating the Modern Financial Landscape: Challenges for Managers'. The objective of the study was focused on the topic of globalization and international financial strategies. In respect of market entry strategy, it is analyzed that the process of decision-making is challenging due to the uncertainty that is involved in the international expansion of the company as the foreign environment is complex, and the domestic organisation is less aware of the environment. Besides, the choices are rational and highlight that the decision-maker can evaluate a set of options, have a goal through which these options can be ranked and also have the capability of identifying the top-ranked options and selecting the same. Further, learnings from the case study show that in the case of McDonald's, the market entry strategy failed due to the uncertain business environment. The company has failed in bringing new customers and managing the competition. Thus, this has been one of the reasons why McDonald's left Jamaica.

For currency risk management techniques, there are different types of exchange rate risk which consist of transaction risk, translation risk and economic risk. Changes in the exchange rate in the currency of the denomination can result in a direct transaction exchange rate risk to the organization. Managers apply different techniques for hedging against currency risk, which mainly relates to the future, forward contracts and options. Hedging is one of the most effective tools for managing the foreign exchange exposure. Organizations have given attention to foreign exchange exposure as it impacts the decision of the practice of hedging.

In respect of globalization, challenges for the managers relate to the managerial adaptations to global cultures. Managers are required to be sensitive to the cultures and make sure that the communication styles and strategies are according to the local preferences. One of the most required skills relates to the development of the capability in translating, learning to speak new languages and mastering the key phrases. An example suggests that cultural differences need to be managed. The study identifies that a diverse multicultural group of people offers both challenges and opportunities to the organization. When the experiences of people from different cultural backgrounds are put together, the result is related to a rich variety of ideas and approaches for solving specific issues. Another opportunity for a multicultural team relates to improvement in productivity and reputation.

6. Practical Recommendations

It is recommended to follow the set of learnings from the study for the managers.

Continuous learning: As managers have increasing challenges related to the uncertain international business environment, market entry strategies and changing regulations, it is recommended that the managers focus on continuous learning. The managers of international companies are required to focus on that global business environment, which has diverse cultural effects, technological advancements and shifting regulatory landscapes. The first point is considering cross-cultural training. Cross-cultural training for managers can help in effectively respecting and understanding cultural differences, which can enhance collaboration communication, and decision-making processes. The recommendation is to engage in courses or workshops that can effectively focus on the cross-cultural management of communication. This can help the managers in facing challenges by allowing them to experience various cultural backgrounds. Other points that can be considered for continuous learning can be following compliance and regulatory updates, leadership and soft skills development, and technological advancements.

Engaging with local experts: Engagement with local experts in the international business environment can be one of the strategic moves for international companies. The first way we will be to find the right expert as it will be important for identifying the entities or the individuals that have high-quality track records in respect of the particular field. Recommendations can be conducting due diligence, checking references and seeking referrals before engaging with an expert in the local market. Other ways can be collaborative brainstorming and workshops, integrating local insights in the process of decision-making, leveraging local networks and maintaining open communication.

Embracing diversity: Embracing diversity can be one of the crucial aspects for international organizations that want to bring a broad range of perspectives, creativity, experiences and innovation into the process of decision-making. The first way can be through leadership commitment, where the diversity initiative can be helpful for the leaders. Recommendations can be to the managers to led by example, strategic goals, mission statement and company values. Another way can be comprehensive diversity training, where the recommendation can be conducting regular training for including elements like business case for diversity, cultural competence and others.

International regulatory compliance management: International regulatory compliance management can be effective in helping the managers from international companies to be able to follow the international and local regulations in the complex business environment. The recommendation can be developing a global compliance framework by outlining the policies, commitments, responsibilities and procedures of the company. Another recommendation is utilizing the technology for compliance management. Today in the current business, environment technology has been playing a major role. Technology is influencing the ways through which people work. Technology can monitor, automate and report compliance activities which can be helpful in efficient processes. Thus, the recommendation can be investing in some compliance management software, which can be effective in continuously tracking the changes in the regulation, generating details for auditing and also can be helpful in the management of compliance tasks. The last recommendation is conducting regular audits and assessments by complying with and identifying the gaps so that adjustments can be made.

References

Brewster, C., Mayrhofer, W., & Farndale, E. (2018). *Handbook of research on comparative human resource management* (2nd ed.). Edward Elgar Publishing. https://books.google.com.my/books?hl=zh-CN&lr=&id=8ChWDwAAQBAJ&oi=fnd&pg=PA48&dq=Reiche

Buckley, P. J., & Casson, M. C. (2009). The internalisation theory of the multinational enterprise: A review of the progress of a research agenda after 30 years. *Journal of International Business Studies, 40*(9), 1563–1580. https://doi.org/10.1057/jibs.2009.49

Caldara, D., & Iacoviello, M. (2022). Measuring geopolitical risk. *The American Economic Review, 112*(4), 1194–1225. https://doi.org/10.1257/aer.20191823

Chilton, A., & Linos, K. (2021). Preferences and compliance with international law. *Theoretical Inquiries in Law, 22*(2), 247–298. https://doi.org/10.1515/til-2021-0023

Christensen, B. J., & Kowalczyk, C. (2017). Introduction to globalization: Strategies and effects. *Globalizations*, 1–16. https://doi.org/10.1007/978-3-662-49502-5_1

Doukanari, E., Ktoridou, D., Efthymiou, L., & Epaminonda, E. (2021). The quest for sustainable teaching Praxis: Opportunities and challenges of multidisciplinary and multicultural teamwork. *Sustainability, 13*(13), 7210. https://doi.org/10.3390/su13137210

Engle, R. F., & Campos-Martins, S. (2020, September 1). Measuring and hedging geopolitical risk. https://papers.ssrn.com/sol3/papers.cfm?abstract_id=3685213

Graham, D., & Woods, N. (2006). Making corporate self-regulation effective in developing countries. *World Development, 34*(5), 868–883. https://doi.org/10.1016/j.worlddev.2005.04.022

Guercini, S., & Milanesi, M. (2022). Foreign market entry decision-making and heuristics: A mapping of the literature and future avenues. *Management Research Review, 45*(9). https://doi.org/10.1108/mrr-11-2021-0806

Harzing, A., & Feely, A. J. (2008). The language barrier and its implications for HQ-subsidiary relationships. *Cross Cultural Management: International Journal, 15*(1), 49–61. https://doi.org/10.1108/13527600810848827

Hoskisson, R. E., & Busenitz, L. W. (2017). Market uncertainty and learning distance in corporate entrepreneurship entry mode choice. *Strategic Entrepreneurship*, 151–172. https://doi.org/10.1002/9781405164085.ch8

Iberdrola. (2023). *We drive the creation of multicultural teams in our search for a global corporate culture*. Iberdrola. https://www.iberdrola.com/talent/multicultural-teams

Jayanthi, M., & Rajandran, R. (2015). *Diversity challenges: From multicultural team perspective*. https://scholar.googleusercontent.com/scholar?q=cache:cA9lPvcLcvIJ:scholar.google.com/+JAYANTHI

Kai Liao, Y., Wu, W.-Y., Dao, T. C., & Ngoc Luu, T.-M. (2021). The influence of emotional intelligence and cultural adaptability on cross-cultural adjustment and performance with the mediating effect of cross-cultural competence: A study of expatriates in Taiwan. *Sustainability, 13*(6), 3374. https://doi.org/10.3390/su13063374

Marketa, R. (2022). *Managing International Teams: How to address the challenges and realize the benefits of National Diversity in a Team under a Creative Commons Attribution-NonCommercial-ShareAlike 4.0 International License (CC BY-NC-SA 4.0)*. https://libres.uncg.edu/ir/uncg/f/M_Rickley_Managing_2022.pdf

Molinsky, A., & Moriarty, R. (2016, October 7). Adapting your organizational processes to a new culture. *Harvard Business Review*. https://hbr.org/2016/10/adapting-your-organizational-processes-to-a-new-culture?registration=success

O'Brien, B. (2015, June 5). *4 lessons learned from famous market entry failures*. Trade Ready. https://www.tradeready.ca/2015/trade-takeaways/4-lessons-learned-famous-market-entry-failures/

Papaioannou, M. G. (2006). Exchange rate risk measurement and management: Issues and approaches for firms. *SSRN Electronic Journal.* https://doi.org/10.2139/ssrn.947372

Sogancilar, N. & Ors, H. (2018). Understanding the challenges of multicultural team management. *Journal of Business Economics and Finance, 7*(3), 259–268. https://dergipark.org.tr/en/pub/jbef/issue/39653/469246

Vigneau, L., Humphreys, M., & Moon, J. (2014). How do firms comply with international sustainability standards? Processes and consequences of adopting the global reporting initiative. *Journal of Business Ethics, 131*(2), 469–486. https://doi.org/10.1007/s10551-014-2278-5

Wahab, A., Rahim, A., & Janor, H. (2019). Role of foreign exchange exposure in determining hedging practises in Malaysia. *International Journal of Economics and Management, 13*(1), 79–91. http://www.ijem.upm.edu.my/vol13no1/6)%20Role%20of%20Foreign%20Exchange%20Exposure.pdf

Watson, G. F., Weaven, S., Perkins, H., Sardana, D., & Palmatier, R. W. (2018). International market entry strategies: Relational, digital, and hybrid approaches. *Journal of International Marketing, 26*(1), 30–60. https://doi.org/10.1509/jim.17.0034

Wever, M., Wognum, N., Trienekens, J., & Omta, O. (2012). Managing transaction risks in interdependent supply chains: An extended transaction cost economics perspective. *Journal on Chain and Network Sciences, 12*(3), 243–260. https://doi.org/10.3920/jcns2012.x214

Zachary, M. A., Gianiodis, P. T., Payne, G. T., & Markman, G. D. (2014). Entry timing. *Journal of Management, 41*(5), 1388–1415. https://doi.org/10.1177/0149206314563982

Chapter 4

Financial Risk Management in the Digital Age

Zhang Xiaoqi[a] and Muhammad Ali[b]

[a]UCSI University, Malaysia
[b]Taylor's University, Malaysia

Abstract

The financial industry is becoming more intelligent and digital, and the adoption of new technologies is promoting financial innovation while making financial security subject to disruption. Internet finance, as a product of the rapid development of information technology and the financial industry, has ushered in major changes in the development of the financial industry. The application of new technologies in the financial sector will bring about the development of intelligent investment consulting businesses for financial institutions The development of such a business reduces the threshold at which a customer can obtain financial services and improves the convenience and accessibility of financial services. Under the complex domestic and international economic situation, enterprises need to pay attention to financial risks and reasonably control financial risks. Applying blockchain technology to supply chain financial risk management has a natural match for solving the traditional difficulties in supply chain risk. This chapter mainly describes the types, assessment methods and existing problems of financial risks, as well as the prevention and control of network security risk management and Internet financial risk management arising therefrom, and also involves stress testing and scenario planning, blockchain-based financial risk management and risk culture, among which financial risk assessment and Internet financial risk management are mainly the content. With the help of information technology, we can effectively identify and prevent all kinds of risks and effectively promote the sustainable and healthy development of the financial industry.

Keywords: Financial risk; Internet financial risk; risk management; stress testing; risk culture

Strategic Financial Management, 49–69
doi:10.1108/978-1-83608-106-720241004

1. Introduction

After integrating with new technology, the financial industry is becoming more intelligent and digital, and fintech has recently emerged as the most significant area of financial innovation. On the other hand, the adoption of new technology exposes network security to subversive influence and significant impact. As a result of these vulnerabilities becoming more widely known, the security issue becomes more serious, making it necessary to redefine regulatory boundaries. Network security has improved in terms of the legal framework, new systems and technological specifications as a result of the new technology (Duan et al., 2022).

Internet finance, as a product of the rapid development of information technology and the financial industry, has become an effective supplement to the traditional financial industry, making the development of the financial sector usher in major changes. The arrival of the big data era has promoted the continuous development of various industries and also brought greater opportunities for the development of Internet finance but also further aggravated the risks of Internet finance. With the help of big data and other information, technology can realize the effective identification and analysis of all kinds of risks of Internet finance, and on this basis, it can formulate scientific risk prevention strategies and effectively promote the sustainable and healthy development of the Internet financial industry.

Under the complex domestic and international economic situation, enterprises need to pay attention to financial risks and reasonably control financial risks. Otherwise, enterprises will easily fall into the survival and development crisis and hinder their development. Financial risk management involves a lot of work, so enterprises need to combine financial risk management matters, build financial risk management programs and comprehensively control financial risks. In the process of operation, it is necessary for enterprises to appropriately reduce commercial loans to avoid the emergence of major financial risks, which in turn jeopardize their healthy development.

Blockchain technology, due to its revolutionary data storage and dissemination characteristics, has been used in many fields, especially in the financial aspect, showing an obvious bright future for various operations of banks. Applying blockchain technology to supply chain financial risk management, the combination of both features and needs has a natural match for solving the traditional difficulties in supply chain risk.

The development of digital finance can play a good complementary role to the insufficiency of enterprise credit, which can solve the trust problem between the two parties of transactions in the financial field and reduce the cost of obtaining information for financial market participants to promote the development of inclusive fintech does not only play a role in the process of development to reduce the operating costs but also plays a role in the development of fintech technology to increase the efficiency of financial operations, which is the principle that the development of fintech follows. The development of such a business reduces the threshold at which a customer can obtain financial services and improves the convenience and accessibility of financial services.

The need for organizations and regulators to invest significant time and resources in understanding the significance of risk culture as a driver of risk-appropriate behavior has been brought to light by global and national crises in the finance sector (Osman & Lew, 2021). These crises highlighted concerns with inadequate risk management systems and controls as well as inadequate institutional attitudes toward risk, which resulted in substantial losses, institutional failures and a decline in public confidence.

The phenomenon of shadow banking of non-financial enterprises stems mainly from the imbalance between the development of the financial sector and the real sector and the irrational layout of financing. This serious mismatch between the rapid development of the financial sector and the slow development of the real economy shows that the financial sector has not fully performed its function of serving the real economy. Not only has it failed to promote the rational allocation of resources and enhance market vitality but it has also accumulated systemic risks under high leverage. In this case, the rate of return of the financial sector is much higher than that of the real sector.

2. Modern Risk Assessment Techniques

2.1 Concept of Financial Risk

Financial risk refers to risks related to finance, such as financial market risk, financial product risk, financial institution risk and so on. If financial risk occurs in the operation of financial institutions, it is not only easy to affect their stable development but also easy to spread to the whole financial market, leading to the collapse of the financial system (Wang, 2021). In addition, financial risks can also occur when enterprises are unable to regulate their business activities well so the enterprises themselves face economic losses and affect their business efficiency.

2.2 Types of Financial Risk

First, interest rate risk. Yield risk, option risk and pricing risk are all risks arising from changes in interest rates. Analyzed from the perspective of yield risk, if interest rates become higher, the cost of business activities will increase, thus giving rise to yield risk. Analyzing from the perspective of risky options, some enterprises lack an understanding of the relationship between options and interest rates, and if interest rates change, enterprises are likely to experience operational problems, thus reducing their level of operating income or even preventing them from operating normally (Aven & Renn, 2009). Analyzed from the perspective of pricing risk, after the change in interest rates, enterprises need to re-pricing products and services, which will lead to a large difference from the original time, thus increasing the probability of financial risk. Second, market risk. The entire operation of the enterprise in the market environment, if the market risk, it is easy to affect the development of business operations. For the enterprise for inflation is difficult to sell goods, thus affecting sales and economic benefits, and in the deflationary market, economic environment will reduce the amount of money in the market, affecting the normal operation of the enterprise. Third, the exchange rate risk. In the case of exchange rate changes, enterprises are very prone to translation risk, resulting in book losses, which is not conducive to ensuring their level of economic development (Xinyue, 2021).

Financial risk can be categorized into systemic and non-systemic risk according to the nature of the risk and the response to it. Quantitatively financial risk is equal to the sum of the two. First of all, systemic risk is what people call macro-risk; usually, it is the global factors that lead to changes in investment returns, such risk will also have an impact on the returns of foreign exchange, securities and other financial investments, is any investor to bear and it is difficult to avoid. Non-systematic risk, on the other hand, refers to the micro-risk, and the entire financial investment market is not necessarily linked (Bryce, et al., 2016). It is the risk brought about by the individual financing subject's unique situation, which has nothing to do with the market as a whole. This is a type of risk that can spread the investment risk through the investment operation, so it is possible to carry out reasonable control and management of non-systematic risk, and then effectively reduce the possibility of financial investment for the enterprise to bring risk and increase economic benefits.

2.3 Financial Risk Assessment Methods and Existing Problems

The management of financial risk is the most important part of the financial investment management of enterprises and is of great significance to the financial security of enterprises. Financial risk assessment is the most important part of financial investment management, the correct assessment of risk can give the enterprise a full understanding of the risk and understanding, to a large extent, can help the enterprise to effectively avoid financial risk, reduce the financial loss of the enterprise and enhance the enterprise's return on investment (Gungoraydinoglu & Öztekin, 2022). Enterprise financial risk assessment refers to the financial risk before or when the risk occurs, the impact of the risk event and the possibility of loss of property for quantitative assessment work. That is, risk assessment is to carry out specific numerical statistics, the degree of loss and the impact of funds to clarify and measure.

2.3.1 Assessment Methods

2.3.1.1 Beta Coefficient Measurement Methodology. The β coefficient, also known as the β coefficient balance method, is a commonly used indicator for measuring market risk, i.e. systematic risk, according to the capital asset pricing model, which is the degree of risk in the capital market. Its advantage lies in the use of mathematical and statistical theories with a strong scientific basis and can express the linear relationship between the expected return of a risky asset and the market risk it bears (Bavoso, 2021). β coefficient can be used to measure the volatility of individual securities or portfolios of securities relative to the overall market.

2.3.1.2 Mean–Variance Measures. The magnitude of risk depends on the magnitude of uncertainty, and in measuring risk since risk reflects the deviation of actual loss or return from expected loss or return, we can measure it with the help of some mathematical indicators. Variance reflects the degree of dispersion of a random variable from mathematical expectations, defining the risk of an investment as the deviation of the actual rate of return from the expected rate of return (Bao et al., 2019). The standard deviation can be used to measure the extent to which a measurement deviates from the mean. The larger the standard deviation, the greater the deviation, the more dispersed the data and the greater the likelihood of larger losses. However, when there is a significant difference between two sets of data, the standard deviation alone cannot distinguish the magnitude of the risk, and the coefficient of variation is used to compare the dispersion of the data (Perron, 1990). Typically, the coefficient of variation varies in the same direction as the likelihood of risk, the smaller the coefficient of variation, the less likely a significant risk will occur and the greater the risk.

2.3.1.3 VaR Methodology. VaR (Value at Risk) refers to the value at risk of financial security or a portfolio of financial assets if a loss occurs during normal fluctuations in the financial markets, and the maximum possible loss is the value at risk (Buckshaw, 2008). It can also be understood that under a certain confidence level if a financial asset is likely to incur a loss in a certain period in the future, the maximum amount of its loss is the insured value. the formula for the VaR measurement method is $\text{Prob}(\Delta p > \text{VaR}) = 1 - c$. When utilizing this method to conduct a risk assessment, it is necessary to select the appropriate parameters.

2.3.2 Problems With the Assessment

All three methods mentioned above have some problems in practice, which will have an impact on the correct assessment of financial risks. First, due to the differences in sample data and theoretical foundations, there may be bias when assessing the same financial investment program (SKYbrary, 2021). For example, when using the ranking method to compare and analyze different financial investment risks, the beta coefficient measure and the mean–variance assessment method, the measured results are likely to be in conflict and the situation in which the assessment results deviate from the actual risk situation occurs. Second, no matter which risk assessment technique is used, a certain amount of sample data must be selected, which is only a representative of the sample as a whole, and the selection of the sample has a different focus (Bavoso, 2021), which will lead to different investors to grasp risk-related information for different purposes, which will have a significant impact on risk assessment.

2.4 Recommendations for Assessment Methodology

2.4.1 Combining Qualitative and Quantitative Analysis

When carrying out financial investment risk assessment, in addition to using various risk measurement models to quantitatively analyze the size or degree of risk, it is also necessary to combine effective qualitative analysis methods to evaluate risk (Yu & Wei, 2019). Commonly used qualitative analysis tools include the risk map evaluation method, risk degree evaluation method and management scoring method. The risk map evaluation method is most commonly used in the qualitative assessment of financial investment risks.

2.4.2 Stress Testing of VaR Calculation Models

Stress testing is an important part of the risk management process and is a scenario analysis method, where some unfavorable market environments are hypothesized so that the value at risk of an asset or portfolio of assets in that environment can be calculated and the possible change in value can be assessed (Posch, 2020). Once a reasonable scenario has been validated, the financial institution will take appropriate measures to mitigate the impact of the unfavorable scenario on itself.

3. Cybersecurity Risk Management

3.1 Risks and Challenges Facing Internet Finance in the Context of Big Data

The development of Internet finance should not only be carried out from the perspective of the soundness of its service functionality, but also strengthen risk management, and it is necessary to clarify the content of different aspects of the risk, to specifically put forward a reasonable solution strategy.

3.1.1 Risks of Basic Technology and Business Development

The acceleration of the speed of information flow, the need to find and store massive amounts of information, and the relevant financial content need to be in a large number of network information queries, to a large extent, increasing the workload of information collectors, need to use the professional management platform system for effective search (Adla & Frendi, 2021). The lack of technology has caused more problems in information protection, and many financial institutions are actively studying these information leakage problems and optimizing the application of various technologies. The financial industry is characterized by a certain degree of exhibition and logic, and when carrying out Internet innovation, the work in data and information analysis needs to be more careful. Financial institutions typically construct their own data centers because they must maintain the security of their information services (Kemp, 2017). Thus, when the banking and securities industries grow quickly, information security concerns also do so. As a result, managers are increasingly worried about data security and service access efficiency (Refer Fig. 4.1).

3.1.2 Integrity Risk

The integration of the financial industry and the Internet has led to the innovative development of Internet financial enterprises. In earlier times, the development of

Fig. 4.1.   Financial Data Life Cycle Management. *Source:* Author's work.

Internet financial enterprises would utilize debts, and to increase earnings and expand the scale of the enterprise, it is necessary to constantly add new projects and investors to ensure the conservation of the enterprise's capital flow (Fan, 2022). However, the addition of too many investors can cause unsuitable claims to be introduced without effective screening, causing problems in the development of Internet finance. Based on this kind of situation, because the credit audit and assessment work of the Internet financial enterprises is not in place, the corresponding selection standard is insufficient, and the rough credit evaluation management work has led to the development of Internet financial enterprises with risks in terms of integrity (Niu* et al., 2019), and the risk of credit defaults and frauds is also increasing under the successive influence.

Another thing that needs to be paid attention to is the problem of legal risk. In the working environment of Internet financial enterprises, the content of legal risk is mainly manifested in the virus invasion of the internal network and the use of the Internet platform by all kinds of lawless elements and hackers to damage and tamper with information financial transactions, steal and transfer funds to achieve the purpose of money laundering (Werbach, 2018). The emergence of such legal risks can cause Internet financial enterprises to face greater risks of capital loss and even the phenomenon of corporate bankruptcy, which undermines the stability of social and economic development.

3.1.3 Policy and Management Content Risk

Internet financial enterprises cooperate with various banks, and a lot of funds for trusteeship, but only the form of trusteeship, in the payment link, the investor's funds are still stored in the enterprise's account opened in the bank, and did not detach from the Internet enterprise, and the bank to produce the storage link, there is still the risk of misappropriation of the enterprise, and the corresponding supervisory and management work is missing, management mechanism is not sound enough, so that the funds storage problems occur with a higher probability (Chinazzi et al., 2013). Many financial enterprises will choose to advertise to expand their popularity, spend a lot of money to improve their credibility with the authority of well-known media, set up branches and affiliates in different regions, broaden their service surface, attract more investors and social masses, provide funds for investment or blind consumption and provide more loopholes for lawless elements to commit economic crimes(Hasan et al., 2021), which results in the development of Internet financial enterprises or organizations not in line with the social and economic development of the Internet, which results in the development of Internet financial enterprises or organizations not in line with the social and economic development of the Internet. The development of organizations and institutions does not meet the requirements of the social and economic market (Gelles, 2016). In addition, due to insufficient supervision and control by the relevant units, no supervision and control have been carried out on the relevant Internet financial platforms, and during their operation and development, the risks of capital management cannot be detected in time, leading to the further spread of more risks.

A high-risk security incident that worries financial organizations and their regulators is the leakage of sensitive data. The characteristics of high data sensitivity and high black market value will encourage the incidence of malicious data leakages events, such as theft and other network attacks and purposeful behavior of internal staff, for financial institutions due to their unique industry background (Kang et al., 2021). Additionally, when internal people use network platforms for data transmission and storage, such as cloud discs, libraries and code warehouses, they frequently leak sensitive internal data to the public network as a result of carelessness or data insensitivity.

3.2 Prevention and Control of Internet Financial Risk Management in Big Data Environment

To make the development of Internet financial enterprises or institutions more reasonable and scientific, so that their development is sustainable, it is necessary to carry out effective risk management from different development perspectives, combined with the social reality, implement a variety of management policies and then realize the reduction of risk.

3.2.1 Establishment of a Sound Risk Prevention System

Financial institutions in the digital age should fully define the main content, scope, responsibility and specific units of responsibility for Internet financial risk management and then establish a sound risk prevention system on this basis. In this process, the Internet financial risks and their impact should be scientifically assessed, and the transparency of risk management should be accurately grasped to effectively reduce the negative impact of risk and loss (Brignoli et al., 2021). In addition, it is necessary to comprehensively implement the pre-risk control measures, the relevant institutions and departments should comprehensively analyze the characteristics of Internet finance and its main types of risk, improve the scientific and targeted nature of risk prediction, risk identification, risk analysis, risk prevention and adhere to the perspective of pre-control to build a perfect Internet financial risk prevention system, to provide the necessary decision-making support for the further implementation of risk prevention and then comprehensively improve the effect of risk identification and prevention and provide the necessary guarantee for the development of Internet finance in the era of big data (Tikk, E.,2021).

3.2.2 Create the Ideal Regulatory Framework for Network Security

Some nations create third-party entities to oversee the risk assessment and vulnerability of financial institutions' data security capabilities. Countries also continue to promote financial data safety standards and improve the highest level of domestic financial data security (Kang et al., 2021). Digital currency and other encrypted assets have come under the scrutiny of financial network security supervision due to the advancement of digital technology (Varga et al., 2021). Global regulation of private or corporate issuing of non-sovereign digital currencies is likewise more strict. The ongoing monitoring of financial network security supervisory measures is a result of the digital transformation of the financial infrastructure. International financial supervision is more concerned with the growth of the financial infrastructure of the financial industry as a result of the deepening financial technology scenario, the digital transformation of financial infrastructure areas like the settlement of the clearing, the settlement of securities and the network system, as well as the continuous acceleration of the digital transformation of the financial sector (Bat & Houben, 2020).

3.2.3 The Emphasis of Financial Network Security Management Is on the Use of Technology

Network encryption security protocol SSL, SET, firewall technology and intrusion detection technology (IDS) are some of the network financial security technologies that are evolving along with the network. The log is processed by the local traffic manager using the SSL and decryption mechanism (Gelles, 2016). The site's load balancing software can load balance the web front server, application server, database server, cache server and other servers all at once.

The security protection of all types of servers is the key to the customer's main concern, and it is advised that they be protected by a web firewall, use a security audit platform to alarm all types of database operations, data table calls and modified actions (Wang & Wang, 2022) and make sure that a lot of users can audit the database in their current circumstances. The user account and password for the online trading system are protected by the dynamic password authentication method.

3.2.4 Strengthen the Ability to Apply Big Data

Internet financial enterprises should make full use of big data, the Internet, artificial intelligence and other information technologies to collect, analyze and process a wide range of various types of risk information data, based on which they can form a database of Internet financial risk information and realize effective prevention and control of risks, to fully ensure the safe operation and cost-effectiveness of Internet finance in the context of big data and form an operable report for further implementation of the risk prevention to provide the necessary reference (Wen, 2019). At the same time, Internet financial enterprises should make full use of the big data software system to carry out comprehensive and accurate analysis of all kinds of investment portfolios and to improve the quality of Internet financial investment. In addition, Internet financial enterprises should make full use of the view and automation mode to realize effective identification and prediction of Internet financial risks and implement targeted risk prevention measures on this basis (Wang, 2021).

3.2.5 Cultivate Professional Internet Financial Risk Management Personnel

To improve the quality of Internet financial risk management, talents more in line with the needs of the industry are needed to make significant contributions so that the safety and reliability of Internet finance can be improved. Therefore, what needs to be paid attention to is the skills training for new and old employees, according to the characteristics of different work groups, setting up appropriate skills training strategies and then strengthening the overall service capacity of Internet financial institutions, to avoid more financial risks (Li, 2021). The generation of professional talents not only requires the improvement of training programs and measures but also requires a corresponding assessment system as a constraint to check the staff's learning at the right time and to improve the quality of the Internet financial risk management work.

4. Scenario Planning and Stress Testing

4.1 Stress Testing

Bank managers need to estimate potential losses to consider the level of capital that banks must hold to meet the liquidity needs of their customers and creditors. Stress testing is currently used as a risk management tool by many financial institutions to determine the extent to which stress in a given scenario affects the value of their portfolios (Lu et al., 2019). For example, commercial banks use stress tests to weigh the risks inherent in their portfolios against their expected returns. Nonetheless, stress testing also enables policymakers to assess a bank's resilience to macroeconomic shocks and to ensure that sufficient capital is available to deal with these shocks. Having sufficient capital not only protects banks from the risk of insolvency but also prevents a banking crisis from spreading into an overall economic crisis, so although stress tests are usually conducted at the level of individual financial institutions, central banks are also interested in aggregate stress tests because monetary authorities are more concerned about the stability of the financial system as a whole than they are about individual banks or portfolios (Abdolshah et al., 2020).

4.2 Scenario Usage

Central banks can assess the risk tolerance of the banking system under different scenarios through aggregate stress tests. While the purpose of stress tests for commercial banks is to determine how much risk is acceptable for a given level of expected return on a portfolio, central banks conduct stress tests to analyze structural vulnerabilities in the financial system as a whole. These aggregate stress tests are important for monetary authorities because it allow them to fully understand these vulnerabilities, enabling them to take countermeasures to avoid financial crises that would have repercussions for the economy as a whole (Kalirai & Scheicher, 2002).

Thus, these scenarios can serve as a guide for policymakers and financial markets in developing business strategies, helping to shape market expectations and realizing benefits from all aspects of the transition. To be effective, scenario users must be able to predict future narratives and the range of potential outcomes that could occur given the economic-social–climate nexus and possible policy actions. This can also help financial institutions optimize their strategic decisions relative to the market to benefit from and support the transition (Hopkin, 2017). For short- and medium-term business planning by financial institutions, scenarios should reflect reasonably expected scenarios that are central to the distribution. This is to provide insights into tactical business decisions. Most high-level scenarios provide limited insights into the effects of transformation at a more granular level, such as between individual firms or institutions that behave differently in the broader system, and therefore often need to be complemented with other data and analysis for a more refined assessment.

In contrast, for stress testing and broader financial risk management purposes, scenarios should reflect plausible worst-case scenarios, which are located in the tails of the distribution (Kemp, 2017). This is to ensure that balance sheet risk is captured under classical financial risk logic. Such scenarios need to be inherently different from the central case or best-case scenarios used for long-term planning (Baer et al., 2023). However, most scenarios explored by financial institutions for risk management purposes are long-term scenarios that do not reflect the associated transition dynamics and volatility and thus are unlikely to make a meaningful difference to financial risk outcomes when used by financial institutions to inform risk management and may miss the big picture of associated tail risks.

5. Financial Risk Management Methods with Blockchain Technology

5.1 Problems Faced by Supply Chain Finance Risk Management Methods Before Using Blockchain Technology

The risk management measures of traditional supply chain finance are inherited from ordinary credit risk management experience, and combined with the practical experience of banks in supply chain finance, they have a certain degree of rationality and effectiveness (Abbasi et al., 2019). However, unlike ordinary credit, supply chain finance involves a large number of enterprises and institutions, complex types of actual supply chains and variable contract documents, which requires more prominent personalized and differentiated characteristics of the management measures of supply chain finance and creates more pressure and higher costs for the banks' supply chain finance risk control management.

5.1.1 Information Asymmetry

Various risk management measures taken by the bank in the supply chain financial business are essentially through the investigation to obtain information, summarize and analyze the data and then according to the information obtained to take corresponding risk management means, so the acquisition of accurate and timely information is the essential requirement of supply chain financial risk management (Rijanto, 2021). Compared with general credit, the information asymmetry phenomenon existing in each link is not eliminated or weakened but increased. Because supply chain finance involves more participants, longer processes and more complicated situations. The supply chain production enterprises, assessment organizations and logistics companies, including various subjects, each master their subject information, but the data lack effective means of mutual communication, the bank to the scattered and messy data collected without error, need to pay more human and material resources (Renduchintala et al., 2022).

From another point of view, in the risk management of supply chain finance, banks have a primitive way of obtaining information and recognizing risks, and it is difficult to understand the whole picture of supply chain flow and the real operation situation of enterprises. Meanwhile, in the process of information transmission, there is the possibility of tampering and falsification due to human operation, and moral risk still exists (Bryant & Camerinelli, 2013). In addition, when the bank identifies and measures the risk, the information obtained lacks timeliness, and the enterprise may lose its solvency with the changes in the market environment, production and operation, thus generating risks. Therefore, the phenomenon of information asymmetry is more prominent in traditional supply chain finance risk management methods.

5.1.2 High Cost and Low Efficiency of Risk Management

In the process of obtaining supply chain information, because the participants involved in the supply chain have increased a lot compared with the general credit, the investigation procedure is more cumbersome and the operation is more complicated, which results in the supply chain financial risk management needs to pay higher costs and low efficiency (Rozario, & Thomas, 2019). In many supply chain financial businesses, the bank needs enterprises and logistics companies to conduct field investigations, involving the place may be all over the world, the enterprise's financial information management level may also be uneven, the bank to fully grasp the information and to do a timely update, it is bound to pay a high cost of an investigation. These costs are naturally transferred to the financing enterprises, leading to a reduction in the efficiency of supply chain financing.

5.1.3 Insufficient Operational Risk Avoidance

In the approval of supply chain finance, there will be a set of standardized approval processes before, during and after the loan; no matter it is whether it is the verification and investigation of contract documents or the field visit of logistics and warehousing, it requires a lot of professional staff to complete. Banks usually address operational risks by standardizing procedures and strengthening the implementation of responsibilities (Wuttke et al., 2019). But in actual operation, the investigators need to have strong professional ability and high professional responsibility. In the process of developing of supply chain finance business, banks cannot guarantee the construction of professional talents to keep pace with the rhythm. Specific operation personnel even turn a blind eye to doubtful situations and submit results in violation of the law to pursue performance. To a certain extent, the business ability and ethical level of risk management professionals have become important factors in supply chain finance risk management.

5.2 The Solution of Blockchain Technology to Traditional Supply Chain Finance Risk Management Problems

5.2.1 Breaking the Information Asymmetry Effect

With the support of blockchain technology, banks can obtain complete accounts receivable financing business information through the accounts receivable chain platform and realize the integration and sharing of business flow, logistics and capital flow information, thus breaking the information island effect between various subjects of supply chain finance and reducing the occurrence of information asymmetry (Qian & Xi, 2023). In this new type of supply chain financial service platform, accounts receivable are transformed into digital asset certificates, and the core enterprises in the supply chain are directly obligated to repay the electronic certificates. The electronic certificates can be split and circulated at will, and under the assumption that the credit risk of the core enterprise is small enough, such electronic certificates can be approximated to be used as cash (Lee, 2023). Moreover, there is no difference in the realization of digital certificates held by end-of-supply chain suppliers and first-tier suppliers of the core enterprise, thus fundamentally constructing a supply chain finance trust transfer mechanism that enables end-of-supply chain enterprises to obtain the same financing capability as first-tier suppliers.

5.2.2 Reduce the Cost of Risk Management

Restricted by the limitations of information access, and the traditional supply chain financial risk management, the cost remains high. The carrier of traditional information is a variety of paper contracts, logistics documents, warehousing and storage lists, etc. If enterprises collude to cheat loans, it is much easier to forge evidence, and banks need to increase the investigation procedures and increase the cost of wind control just by investigating and verifying these credentials.

On the accounts receivable service platform based on blockchain technology, the characteristics of blockchain technology, such as distributed storage and hash algorithm, ensure the absolute authenticity of the transaction and financing information on the platform (Sun, 2022). The characteristics of blockchain technology, such as timestamp and traceability, leave traces of the whole record of the enterprise's financing transaction information, which is very convenient to be tracked by the bank in real-time; the characteristics of digital signature, asymmetric encryption and other technologies satisfy the privacy and confidentiality of the information circulating on the platform (Deng et al., 2021). The digital signature, asymmetric encryption and other technical features satisfy the privacy and confidentiality requirements of the information circulating on the platform; smart contracts and other technical features greatly reduce the moral risk of corporate repayment and the operational risk of the whole business.

5.2.3 Simplify the Process and Reduce Operational Risk

Operational risk exists in all procedural aspects of supply chain finance, in the process of pre-approval and supervision of loans, the most essential requirement for risk management by banks is to obtain true and complete information to break the phenomenon of information asymmetry in the supply chain, so a large number of investigators are required to obtain and verify the business and financial situation of enterprises, and to investigate whether the transaction is real on the spot, etc. In this human operation, mistakes are likely to be made (Adams et al., 2023). In this human operation is very likely to make mistakes and hidden huge operational risks. Once the information obtained by the bank due to human negligence is wrong, then the decision taken based on this information may be contrary to reality. However, on a blockchain platform based on supply chain technology, the probability of these problems occurring will be greatly reduced with the support of blockchain technology (Chen & Bellavitis, 2020). For example, the data on the blockchain will be cross-validated and co-maintained at various nodes across the network after entry, and once the data are entered incorrectly, inconsistency with the copies of data kept by other nodes will result in invalidation of that input. Furthermore, on the receivables chain platform, the circulation of data is very convenient, and banks only need to guarantee that the core enterprises can fulfill their repayment obligations on time, so they can simplify the setup of other risk management processes, thus reducing the operational risks in the implementation of the system (Abdulhakeem & Hu, 2021). Finally, due to the technical characteristics of the smart contract of the blockchain, the repayment terms and conditions can be set in advance on the platform when the enterprise is financed, so that the fund settlement can be executed through the computer, avoiding human intervention in the execution, and reducing the operational risk in the whole process of the supply chain finance receivables business.

6. Risk Culture and Communication

6.1 Risk Culture

The conventions, behaviors, sense-making techniques and priorities that influence risk-related practices inside a company or industry can all be categorized as part of the risk culture. Between 2007 and 2011, professional bodies and consultants in the British financial industry used the term more than seven times as often (Power et al., 2013). On the premise that managers don't take enough risks and that incentives must be created to combat this risk aversion, a significant body of research, originating with (Jensen & Meckling, 1976), aims to address the agency problem of "managerial risk aversion." As long as it is properly defined and effectively controlled, regulators tend to view risk aversion as ethically neutral. This perspective conflicts with the claim that risk cultures are a component of a complex, developing financial system that is characterized by dominant, shared and socially formed modes of thought.

6.2 Organizations

An important component of the framework in which moral behavior is either encouraged or discouraged is provided by organizational cultures. According to Loseke (2007), the socially organized components of culture can collectively make up an overarching "narrative" or identity trait, which can then be connected to specific virtues. As was already said, risk culture is essential to risk management and influences the behavior of those involved in the finance sector. Sheedy and Grifn (2014) have demonstrated that they can vary widely within organizations in the finance sector and can promote beneficial behavior, but they can also contribute to the promotion of detrimental practices (Darley, 2005). Finance-related organizations can be seen as tools for achieving the good life, but they also have a life of their own that goes beyond the lives of their members, who may not have much power to alter the organizations' structures (Sison, 2000). Their integration into local, global, market and non-market networks of social ties must be addressed (MacIntyre, 1999).

Therefore, it is reasonable to define virtuous finance organizations as those who manage risk and protect the interests of all of their stakeholders. Such organizations have managerial practices that "allow people to find meaning and fulfillment in excellence" as well as "appropriate and efficient decision-making structures in the face of internal and external pressures" (Collier, 1995). The understanding that organizations are 'practice institution combinations' is essential to Moore's definition of virtue-based organizations. Therefore, a virtuous financial organization's main duty is to concentrate on its core activity.

6.3 Management

According to Power (2009), risk management has never been neutral or free of values. The norms, attitudes and sense-making inherent to financial risk cultures mirror the underlying mechanical paradigm and financial logic. We support the idea that risk culture should be founded on a revitalized heritage of virtue ethics within mostly collaborative societies rather than on mechanistic tales of ambition and the pursuit of self-interest in a predominantly competitive society (Agarwal & Kallapur, 2018). Risk cultures inside organizations are an emergent characteristic of leadership cultures, which are in turn shaped but not solely dictated by financialized capital. Numerous initiatives to modify the culture of risk center on the technological scientific quantification of the inherently unknowable future. As a result, it is advised to take a different, normative approach that plays to people's goals. Managers and finance experts who are committed to gaining a thorough understanding of the driving causes behind the situation and acting properly are what are required (Llewellyn et al., 2014).

To establish an ethical framework that may be used for financial risk management, we have relied on the development of MacIntyrean virtue ethics by Moore (2015, 2017), Rocchi et al. (2021) and Sison et al. (2019). We have argued in favor of a risk management strategy that acknowledges that risk cultures are a component of a complex, dynamic risk system. The promotion of virtue in the finance sector is more likely to be successful than external control measures based on reductionist principles. Additionally, if we analyze the risk system via the prism of virtue ethics, we arrive at a different understanding of the potential for change. If risk and leadership cultures have been dysfunctional, virtue ethics offers a way to define what "functional" might entail. To achieve this, we have used a virtue ethics framework that is widely recognized, allows for a wide range of interpretations and implementations and can be applied to both specific financial professionals and to cultures of financial risk in general.

7. Conclusion

In conclusion, efficient risk management is still critical for protecting against possible risks and optimizing opportunities as financial systems continue to change in the digital era. Real-time risk identification, assessment and mitigation are made possible by the unparalleled capabilities provided by the integration of cutting-edge technologies like block chain, artificial intelligence and big data analytics. But these developments also bring with them new risks and complexities, necessitating creative thinking and proactive risk management techniques. Organizations can ensure sustainable growth and long-term success in the digital era by cultivating a culture of vigilance, collaboration and continuous improvement. This will enable them to negotiate the shifting landscape of financial risk with confidence, resilience and agility.

References

Abbasi, W. A., Wang, Z., Zhou, Y., & Hassan, S. (2019). Research on measurement of supply chain finance credit risk based on internet of things. *International Journal of Distributed Sensor Networks, 15*(9). https://doi.org/10.1177/1550147719874002

Abdolshah, F., Moshiri, S. & Worthington, A. (2020). Macroeconomic shocks and credit risk stress testing the Iranian banking sector. *Journal of Economic Studies, 48*(2), 275–295. https://doi:10.1108/jes-11-2019-0498

Abdulhakeem, S. A., & Hu, Q. (2021). Powered by Blockchain Technology, DEFI (decentralized finance) strives to increase financial inclusion of the unbanked by reshaping the World Financial System. *Modern Economy, 12*(01), 1–16. https://doi.org/10.4236/me.2021.121001

Aburumman, M., Newman, S., & Fildes, B. (2019). Evaluating the effectiveness of workplace interventions in improving safety culture: A systematic review. *Safety Science, 115*, 376–392. https://doi.org/10.1016/j.ssci.2019.02.027

Adams, R. M., Brevoort, K. P., & Driscoll, J. C. (2023). Is lending distance really changing? Distance dynamics and loan composition in small business lending. *Journal of Banking & Finance*, 107006. https://doi.org/10.1016/j.jbankfin.2023.107006

Adla, A., & Frendi, M. (2021). A decision support Systemfor commercial lending. In *2021 International Conference on Decision Aid Sciences and Application (DASA)*. https://doi.org/10.1109/dasa53625.2021.9682296

Agarwal, A., Gupta, A., Kumar, A., & Tamilselvam, S. G., (2019). Learning risk culture of banks using news analytics. *European Journal of Operational Research, 277*(2), 770–783. https://doi.org/10.1016/j.ejor.2019.02.045

Agarwal, R., & Kallapur, S. (2018). Cognitive risk culture and advanced roles of actors in risk governance: A case study. *The Journal of Risk Finance 19*(4), 327–342. https://doi.org/10.1108/JRF-11-2017-0189

Australian Prudential Regulation Authority. (2021). Building a culture for success. https://www.apra.gov.au/news-and-publications/apra-executive-director-superannuation-division-suzanne-smith-speech-to-asfa. Accessed on August 16, 2022.

Aven, T., & Renn, O. (2009). On risk defined as an event where the outcome is uncertain. *Journal of Risk Research, 12*(1), 1–11. https://doi.org/10.1080/13669870802488883

Baer, M., Gasparini, M., Lancaster, R., & Ranger, N. (2023). "All scenarios are wrong, but some are useful"—Toward a framework for assessing and using current climate risk scenarios within financial decisions. *Frontiers in Climate, 5*. https://doi.org/10.3389/fclim.2023.1146402

Ban, Y. (2019). Supply chain financial risk management strategies in the big data environment. *Management Observation*, (20), 167–168.

Bao, W., Lianju, N., & Yue, K. (2019). Integration of unsupervised and supervised machine learning algorithms for credit risk assessment. *Expert Systems with Applications, 128*, 301–315. https://doi.org/10.1016/j.eswa.2019.02.033

Bats, J. V., & Houben, A. C. F. J. (2020). Bank-based versus market-based financing: Implications for systemic risk. *Journal of Banking & Finance, 114*, 105776. https://doi.org/10.1016/j.jbankfin.2020.105776

Bavoso, V. (2021). Financial intermediation in the age of Fintech: P2p lending and the reinvention of banking. *SSRN Electronic Journal*. https://doi.org/10.2139/ssrn.3849577

Bloor, G., & Dawson, P. (1994). Understanding professional culture in organizational contexts. *Organization Studies, 15*(2), 275–295. https://doi.org/10.1177/017084069401500205

Borg, K., Boulet, M., Smith, L., & Bragge, P. (2019). Digital inclusion & health communication: A rapid review of literature. *Health Communication, 34*(11), 1320–1328. https://doi.org/10.1080/10410236.2018.1485077

Brignoli, M. A., Caforio, A. P., Caturano, F., D'Arienzo, M., Latini, M., Matta, W., Romano, S. P.,& Ruggiero, B. (2021). A distributed security tomography framework to assess the exposure of ICT infrastructures to network threats. *Journal of Information Security and Applications, 59,* 102833. https://doi.org/10.1016/j.jisa.2021.102833

Bryant, C., & Camerinelli, E. (2013). *Supply chain finance.* EBA (Euro Banking Association).

Bryce, C., Webb, R., Cheevers, C., Ring, P., & Clark, G. (2016). Should the insurance industry be banking on risk escalation for solvency II? *International Review of Financial Analysis, 46,* 131–139. https://doi.org/10.1016/j.irfa.2016.04.014

Buckshaw, D. L. (2008). Use of decision support techniques for information system risk management. *Encyclopedia of Quantitative Risk Analysis and Assessment.* https://doi.org/10.1002/9780470061596.risk0245

Cane, J., O'Connor, D., & Michie, S. (2012). Validation of the theoretical domains framework for use in behavior change and implementation research. *Implementation Science, 7*(37). https://doi.org/10.1186/1748-5908-7-37

Carretta, A., Farina, V., & Schwizer, P. (2017). Risk culture and banking supervision. *Journal of Financial Regulation and Compliance, 25*(2), 209–226. https://doi.org/10.1108/JFRC-03-2016-0019

Chen, Y., & Bellavitis, C. (2020). Blockchain disruption and decentralized finance: The rise of decentralized business models. *Journal of Business Venturing Insights, 13.* https://doi.org/10.1016/j.jbvi.2019.e00151

Chinazzi, M., Fagiolo, G., Reyes, J. A., & Schiavo, S. (2013). Post-mortem examination of the International Financial Network. *Journal of Economic Dynamics and Control, 37*(8), 1692–1713. https://doi.org/10.1016/j.jedc.2013.01.010

Collier, J. (1995). The virtuous organization. *Business Ethics: A European Review, 4*(3), 143–149.

Darley, J. M. (2005). How organizations socialize individuals into evildoing. In S. Collins-Chobanian (Ed.), *Ethical challenges to business as usual* (pp. 211–223). Pearson Prentice Hall.

Deng, L., Lv, Y., Liu, Y., & Zhao, Y. (2021). Impact of fintech on bank risk-taking: Evidence from China. *Risks, 9*(5), 99. https://doi.org/10.3390/risks9050099

Domańska-Szaruga, B. (2020). Maturity of risk management culture. *Entrepreneurship and Sustainability Issues, 7*(3), 2060–2078. https://doi.org/10.9770/jesi.2020.7.3(41)

Doughty, K. (2011). The three lines of defense related to risk governance. *ISACA Journal, 5,* 1–3.

Duan, H., Sun, M., & Jackson, I. (2022, June). Financial cyber security risk and prevention in digital age. In *International Conference on Applications and Techniques in Cyber Intelligence* (pp. 648–653). Springer International Publishing.

Dun and Bradstreet. (2006). *Financial risk management.* Tata McGraw-Hill.

Fabozzi, F., & Peterson, D. P. (2009). *Finance: Capital markets, financial management, and investment management.* Wiley and Sons.

Fan, Q. (2022). An analysis of supply chain finance and small and medium-sized enterprises financing pressure relief. In *Proceedings of the 2nd International Conference on Public Management and Big Data Analysis.* https://doi.org/10.5220/0012069400003624

Gelles, M. G. (2016). Robust cyber risk management. *Insider Threat*, 125–136. https://doi.org/10.1016/b978-0-12-802410-2.00009-5

Gungoraydinoglu, A., & Öztekin, Ö. (2022). Financial crises, banking regulations, and corporate financing patterns around the world. *International Review of Finance*, *22*(3), 506–539. https://doi.org/10.1111/irfi.12381

Hasan, S., Ali, M., Kurnia, S., & Thurasamy, R. (2021). Evaluating the cyber security readiness of organizations and its influence on performance. *Journal of Information Security and Applications*, *58*, 102726. https://doi.org/10.1016/j.jisa.2020.102726

Hopkin, P. (2017). *Fundamentals of risk management: Understanding, evaluating and implementing effective risk management.* Kogan Page.

Horcher, K. A. (2011). *Essentials of financial risk management.* John Wiley and Sons.

Ji, L. (2020). Research on supply chain financing risk identification and control of technology-based small and medium-sized enterprises under the Internet of Things financial model. *China Management Informatization*, (4), 125–127.

Kalirai, H., & Scheicher, M. (2002). Macroeconomic Stress Testing: Preliminary Evidence for Austria in: OeNB. *Financial Stability Report*, *3*, 58–74.

Kang, Q., Wu, J., Chen, M., & Jeon, B. N. (2021). Do macroprudential policies affect the bank financing of firms in China? Evidence from a quantile regression approach. *Journal of International Money and Finance*, *115*, 102391. https://doi.org/10.1016/j.jimonfin.2021.102391

Kemp, M. H. D. (2017). Individual elements of the financial system. *Systemic Risk*, 111–217. https://doi.org/10.1057/978-1-137-56587-7_4

Lam, J. (2014). *Enterprise risk management: Form incentives to controls.* John Wiley and Sons.

Lee, G. (2023). Blockchain for product traceability in the supply chain. In *Blockchain in supply chain digital transformation* (pp. 143–160). https://doi.org/10.1201/9781003256755-7

Li, C. (2021). Current status of the development of Internet finance and financial technology. *Modern Business*, (1), 111–113. https://doi.org/10.14097/j.cnki.5392/2021.01.034

Lin, T. (2022). Internet financial risk supervision and government governance mechanism transformation. *Economic Research Guide*, (27), 110–112.

Llewellyn, D., Steare, R., & Trevellick, J. (2014). *Virtuous banking: Placing ethos and purpose at the heart of finance.* ResPublica Trust.

Loseke, D. R. (2007). The study of identity as cultural, institutional, organizational, and personal narratives: Theoretical and empirical integrations. *The Sociological Quarterly*, *48*(4), 661–688.

Lu, Y., Zhao, H., & Zhang, M. (2019). Research on risk management performance evaluation of commercial banks - evaluation framework based on AHP-DEA method. *Financial Supervision Research*, (9), 83–98. https://doi.org/10.13490/j.cnki

MacIntyre, A. (1999). Social structures and their threats to moral agency. *Philosophy*, *74*(3), 311–329.

Martin, J. (1992). *Cultures in organizations.* Oxford University Press.

McConnell, P. (2012). The governance of strategic risks in systemically important banks. *Journal of Risk Management in Financial Institutions*, *5*(2), 128–142.

Mearns, K., Kirwan, B., Reader, T. W., Jackson, J., Kennedy, R., & Gordon, R. (2013). Development of a methodology for understanding and enhancing safety culture in Air Traffic Management. *Safety Science*, *53*, 123–133. https://doi.org/10.1016/j.ssci.2012.09.001

Millo, Y., & MacKenzie, D. (2009). The usefulness of inaccurate models: Towards an understanding of the emergence of financial risk management. *Accounting, Organizations and Society*, *34*(5), 638–653.

Mohammed, A., & Sykes, R. (2012). Sharpening strategic risk management: Resilience: A journal of strategy and risk. www.pwc.com/gx/en/services/advisory/consulting/risk/resilience/publications/sharpening-strategic-risk-management.html

Moore, G. (2015). Corporate character, corporate virtues. *Business Ethics: A European Review*, *24*(S2), S99–S114.

Moore, G. (2017). *Virtue at work: Ethics for individuals, managers and organizations.* Oxford University Press.

Niu*, B., Ren, J., & Li, X. (2019). A peer-to-peer lending credit risk prediction method: Application of Balanced Relative Margin Machine. In *Risk analysis based on data and crisis response beyond knowledge* (pp. 156–162). https://doi.org/10.1201/9780429286346-23

Olukoya, O. (2021). Distilling blockchain requirements for digital investigation platforms. *Journal of Information Security and Applications*, *62*, 102969. https://doi.org/10.1016/j.jisa.2021.102969

Osman, A., & Lew, C. C. (2021). Developing a framework of institutional risk culture for strategic decision-making. *Journal of Risk Research*, *24*(9), 1072–1085.

Perron, P. (1990). Testing for a unit root in a time series with a changing mean. *Journal of Business & Economic Statistics*, *8*(2), 153. https://doi.org/10.2307/1391977

Philippon, T. (2019). *On fintech and financial inclusion (No. w26330).* National Bureau of Economic Research.

Posch, A. (2020). Integrating risk into control system design: The complementarity between risk-focused results controls and risk-focused information sharing. *Accounting, Organizations and Society*, *86*, 101126. https://doi.org/10.1016/j.aos.2020.101126

Power, M. (2009). The risk management of nothing. *Accounting, Organizations and Society*, *34*(6), 849–855.

Power, M., Ashby, S., & Palermo, T. (2013). *Risk culture in financial institutions: A research report.* Economic and Social Research Council.

Pritchard, C. L. (2015). *Risk management: Concepts and guidance.* CRC Press.

Qian, Y., & Xi, X. (2023). Application analysis of block chain technology in Supply Chain Finance. *Internet Finance and Digital Economy*. https://doi.org/10.1142/9789811267505_0047

Renduchintala, T., Alfauri, H., Yang, Z., Pietro, R. D., & Jain, R. (2022). A survey of blockchain applications in the fintech sector. *Journal of Open Innovation: Technology, Market, and Complexity*, *8*(4), 185.

Renn, O. (1998). Three decades of risk research: Accomplishments and new challenges. *Journal of Risk Research*, *1*(1), 49–71.

Rijanto, A. (2021). Blockchain technology adoption in supply chain finance. *Journal of Theoretical and Applied Electronic Commerce Research*, *16*(7), 3078–3098.

Rocchi, M., Ferrero, I., & Beadle, R. (2021). Can finance be a virtuous practice? A MacIntyrean account. *Business Ethics Quarterly*, *31*(1), 75–105.

Rozario, A. M., & Thomas, C. (2019). Reengineering the audit with blockchain and smart contracts. *Journal of Emerging Technologies in Accounting*, *16*(1), 21–35.

Sharma, B., Thulasiram, R. K., & Thulasiraman, P. (2015). Computing value-at-risk using genetic algorithm. *The Journal of Risk Finance*, *16*(2), 170–189.

Sheedy, E., & Grifn, B. (2014). *Empirical analysis of risk culture in financial institutions.* https://www.lse.ac.uk/accounting/CARR/events/Sheedy-Risk-Culture-Paper-Nov-14.pdf

Sison, A. J. (2000). Integrated risk management and global business ethics. *Business Ethics: A European Review, 9*(4), 288–295.

Sison, A., Ferrero, I., & Guitián, G. (2019). Characterizing virtues in finance. *Journal of Business Ethics, 155*(4), 995–1007.

SKYbrary. (2021). Assessing safety culture in ATM. https://www.skybrary.aero/index.php/Assessing_Safety_Culture_in_ATM. Accessed on July 20, 2021.

Sun, J. (2022). Factors affecting the non-performing loan ratio of commercial banks under the new normal. *Economic Research Guide,* (21), 92–94.

Tikk, E. (2021). Future normative challenges. In *The Oxford handbook of cyber security* (pp. 750–768). https://doi.org/10.1093/oxfordhb/9780198800682.013.50

Varga, S., Brynielsson, J., & Franke, U. (2021). Cyber-threat perception and risk management in the Swedish financial sector. *Computers & Security, 6*(105), 102239.

Wang, W. (2021). Potential security risks and countermeasures in the Internet financial model. *Business Exhibition Economics,* (1), 52–54.

Wang, N., & Wang, K. (2022). Internet financial risk management in the context of big data and artificial intelligence. *Mathematical Problems in Engineering.* https://doi.org/10.1155/2022/6219489

Wen, J. (2019). Risk management of the Internet financial industry under the background of big data. *Business Economics,* (9), 171–172. https//doi.org/10.19905/j.cnki.syjj1982.2019.09.063

Werbach, K. (2018). Trust, but verify: Why the blockchain needs the law. *Berkeley Technology Law Journal, 33*(2), 487–550.

Wuttke, D. A., Rosenzweig, E. D., & Heese, H. S. (2019). An empirical analysis of supply chain finance adoption. *Journal of Operations Management, 65*(3), 242–261.

Xiang, J. (2021). Internet financial risks and the transformation of government governance mechanisms. *Social Science Research,* (1), 74–82.

Yu, T., & Wei, S. (2019). Funds sharing regulation in the context of the sharing economy: Understanding the logic of China's P2P lending regulation. *SSRN Electronic Journal.* https://doi.org/10.2139/ssrn.3310288

Chapter 5

Corporate Governance for SMEs: Theory, Problem and Implications

Muhammad Faisal Sultan[a], Muhammad Raghib Zafar[a] and Kashif Riaz[b]

[a]KASB Institute of Technology, Pakistan
[b]Shaheed Zulfiqar Ali Bhutto University of Law, Pakistan

Abstract

Corporate governance is one of the most important topics available in the literature related to large-sized companies. However, the topic has rarely been discussed in the case of SMEs. However, the importance of the topic and mechanism has been in the limelight for more than one and a half decades. Although lack of knowledge especially regarding theoretical implications, literature and implications is still required to optimize the mechanism as well as its implications for SMEs. Therefore, this chapter has been formulated specifically concerning corporate governance mechanisms and their implications for SMEs. Hence, the scope of this study is much broader than those studies that focused on quantitative examination of variables of interest. Thus, the significance of this study has multiple folds as it is not only important for academicians and researchers but also for managers, entrepreneurs and policymakers.

Keywords: Corporate governance; SMEs; firm size; directors; board; board size; independent director

1. Background

Since the last century, researchers and investigators have been trying to understand the concept of corporate governance (Dube et al., 2011; Hakimah et al., 2019). The concern increases due to the dilution and failure of several well-known large organizations (Hakimah et al., 2019). Therefore, several attempts have been made by a panel of experts to define corporate governance in the light of social, cultural, political and economic factors (Dube et al., 2011). Hence, corporate

Strategic Financial Management, 71–82
doi:10.1108/978-1-83608-106-720241005

governance can easily be defined as the set of policies and processes that are used to solve agency problems by drawing lines between owners and managers. Thus, corporate governance is viewed as a set of procedures that are used to resolve conflict among diverse stakeholders (Hakimah et al., 2019). Corporate governance is not only beneficial for managers and owners, but it is also beneficial for stakeholders as its implementation also ensures transparency as well as disclosure of information (Htay & Salman, 2013).

Therefore, corporate governance becomes an expedient mechanism that seems essential for running any business in the modern world. The ultimate aim of corporate governance is to increase the shareholder equity and the firm's value without sacrificing the value of other stakeholders. Most of the prior studies reflected a positive association between corporate governance and a firm's performance. However, some studies indicated the reverse as well as no relationship between corporate governance and a firm's performance (Essel & Addo, 2021).

1.1 Introduction

SMEs have a direct impact on the country's economy and workforce, but these firms are not only suffering from a lack of funds & higher cost of operations but poor management of resources is also threatening SMEs and their growth (Dube et al., 2011). Still, SMEs don't need separation of management from ownership as SMEs have limited liability until or unless the firm is indexed in the stock exchange (Banerjee, 2005). Although SMEs are the top contributor to the employment sector of developing countries, their dilution has a significant negative impact on the country's socio-economic condition. Though SMEs do not apply a code of corporate governance as indicated by prior research, SMEs seem to have overestimated the role of corporate governance and risk management abilities (Crossan & Henschel, 2012). Although recent studies on the role of corporate governance signify the use of corporate governance practices in SMEs and due to the role of SMEs in economic growth, governments of the developing world are also paying due concern to the growth and development of the SME sector (Hakimah et al., 2019).SMEs may leverage their growth through applying codes of corporate governance. However, the lack of information may affect the process of corporate governance at SMEs as the lack of information creates issues of reliability either due to unavailability or unauthentic information (Banerjee, 2005). Although a need for research on corporate governance practices, its type and implications are legitimate, that will become more substantiated when we consider the fact that most of the prior research is either associated with practices of large corporations & also with the developed world (Hakimah et al., 2019).

1.2 Benefits of Corporate Governance for SMEs

Studies like Subbarao et al. (2013) indicate multiple benefits that SMEs may attain through applying effective practices of corporate governance. Some major benefits that SMEs may attain are as follows:

- Increase of internal control, accountability and higher chances of profitability due to lower chances of fraudulent activities.
- Lower chances of conflict among owners and management.
- Raising funds for SMEs may also become easy.
- Implementing corporate governance in SMEs links the management of SMEs with the financial markets. This linkage may also help SMEs through the increase in the quality of the firm's management.

1.3 Gray Area

Studies reflect that SMEs are one of the most considerable areas of research special focus has been given to empirical investigation for exploring areas like business planning, management systems, etc (Crossan & Henschel, 2012).

Therefore, the investigation of corporate governance that varies for different companies and size of the firm (Akbar et al., 2020) is imperative for SMEs, especially to understand the type that may effectively be implemented in SMEs (Htay & Salman, 2013). The need for research on corporate governance mechanisms was also highlighted by prior studies, e.g. Sarvikivi et al. (2012).

Hence in recent times, studies are trying to explore corporate governance practices concerning SMEs (Hakimah et al., 2019). However, studies that are conducted about the corporate governance mechanism of SMEs are very limited. On the other side, most of the work was based on SMEs from the developed world, e.g. Europe, the USA, etc. Hence there is a need to conduct further studies on the corporate governance mechanism of SMEs (Essel & Addo, 2021; Teixeira & Carvalho, 2023). Special consideration may also be given to the inclusion of all the relevant variables to provide a more thorough and rigorous understanding of the implementation of corporate governance practices for SMEs (Ciampi, 2015).

2. Theoretical Underpinning

Most of the time corporate governance has been studied through the lens of large corporates. Therefore, the theory that underlines the concept of corporate governance is contract theory that is associated with agency problems Therefore, almost all the research papers, reviews and business committee reports are focused on agency problems (Dube et al., 2011). Although other than agency theory several theories are found to be associated with the concept of corporate governance, e.g. stewardship theory, resource dependency theory, transaction cost theory and political theory (Essel & Addo, 2021).

However, Hakimah et al. (2019) quoted the reference of Mulili and Wong (2011) that two major theories associated with the concept of corporate governance are agency theory and proprietorship theory. The agency theory lies in the assumption that management is working for the increase in the worth of shareholders' equity. The theory is also used to resolve the contradiction between the interest of management and shareholders, but due to this assumption, agency theory is only limited with the public limited or large corporations and cannot be implanted to the SMEs. On the other side, most of the SMEs are owned by entrepreneurs and controlled by entrepreneurs and the family of entrepreneurs. Therefore, there is no concept of agency theory and entrepreneurs are very concerned about the growth and sustainability of the business to increase their equity as well as to secure the future of their families (Hakimah et al., 2019).

Although effective management needs consultation, we cannot ignore the presence of a strong board in SMEs. Hence, it is effective to relate stewardship theory with the corporate governance mechanism in SMEs (Htay & Salman, 2013). Hence in line with Hakimah et al. (2019), stewardship theory is highly associated with the corporate governance mechanism at SMEs. SMEs are composed of family members, and the use of stewardship is to maintain effective checks and balances to ensure maximum benefits of stakeholders. The second name of stewardship theory is stakeholder theory which indicates that an organization is not only for profit making. This point is also supported by the example in which an organization is posited as an example of a social setup that has a significant impact on the welfare of several stakeholders. Hence, the study is also supported by the latest studies, e.g. Essel and Addo (2021) for implementation of corporate governance practices in SMEs.

The stewardship theory of corporate governance originated from the grounds of social sciences, particularly from the disciplines of sociology and psychology. Moreover, the gist of the theory is to increase the owner's wealth by increasing the performance of the business. Therefore, top-level employees must assume the role of stewards while other members are required to take ownership of the allocated tasks to provide maximum return on shareholder investment (Essel & Addo, 2021). This theory is also supported for the effective governance mechanism in family-owned firms as following stewardship behavior motivates managers to work best in the interest of the firm and follows collectivism and trustworthiness (Latif et al., 2014).

2.1 Literature Review

SMEs are perceived as fuel for the developing economies. SMEs are used to ignite several economies across the globe by contributing significantly in the areas of income generation, employment generation and poverty reduction (Hakimah et al., 2019). However, survival is not easy for SMEs and therefore need proper guidance and advice from experts to sustain themselves in the extensive competitive environment. SMEs need innovative ideas that may make them flourish through taking strategic maneuvers for sustaining as well as for acquiring venture capital. Thus, the need for a corporate governance mechanism in SMEs is legitimate to make the board work in the desired manner which in the long term embarks multiple ways for making SMEs succeed (Htay & Salman, 2013).

Dube et al. (2011) highlighted some of the major benefits of good corporate governance, e.g. an increase in the confidence of investors and financers due to the improvement in the book of accounts. In addition to the growth-related benefits, the use of corporate governance also reduces risks of insolvency for SMEs. Hence, it is optimal to state that the use of corporate governance is beneficial for SMEs, but there is a need to understand the approach that may induce effective policy-making and the firm's performance (Singh & Pillai, 2022). However, the approach of corporate governance for SMEs must be different from large-sized organizations as the organizational structure for SMEs is much simpler as compared to the public-listed companies (Mahzan & Yan, 2014). Although the importance of elements of corporate governance may vary to different forms of companies, countries' locations, etc (Essel & Addo, 2021), the presentation of these elements (variables) in an adequate manner for the growth and betterment of SMEs is the major purpose of this study. Hence, in line with the previous claims, the literature review will discuss important elements of corporate governance for SMEs.

2.1.1 Family Ownership

Most of the SMEs are operated by one member of one family. The situation is the same in the developing world where most SMEs are operated by family members. Hence, the control of the firm is with the family, and they mostly do not practice corporate governance (Umrani et al., 2015). Family businesses rely on love and commitment which increases the affection of managers toward the firm and reduces agency costs (Abor & Biekpe, 2007). Hence, the management of a small is highly concentrated as the majority of shareholders in the board result in lower conflicts and provide stability to the firm (Ciampi, 2015). Evidence also supported the associations and impact of these associations and inclinations toward the firm and increased firm performances (Abor & Biekpe, 2007).

However, a few recent studies also highlight the negative association between family ownership and the profitability and performance of business (Hakimah et al., 2019). The major reason for the negative association hinges upon the lack of competitiveness, skills and abilities of business owners as well as managers holding key positions. Evidence from Malaysian SMEs indicated concentrated ownership which also causes a decline in the profitability of the firm due to fraudulent activities of shareholders (Umrani et al., 2015). Similar sort of findings were reflected by Ehikioya (2009) for family-owned businesses that the addition of more than one family member to the board will affect firm performance negatively.

2.1.2 Board Size

Previously wider boards are perceived as the better choice for effective implementation of corporate governance practices. However, recent studies are indicating that smaller sizes of the board are better for better cooperation, communication and control. On the other side for SMEs, it is entirely a new experience to be shifted from a single owner to a larger board (Abor & Biekpe, 2007). Although in recent times SMEs have been operating in highly competitive environments, the role of the board is extremely important in advising management and formulating effective strategic plans for making SMEs grow and fostering the probability of equity investment and venture capital from banks (Htay & Salman, 2013). Therefore, the real job of board members in SMEs is to make the company attractive to investors, customers and employees. This may look optimal through following stewardship behavior for devising optimal guidelines and directions (Htay & Salman, 2013). Introducing corporate governance to SMEs may also result in the definition of choices for business and its operations and also optimize the firm's internal structure and human relations. This change in the philosophy of management tends to produce a positive impact on a firm's performance (Abor & Biekpe, 2007). Similar to one of the initial studies, Hakimah et al. (2019) reflected the positive association between board size and the performance of SMEs. However, Bennett and Robson (2004) highlighted that it is much more subjective to discuss the relationship between board size and a firm's performance as it varies for the size of the firm. This argument is also supported by studies like Eisenberg et al. (1998) and Dahya et al. (2008) indicated a negative association between board size and a firm's performance. It is useless for SMEs to have larger boards as the cost of having larger boards may overcome the benefits obtained. Other than that coordination problems along with issues in monitoring of managers may also create difficulties for SMEs (Afrifa & Tauringana, 2015).

2.1.3 Independent Directors

The inclusion of independent directors on the board is positively evaluated by the market. It provides the sense of strong sense of monitoring. Therefore, the inclusion of independent directors influences investors' inclination positively as the presence of more independent directors in the firm is perceived as the guarantee of protection of shareholder interest (Georgiou, 2010). Adding to the literature research also indicated that CEOs of family-owned businesses are reluctant to add independence due to the threat of losing control over business (Latif et al., 2014). However, SMEs are a special form of business, and due to their nature, the inclusion of independent directors may cause a decline in the firm performance. Therefore, there must be a difference that inclusion of independent directors may create for small- and medium-sized corporations. Studies also indicate that when the company has an influential CEO, then the hiring of the independent director may be based on political association (Afrifa & Tauringana, 2015).

Thus, independent directors may not be able to perform their duties with due diligence. Hence, their observations on the activities of the executive director are full of leniency (Afrifa & Tauringana, 2015). However, one of the studies by Htay and Salman (2013) reflected a positive association between the inclusion of independent directors on boards may also optimize the performance of SMEs.

Similar findings are given by Ciampi (2015) through the reference to small-sized firms in Italy that negative association between concentrated board and firm's default. Hence, it is legitimate to believe that in Italy small firms do not include much of independent directors on the board. Contradictory to these, findings, the findings of Ehikioya (2009) indicated that family-owned businesses are less focused on including non-executive (independent directors) in the board as compared to the non-family-owned businesses. A similar has been indicated by the study of Rashid (2009) concerning SMEs from Bangladesh indicated the inclusion of independent directors does not add any value to the firm. Similar is the case of Pakistan where non-executive directors and independent directors do not seem to be independent in decision-making. Other than these reasons one of the other reasons for the non-serious attitudes of independent directors is the nominal remuneration which does not motivate these directors to pay full diligence (Latif et al., 2014).

2.1.4 Females on the Board of Directors

The resource-based view indicated that it is better to have diversity in the board of governors. Diversity may provide better understanding and quality, innovation as well as better evaluation and control (Arzubiaga et al., 2018). The inclusion of female directors on board is found to be correlated with the performance of large-sized firms and may also be positively correlated with the performance of SMEs (Hakimah et al., 2019). A similar was postulated by Lim and Envick (2013) that the inclusion of females on the board of directors is positively associated with the performance of SMEs. Females are also found to be more motivated in working in high positions in family-owned SEMs, and they also do not possess any fear of glass ceilings. However, females also tend to learn and perform in non-family businesses. However, studies like Ali et al. (2014) indicated that it is better to mention the debate on the inclusion of female directors on the board as inconclusive. However, the inclusion of different genders on the board may trigger different benefits to the SMEs and their management. Female directors have a high tendency to reduce conflicts in the process of decision-making and also leverage with great ability of multi-tasking (Arzubiaga et al., 2018).

2.1.5 CEO Age

There is a definite relationship between the age of the CEO and the firm's performance. Studies indicated that younger CEOs have a lesser tendency to take risks, and chances of error in decision-making may also be higher due to lack of experience. However, there is a strong probability of differentiated results for SMEs as larger companies have the resources and abilities to hire more skilled and competitive personnel as compared to SMEs (Afrifa & Tauringana, 2015). Afrifa (2013) highlighted the difference in age affects firm performance of medium and small-sized firms in different manners.

2.1.6 CEO Tenure

The tenure of the CEO is also a potent predictor of a firm's performance perhaps the length of tenure for large-sized firms is found to be significantly higher as compared to SMEs. However, generally, the length of CEO tenure is positively associated with the firm performance as the duration assists the CEO in developing rapport and goodwill in the industry. Moreover, the experience of the CEO also assists the CEO in formulating an effective strategy; therefore, CEO tenure is a potent predictor of a firm's performance (Afrifa & Tauringana, 2015).

2.1.7 Foreign Ownership

This is the element that may prove to be very important for corporate governance. Studies highlighted that firms with lower capital may flourish extensively through foreign investment. Moreover, foreign funding also enforces better control through auditing and reporting mechanisms. Prior studies also postulated that foreign ownership is critically important for small-sized organizations in developing areas (Abor & Biekpe, 2007).

2.1.8 Remuneration for Directors

There is a negative association between the directors' remuneration as this may hinder the judgment and expression of the director. Hence, director may hesitate to give his opinion and expression and higher compensation may cause an association between directors and managers, which may positively affect their worth and income. However, it will harm the growth and performance of the firm (Afrifa & Tauringana, 2015).

2.1.9 The Frequency of Board Meetings

Board meetings are necessary for effective assessment and control. However, there are two separate schools of thought. One of which is in support of the increase in the frequency of board meetings while the second one indicated otherwise (Ahmad et al., 2014). However, the family-owned business study of Ahmad et al. (2014) quoted the reference of Yasser et al. (2011) to indicate that the increased frequency of board meetings positively affects the performance of the family-owned business.

3. Research Methodology

This is one of the descriptive studies (Sekaran & Bougie, 2016) that is conducted to develop a detailed understanding of the corporate governance mechanism and tools associated with SMEs. The development of this study is based on the identification of theories, variables and implications from multiple studies. This will provide a detailed understanding to readers about the corporate governance mechanism and its implications for SMEs. Hence, the philosophy associated with this study is epistemology, and the research approach is deductive. The reason behind these postulates is associated with the concept of research onion developed by Saunders et al. (2007) which highlighted that epistemology is the philosophy of knowledge, and the deductive approach is best when there is a need to specify a problem that may be solved to provide significance to stakeholders.

Although the purpose of the study is to collect and disseminate knowledge in detail, the study is not associated with any form of statistical testing. Thus, the best-suited philosophical stance for this study is constructivism which is highlighted by Syed and McLean (2021). The use of constructivism is best for qualitative studies that must be built upon authentic and published data. Hence, the research strategy for compiling this chapter is archival, and the time horizon is cross-sectional. Relating both of these postulates with the research onion, it has been revealed that archival is the strategy of data collection from secondary data sources. Moreover, cross-sectional is the time horizon in which researchers collect and analyze data once (Saunders et al., 2007, 2015). Therefore, this is one of the most interesting studies that combine parameters and concepts from different studies to provide the reader with complete and detailed information. Thus, the study is one of the pervasive that has significance for multiple stakeholders as it is not only in favor of academicism and researchers but also for entrepreneurs, managers and policymakers.

4. Conclusion, Significance and Recommendations

This chapter has been formulated to increase readers' knowledge about the corporate governance mechanism, its implications for SMEs and related theoretical assumptions. Hence, the study is very important for developing countries where managers are unaware of the potential benefits that may be earned by implementing the protocols of corporate governance. This study also highlighted multiple variables, e.g. foreign ownership, the inclusion of female directors and frequency of board meetings that the owners of SMEs or owners of family businesses rarely consider. However, in light of the literature of this study, SMEs may include some new protocols in the corporate mechanisms of SMEs. Therefore, this study has massive significance for policymakers, entrepreneurs and managers. Thus, the scope of implications is not only limited to academia and academic research. Hence, the study is pervasive and may be used by multiple stakeholders for better understanding, practices and implications.

4.1 Policy Implications

Studies indicated that the use of corporate governance mechanisms may be beneficial not only for registered SMEs but also for family-owned smaller firms from developing countries (Abor & Biekpe, 2007). Especially in developing countries like Pakistan the unavailability of data and authentic resources that may be used by researchers to understand and describe the governance mechanism of SMEs (Khurrum et al., 2008). However, the importance of SMEs is massive for developing countries like Pakistan as the SME sector is not the only main employer of the country but also contributes more than 30% to the GDP of the country (Dar et al., 2017). Similar points are raised by initial studies related to the governance mechanism of SMEs, e.g. Abor and Biekpe (2007) that implementation of CG is one of the keys to increase ways to operate business and pertaining opportunities.

Hence, the mechanism may also be used to overcome the lack of management and control as indicated by Dar et al. (2017), which may increase the importance and contribution of SMEs to developing economies like Pakistan. Therefore, the use of this study may provide better policymaking in the area of management and control mechanisms as well as overall designing of an effective code of corporate governance for SMEs and family-owned businesses in developing economies like Pakistan.

References

Abor, J., & Biekpe, N. (2007). Corporate governance, ownership structure and performance of SMEs in Ghana: Implications for financing opportunities. *Corporate Governance: The International Journal of Business in Society, 7*(3), 288–300.
Afrifa, G. (2013). *Working capital management and AIM listed SME companies profitability: a mixed research method approach.* Doctoral dissertation, Bournemouth University.
Afrifa, G. A., & Tauringana, V. (2015). Corporate governance and performance of UK listed small and medium enterprises. *Corporate Governance, 15*(5), 719–733.
Ahmad, N., Iqbal, N., & Tariq, M. S. (2014). Relation of corporate governance with financial performance. *International Letters of Social and Humanistic Sciences, 29*(40), 35–40.
Akbar, M., Hussain, S., Ahmad, T., & Hassan, S. (2020). Corporate governance and firm performance in Pakistan: Dynamic panel estimation. *Abasyn Journal of Social Sciences, 12*(2), 213–230.
Ali, M., Ng, Y. L., & Kulik, C. T. (2014). Board age and gender diversity: A test of competing linear and curvilinear predictions. *Journal of Business Ethics, 125*, 497–512.
Arzubiaga, U., Iturralde, T., Maseda, A., & Kotlar, J. (2018). Entrepreneurial orientation and firm performance in family SMEs: The moderating effects of family, women, and strategic involvement in the board of directors. *The International Entrepreneurship and Management Journal, 14*, 217–244.
Banerjee, P. (2005). Corporate governance and competence in SME's in India. *CACCI Journal, 1*(1), 1–13.
Bennett, R. J., & Robson, P. J. A. (2004). The role of boards of directors in small and medium-sized firms. *Journal of Small Business and Enterprise Development, 11*(1), 95–113.
Ciampi, F. (2015). Corporate governance characteristics and default prediction modeling for small enterprises. An empirical analysis of Italian firms. *Journal of Business Research, 68*(5), 1012–1025.
Crossan, K., & Henschel, T. (2012). Corporate governance: An holistic model for SMEs. *Journal of Management and Financial Sciences, 5*(8), 54–75.
Dahya, J., Dimitrov, O., & McConnell, J. J. (2008). Dominant shareholders, corporate boards, and corporate value: A cross-country analysis. *Journal of Financial Economics, 87*(1), 73–100.
Dar, M. S., Ahmed, S., & Raziq, A. (2017). Small and medium-size enterprises in Pakistan: Definition and critical issues. *Pakistan Business Review, 19*(1), 46–70.
Dube, I., Dube, D., & Mishra, P. (2011). Corporate governance norm for SME. *Journal of Public Administration and Governance, 1*(2).

Ehikioya, B. I. (2009). Corporate governance structure and firm performance in developing economies: Evidence from Nigeria. *Corporate Governance: The international journal of business in society*, *9*(3), 231–243.

Eisenberg, T., Sundgren, S., & Wells, M. T. (1998). Larger board size and decreasing firm value in small firms. *Journal of Financial Economics*, *48*(1), 35–54.

Essel, R., & Addo, E. (2021). SMEs corporate governance mechanisms and business performance: Evidence of an emerging economy. *Journal of Government Information*, *5*(1), 155–169.

Georgiou, A. K. (2010). *Corporate governance and its effect on the performance on family and non-family companies listed on the Cyprus stock exchange*. Doctoral dissertation. Middlesex University.

Hakimah, Y., Pratama, I., Fitri, H., Ganatri, M., & Sulbahrie, R. A. (2019). Impact of intrinsic corporate governance on financial performance of Indonesian SMEs. *International Journal of Innovation, Creativity and Change*, *7*(1), 32–51.

Htay, S. N. N., & Salman, S. A. (2013). Corporate governance: A case study of SMEs in Malaysia. *Middle-East Journal of Scientific Research*, *18*(2), 243–252.

Khurrum, S., Bhutta, M., Rana, A. I., & Asad, U. (2008). Owner characteristics and health of SMEs in Pakistan. *Journal of Small Business and Enterprise Development*, *15*(1), 130–149.

Latif, B., Sabir, H. M., Saleem, S., & Ali, A. (2014). The effects of corporate governance on firm financial performance: A study of family and non-family owned firms in Pakistan. *Research Journal of Finance and Accounting*, *5*(17), 75–89.

Lim, S., & Envick, B. R. (2013). Gender and entrepreneurial orientation: A multi-country study. *The International Entrepreneurship and Management Journal*, *9*, 465–482.

Mahzan, N., & Yan, C. M. (2014). Harnessing the benefits of corporate governance and internal audit: Advice to SME. *Procedia-Social and Behavioral Sciences*, *115*, 156–165.

Mulili, B. M., & Wong, P. (2011). Corporate governance practices in developing countries: The case for Kenya. *International Journal of Business Administration*, *2*(1), 14–27.

Rashid, A. (2010). CEO duality and firm performance: Evidence from a developing country. *Corporate Ownership and Control*, *8*(1), 163–175.

Sarvikivi, E., Roivainen, M., Maunula, L., Niskanen, T., Korhonen, T., Lappalainen, M., & Kuusi, M. (2012). Multiple norovirus outbreaks linked to imported frozen raspberries. *Epidemiology and Infection*, *140*(2), 260–267.

Saunders, M., Lewis, P., & Thornhill, A. (2007). Research methods. *Business students* (4th ed., No. 3, pp. 1–268). Pearson Education Limited.

Saunders, M. N., Lewis, P., Thornhill, A., & Bristow, A. (2015). *Understanding research philosophy and approaches to theory development*. Pearson Education.

Sekaran, U., & Bougie, R. (2016). *Research methods for business: A skill building approach*. John Wiley & Sons.

Singh, K., & Pillai, D. (2022). Corporate governance in small and medium enterprises: A review. *Corporate Governance: The International Journal of Business in Society*, *22*(1), 23–41.

Subbarao, P., Srinivas, P., & Jyothi, G. A. (2013). Problems, procedures and practices in implementing corporate governance in Indian SMEs. *International Journal of Management Research and Development (IJMRD)*, *3*(2).

Syed, M., & McLean, K. C. (2021). Disentangling paradigm and method can help bring qualitative research to post-positivist psychology and address the generaliz-ability crisis. *Behavioral and Brain Sciences, 45*, 58–60.

Teixeira, J. F., & Carvalho, A. O. (2023). Corporate governance in SMEs: A systematic literature review and future research. *Corporate Governance: The International Journal of Business in Society*. https://doi.org/10.1108/CG-04-2023-0135

Umrani, A. I., Johl, S. K., & Ibrahim, M. Y. (2015). Corporate governance practices and problems faced by SMEs in Malaysia. *Global Business & Management Research, 7*(2), 71–77.

Yasser, Q. R., Entebang, H. A., & Mansor, S. A. (2011). Corporate governance and firm performance in Pakistan: The case of Karachi Stock Exchange (KSE)-30. *Journal of Economics and International Finance, 3*(8), 482–491.

Chapter 6

Managing Financial Talent in a Competitive World

Zhang Can

UCSI University, Malaysia

Abstract

Organizations need to strategically manage talent and enhance leadership in this challenging modern business landscape. This chapter provides an in-depth analysis of the complexities faced by financial talent management in the competitive modern business environment and discusses the need for organizations to align their human resource (HR) strategies for growth. It covers the evolution of human resource management (HRM), focuses on the key elements that make up a talent strategy, such as recruitment, selection, employee development and performance appraisal and highlights the application of these elements in finance, in addition to analyzing the importance of the challenges posed by leadership and the need for cross-functional collaboration.

This chapter aims to provide readers with the tools to nurture a diverse-skilled and innovative finance talent that can effectively respond to the complexities of today's business environment and provide the organization with a good supply of excellent financial management talent for future growth.

Keywords: Talent management; financial performance management; leadership management; team building; cross-functional collaboration

1. Introduction

The financial industry is undergoing technological innovation in a global era of increasingly updated information technology (Suryono et al., 2020). This change involves not only the innovation of financial products and services but also the redefinition of core strategies for talent management and organizational development. Being a manager in the financial world requires enhancing teams to

Strategic Financial Management, 83–92

Copyright © 2024 Zhang Can

Published under exclusive licence by Emerald Publishing Limited

doi:10.1108/978-1-83608-106-720241006

remain competitive, ensuring business performance and developing and retaining talent in a diverse environment. Advances in technology, cross-border collaboration and stricter compliance requirements have also made talent management more complex. To succeed in this competitive modern financial environment, managers need to rethink their talent strategy in all aspects. Manpower planning, also known as workforce planning or HR planning, is a critical HR function that deals with the assessment, forecasting and optimization of an organization's human resources to achieve its strategic objectives.

2. History and Development

Frederick Taylor believed in the principle of human management to improve labor efficiency (Taylor, 1911). Barney's (1991) point of view emphasizes that human resources are very competitive. HR planning has become an integral part of strategic planning and involves many complex techniques. The development of human resources has also been developing continuously since its birth, and it has been constantly changing, including artificial intelligence and so on. Therefore, human resources are becoming more and more important in the organization.

2.1 Importance

Talent strategy is closely related to other functions of the company because the company cannot grow without talent. For example, the company's recruitment, talent management, job promotion management and HR goals must be consistent with the organization's goals to keep the company competitive. Becker and Huselid (2010) argue that a firm's organizational workforce needs to be aligned with the firm's goals.

2.2 Definitions

According to the research of relevant scholars, Walker (1992) believes that human resources need to match the organizational field. Bulla and Scott (1994) argue that future workforce needs and strategic goals remain the same. Heathfield (2008) believed that the number of employees and the quality of employees should also be satisfied. Richard D. Johnson (2021) defines HR planning as "the process of analyzing and determining the needs and availability of human resources, and they believe that HR planning includes the position development of employees to enable the organization to achieve its goals" (Johnson et al., 2021).

2.3 Relationship to Other HR Functions

The HRM department is the department of conveying talents for the company. The quality, efficiency and working ability of the company's personnel are closely related to the development of the company. To use talented people, we must have the ability to recognize people. A fair and reasonable salary system should be set for each person to do his or her best. Scholars such as Wright and McMahan (1992) emphasize that talent management is closely related to the wage and performance management (finance department) of enterprises. HR planning is closely related to other resource functions of the company.

2.4 Talent Management

Talent management is a way for the personnel department to introduce and train talents, and it is a necessary condition for the development of enterprises. HR planning supports talent management by anticipating an organization's future workforce needs and identifying potential skills gaps. The core position of the enterprise is the decision-making level, that is the directors of the Board of Directors; these leaders decide the future development dynamics and direction of the company. Of course, senior talents are generally sought by the Ministry of Personnel or commissioned by headhunters, but after the recruitment of talents, training talents and shaping the loyalty of talents is the heavy work of the Ministry of Personnel. Talent management is the process of identifying, attracting, developing and retaining top talent in an organization.

2.5 Recruitment and Selection

Recruitment and selection are the processes of attracting and hiring the most suitable candidates to fill vacant positions within an organization. HR planning plays a significant role in informing these processes by identifying the necessary competencies and skillsets required for each role. HR planning helps organizations develop targeted recruitment campaigns, ensuring that they attract candidates with the appropriate skills and experience.

2.6 Employee Development

The career development stage is the growth process of qualitative change divided into individuals or organizations according to certain standards in the process of career development. Generally speaking, a career experiences growth, exploration, maturity, maintenance and decline are five stages of development, each stage has its characteristics, and career development stage analysis is the basis for the implementation of career planning. Career planning can accelerate employee growth and enhance employee's sense of belonging.

2.7 Performance Management

It's like a customized growth roadmap for each employee. It's a dance journey with employees, starting with setting clear goals, continuing to evaluate performance and giving constructive feedback to find and hone more of their best. "HR planning" is like a conductor behind the stage, making sure that each dancer knows his or her position and role. Only with a deep understanding of the company's long-term strategy and the competencies required for each position we can perfectly align performance management with organizational goals. Every performance data are a powerful reference for HR planning; they tell us what the team has done well and what needs to be corrected. In this way, performance and talent planning can jointly create more possibilities for enterprises.

3. Performance Management in Finance

Performance refers to the specific behavior and performance of the organization or individual at work, which reflects the results or performance of the organization or individual through certain procedures (Gore, 1997). Campbell et al. (1993) believes that performance and behavior are related to a certain extent, considering that the external environment influences the result, while behavior is generated by individual workers.

First, help the company's tactical landing. Performance management is about unbundling the big-picture tactical thinking into each team and individual, ensuring that everyone is on the same page and committed to overall success. Second, the results of accurate control. Performance management is a navigational tool for decision-makers that aligns the progress of each employee with the larger goals of the company. Whether it is the fine-tuning of salary policies, job changes or the timely handling of problems at work, it can provide an efficient and secure information flow.

In this fast-moving business era, financial performance management (FPM) has become a lifesaver for organizations. It ensures that our financial goals are aligned with the big picture, helps the management team make decisions based on real data, optimizes resource allocation, detects and avoids financial risks on time and maintains growth momentum. For those industries that are heavily regulated, FPM also ensures that we follow all regulations and avoid unnecessary hassles. In short, FPM is like a corporate compass, guiding us on the right path in times of calm and storm. Finally, performance management builds a continuous communication bridge, so that the company knows the progress of the work of various departments and employees and ensures that all directions and goals are always in the best state.

The most important link of performance management is the first performance plan, which makes relevant job tasks according to the current strategic plan of the enterprise. The second performance implementation, after the performance plan is clear, needs to follow the time, key nodes and key tasks. This process is performance implementation. Third, performance feedback. In the current implementation of performance appraisal, the implementation method, time and process of performance feedback have been clearly explained. During the implementation of the performance plan, any difficulties or uncertainties that cannot be solved by the employees shall be reported to their immediate superiors. Direct superiors to assist them in solving the problem or give guidance and help. The fourth assessment results can be classified according to grades.

FPM seems to be the compass of an enterprise, drawing the road map of success for the company. It plays an integral role in everything from strategic accountability to decision-making. It's like a complete brand upgrade that makes the entire organization more harmonious and efficient. The highlight here is that when we talk about strategic alignment, it ensures that the finance team is in sync with the broad direction of the company, much like a fashion brand's new collection is closely aligned with market trends. When it comes to accountability and decision-making, this management system acts as our style consultant, helping us set our direction while reminding us to remain professional and responsible. In short, it is a business art that breaks the rules and strives for excellence, which every organization should learn and practice.

4. Leadership Development Programs

Leadership requires the ability to adapt to different teams and lead different types of talent to achieve the strategic goals of the organization. Leadership has attracted much attention in the HR system (Northouse, 2018), and in different practices and academic studies, leadership to achieve common organizational goals has a strong relationship with personal motivation, effective guidance and influence of leadership (Chemers, 2000).

After years of precipitation, the definition and theory of leadership have mushroomed in the literature (Bass & Bass, 2009). Although everyone has a different understanding of leadership, there is a consensus that true leadership does not rely on inherent personality or behavior but requires the leader to adapt flexibly to the specific situation and team needs (Hersey & Blanchard, 1977). A good leader needs a high level of personal and professional quality to ensure the best performance in all situations (Goleman, 2000).

4.1 The Core Elements of Leadership

4.1.1 Situational Awareness

Situational awareness is the ability of leaders to accurately read and interpret the environment in which they find themselves (Osborn et al., 2002). This means that leaders must not only understand the culture and team climate of the organization in which they work but also be able to anticipate and adapt to change. Context-aware leaders can identify which strategies are most effective in a given situation and adjust their behavior accordingly.

4.1.2 Vision and Direction

Behind every successful leader is a keen eye, which not only deeply understands the culture and atmosphere of the team but also can foresee the future and adapt to every change. With this awareness, leaders can accurately grasp every moment and find the most appropriate strategy (Kouzes & Posner, 2012).

4.1.3 Interpersonal Relationships and Communication

The core of interpersonal relationships is trust, which is an essential element of leadership (Covey, 2004). Effective communication is like a transparent window that makes every message shine. As leaders, we need to do more than just speak, we need to listen and make sure that every team member has a voice.

4.1.4 Decision-Making Skills

In this era of rapid change, leaders who can make decisions quickly are the most desirable. Sometimes, we need to make choices quickly with limited time and information and then bravely stand up for the results (Yates & Tschirhart, 2006).

4.1.5 Ethics and Values

Ethics is not only about honesty and integrity but also about how we treat people and things. Every interaction a leader has, whether with team members, customers or other stakeholders, is an opportunity to demonstrate ethical standards (Brown & Treviño, 2006). When we adhere to high ethical standards, we earn the respect and trust of the team, which makes the team more united and efficient.

4.2 Leadership Theory

Trait Theory: Imagine leadership is in your DNA! This is what trait theory tells us – that leaders are "born" (Stogdill, 1948). But times have moved on, and now we know that being a leader also requires environment and training. Just like we often talk about natural star power, some people are born with the charisma and traits to lead. Weber's classic study provides us with a perspective: leadership can be viewed from five dimensions: easygoing, intellectual, reliable, self-control and extroversion. Like each person's personality color, these traits make up a person's unique leadership style. However, this does not mean that everyone's leadership is the same in all situations. As circumstances and industries change, so do they.

Behavior Theory: It's not who you are, it's what you do! (Lewin et al., 1939) This theory looks at the behavior patterns of leaders and tells us that behavior determines everything. The research of this theory mainly focuses on leadership behavior and its influence on leadership behavior. In essence, the theory of leadership behavior aims to verify the influence of leadership behavior on the effectiveness of leadership and emphasize the importance of leadership behavior. The theory of the leading and guiding formula divides leadership into three leading and guiding formulas, authority style, laissez-faire style and democracy style. Quan Wei leadership means that under this leadership mode, the organization strategy and the division of labor among the members are all decided by the leader, and the employees have no right to speak. Democratic leadership means that under this leadership model, people who are willing to listen to the suggestions of the organization and are good at discussing and negotiating with the organization. Discretionary leadership means that under this leadership model, employees have full decision-making rights.

Situational theory: There is a perfect leadership style for every situation! Leadership is not a "one-size-fits-all" approach, but is tailored to local conditions (Hersey & Blanchard, 1977). Leadership is not just a fixed personal trait; it is also about the environment and the people facing it. The leadership situation theory points out that even the same leader may show different leadership effects when facing employees with different maturity levels. Therefore, effective leaders should not only adjust and adapt according to their characteristics but also according to the specific situation to ensure that the leadership behavior is always effectively implemented.

Transformational leadership: This is the kind of leadership that lights up the passion of the team and stimulates the potential of the team! Leaders provide a clear vision for the team and encourage people to step out of their comfort zones and explore new possibilities (Bass & Riggio, 2006). The transformational leadership theory of Kouzes and Posner (1987) subdivides leadership into five aspects that can be observed and learned: (1) Challenge the organization's existing processes; (2) Create a shared vision in the team; (3) Ensure that employees' actions are aligned with this vision; (4) Set clear direction for employees' work and (5) Motivate your employees further by recognizing and rewarding their results.

4.3 Current Challenges to Leadership

In this era of globalization and rapid change, leaders need to become "all-round players". In the face of a variety of teams, cross-cultural leadership becomes very important. At the same time, it is necessary to ensure smooth communication between team members from different cultural backgrounds to avoid misunderstandings. In these challenging times, leaders face many "new normal" challenges. First, thanks to social media and digitization, information travels superfast, so leaders need to not only ensure the accuracy of the message but also pay attention to how they communicate with their team and the public. Moreover, working practices are becoming more flexible, with remote working, flexible hours and collaboration across time zones becoming the norm, and leaders need to understand how to maintain team cohesion and effectiveness in this environment. Also, diversity and inclusion are increasingly valued, and leaders need to know how to appreciate and leverage each unique voice on.their team to create a safe, open and supportive work environment for everyone. Of course, there is also the issue of employee health and well-being, which can never be ignored, and today's leaders need to care more about employee mental health and work–life balance, not just KPIs and performance metrics. In short, modern leaders are like chameleons, constantly adapting and learning to guide the team to a better future.

4.4 Team Building and Cross-Functional Collaboration

In today's work scene, team building and cross-functional collaboration are super critical, and with all kinds of innovative projects and complex tasks, companies can't rely on just one function to do all the work (Parker, 1994). That's the beauty of cross-functional collaboration. Team building and cross-functional collaboration are critical in the fast-paced, efficient modern work scene (Sahebodari et al., 2021). Today, we are not only facing increasingly complex businesses but also looking for the best solution in a variety of cross-departmental collaborations. Think about it, when the product team and the marketing team sit at the same table, discuss and innovate together, the kind of spark that is rubbed out is not just the superposition of knowledge on both sides.

Team building is the cornerstone of team cooperation (Pinto & Pinto, 1990). We develop trust, understanding and rapidity among team members through various training and activities. Cross-functional collaboration requires us to look beyond our professional framework and collaborate with colleagues from other departments to find broader solutions. Organizations need to continuously invest and innovate in team building and cross-functional collaboration (McDonough, 2000). Team building starts with making sure everyone has a common goal and vision. Through a variety of interesting team activities and training, you can strengthen the trust and tacit understanding between the team but also find each other's strengths and weaknesses and better work together. Cross-functional collaboration brings together experts from different departments to leverage their expertise and collaborate on a particular problem or project. For example, marketing and product departments can work together to ensure that the product features and marketing strategies are optimal, but there are many challenges to such cooperation. Different departments have different working cultures and approaches, and communication can be a big problem. Therefore, as a leader, we should pay attention to the training of team communication and cooperation and ensure that everyone can put aside their interests and sincerely work for the ultimate goal of the team and the project. Team dynamics let us discover how the team from the beginning of the unfamiliar to the understanding of the team and finally into a team of efficient cooperation. As we work with our team members, we go through four stages:

(1) Formation stage: The team is beginning to meet, and everyone is exploring their own positions and tasks.
(2) Conflict stage: People begin to express their opinions, one way or another; it is inevitable that there will be a bit of collision.
(3) Normalization phase: When we found the rhythm of the team, we began to establish our "play".
(4) Performance stage: Perfect team running-in, max trust, we sprint together for the goal!

Today's business environment is becoming more complex, and cross-functional teams are like the star teams of enterprises, bringing together a variety of professional talents! The secret to success is clear communication, clear goals and a team leader with leadership. And to respect and recognize the diversity and unique talents of the team, which is the source of power to move the team forward. But as we often say, there are challenges and opportunities. It is cross-departmental collaboration like this that helps us break through old frameworks and see more possibilities. For the long-term development of enterprises, we should pay more attention to and strengthen the training and practice in this area.

5. Conclusion

In the evolving landscape of business and finance, understanding the nuances of leadership, performance management and cross-functional collaboration is paramount. Our journey from the historical developments to the intricate relationships between various HR functions underscores the profound interconnectivity of these domains. Performance management, particularly in finance, stands out as a keystone to organizational success, ensuring that the institution's financial bearings align with its broader goals. Leadership, with its myriad of challenges in the modern era, requires a consistent re-evaluation of its core elements and theories. Moreover, fostering an environment where team building thrives and cross-functional teams collaborate seamlessly remains crucial in today's fragmented and specialized work environments. In wrapping up, this comprehensive review emphasizes the imperative of a holistic approach to HR functions and the undeniable value of leadership development and teamwork in propelling organizations forward in the competitive global marketplace.

References

Barney, J. (1991). Firm resources and sustained competitive advantage. *Journal of Management*, *17*(1), 99–120.

Bass, B. M., & Bass, R. (2009). *The Bass handbook of leadership: Theory, research, and managerial applications*. Simon and Schuster.

Bass, B. M., & Riggio, R. E. (2006). *Transformational leadership*. Psychology press.

Becker, B. E., & Huselid, M. A. (2010). SHRM and job design: Narrowing the divide. *Journal of Organizational Behavior*, *31*(2/3), 379–388.

Brown, M. E., & Treviño, L. K. (2006). Ethical leadership: A review and future directions. *The Leadership Quarterly*, *17*(6), 595–616.

Bulla, D. N., & Scott, P. M. (1994). *Manpower requirement forecasting. Human resources planning society* (pp. 145–155). Plenum Press.

Campbell, J. P., McCloy, R. A., Oppler, S. H., & Sager, C. E. (1993). A theory of performance. *Personnel selection in organizations*, *3570*, 35–70.

Chemers, M. (2000). Leadership research and theory: A functional integration. *Group Dynamics: Theory, Research, and Practice*, *4*(1), 27.

Covey, S. R. (2004). *The 7 habits of highly effective people: Powerful lessons in personal change*. Simon & Schuster.

Goleman, D. (2000). Leadership that gets results. *Harvard Business Review*, *78*(2), 4–17.

Gore, A. (1997). *Serving the American public: Best practices in performance measurement: Benchmarking study report*. National Performance Review. https://books.google.com.my/books?hl=zh-CN&lr=&id=dGbXbdGrxGAC&oi=fnd&pg=PA1&dq=Gore,+A.+(1997).%E2%80%AFServing+the+American+Public:+Best+Practices

+in+Performance+Measurement:+Benchmarking+Study+Report.+National+
Performance+Review.+&ots=12tZ8T16pC&sig=vzz9xQ5Wpp57X065QVqhb5mh
30A&redir_esc=y#v=onepage&q=Gore%2C%20A.%20(1997).%E2%80%
AFServing%20the%20American%20Public%3A%20Best%20Practices%20in%20
Performance%20Measurement%3A%20Benchmarking%20Study%20Report.%
20National%20Performance%20Review.&f=false

Heathfield, S. M. (2008). Twelve tips for team building: How to build successful work
teams. *Human Resources*, 7–11. http://tlmerrill.pbworks.com/w/file/fetch/85213921/
Heathfield%20-%20Twelve%20Tips%20for%20Team%20Building.pdf

Hersey, P., & Blanchard, K. H. (1977). *Management of organizational behavior:
Utilizing human resources*. Prentice-Hall.

Johnson, R. D., Rea, L. M., & Liou, D. D. (2021). *Fundamentals of human resource
management* (2nd ed.). Sage Publications.

Kouzes, J. M., & Posner, B. Z. (1987). *The leadership challenge: How to get
extraordinary things done in organizations*. Jossey-Bass.

Kouzes, J. M., & Posner, B. Z. (2012). *The leadership challenge: How to make
extraordinary things happen in organizations*. Jossey-Bass.

Lewin, K., Lippitt, R., & White, R. K. (1939). Patterns of aggressive behavior in
experimentally created "social climates". *The Journal of social psychology*, *10*(2),
269–299.

McDonough, E. F., III. (2000). Investigation of factors contributing to the success of
cross-functional teams. *Journal of Product Innovation Management: An International Publication of the Product Development & Management Association*, *17*(3),
221–235.

Northouse, P. G. (2018). *Leadership: Theory and practice*. Sage Publications.

Osborn, R. N., Hunt, J. G., & Jauch, L. R. (2002). Toward a contextual theory of
leadership. *The Leadership Quarterly*, *13*(6), 797–837.

Parker, G. M. (1994). Cross-functional collaboration. *Training & Development*,
48(10), 49–53.

Pinto, M. B., & Pinto, J. K. (1990). Project team communication and cross-functional
cooperation in new program development. *Journal of Product Innovation Management: An International Publication of the Product Development & Management
Association*, *7*(3), 200–212.

Sahebodari, M., Soltani, M., & Kordenaeij, A. (2021). Antecedents of formation of
competitive relationships. *Journal of Strategic Management Studies*, *12*(48),
123–143.

Stogdill, R. M. (1948). Personal factors associated with leadership: A survey of the
literature. *Journal of Psychology*, *25*, 35–71.

Suryono, R. R., Budi, I., & Purwandari, B. (2020). Challenges and trends of financial
technology (Fintech): A systematic literature review. *Information*, *11*(12), 590.

Taylor, F. W. (1911). *The principles of scientific management*. Harper & Brothers.

Walker, M. B. (1992). *The psychology of gambling*. Pergamon Press.

Wright, P. M., & McMahan, G. C. (1992). Theoretical perspectives for strategic
human resource management. *Journal of Management*, *18*(2), 295–320.

Yates, J. F., & Tschirhart, M. D. (2006). Decision-making expertise. In *The Cambridge handbook of expertise and expert performance* (pp. 421–438). Cambridge
University Press.

Chapter 7

Data Management and Analytics in Finance

Rabia Sabri[a] and Tehzeeb Sakina Amir[b]

[a]Institute of Business Management, Pakistan
[b]Bahria University, Pakistan

Abstract

The chapters emphasise the importance of data management from the perspective of the business management process, where big data is the most crucial and pressing technical and business issue in the modern realm of technology. The same data has a significant influence on the current financial environment. Organisations are facing challenges in explicating complicated financial data manually and using it to drive their decision-making processes. Data-driven decision-making is a dominant tool for any professional. It enhances precision, alleviates risk, improves efficacy, aids financial management, offers customer insights, provides a competitive edge, supports strategic planning, enables performance tracking, fosters innovation and has predictive capabilities. The power of data makes the organisation more prosperous and resilient in the face of change. By making informed decisions based on data and analytics, organisations can unlock their full potential and achieve sustainable growth. The chapter suggests a data-driven culture in the organisation with the help of strategising in terms of data collection, analytics and data management by establishing governance and regulatory practices to ensure data security and integrity. The latter part covers the forecasting and transformative ability of data by integrating machine learning and deep learning models. The chapter also covers the visualisation perspective of the data by transforming the information into a visual setting, illuminating the hidden insights and making them tangible and relatable. The chapter closes with a suggestion for managers to stay competitive, make more reasoned and sound decisions and adapt to the evolving business environment.

Strategic Financial Management, 93–118
Copyright © 2024 Rabia Sabri and Tehzeeb Sakina Amir
Published under exclusive licence by Emerald Publishing Limited
doi:10.1108/978-1-83608-106-720241007

Keywords: Data management; data-driven culture; data analytics; data security; data visualisation. predictive modelling

1. The Storytelling of Data

Finvilla is a city of tall buildings and busy streets. Max, a financial expert, usually makes decisions and bold, risky investments based on his intuitions and gut feelings without proper fundamental investigations. On the other hand, Lilly is known for making informed and smart decisions based on her mathematical and analytical skills.

They both worked for competitor financial institutions and met each other on different platforms and conferences. Their approaches to making financial decisions always resulted in conflicted arguments.

A startup venture approached Lilly and Max, for the investment opportunity, as a fintech-based innovative solution provider. Max evaluated a company on the basis of his gut feelings and heavily invested the funds in the startup. In contrast, Lilly, with her team, assessed the company's fundamentals and technical and also, with due diligence, evaluated the financial and operational standing of the startup and its business model. From an operational point of view, she also set up smart objectives and benchmarks for performance. She purposely invested a low amount of funds.

Both the participants gained with the growth of the startup, but with the changing environment of the fintec industry, new entrants and regulatory and governance issues arise. Lilly has already forecasted the changes and adjusted her financial decisions to minimise losses, as well as capture other market opportunities.

Max learnt from his experience and the results of his decision and concluded that data analytics may improve intuition and that there should be a balance between instincts and empiricism. Lilly's remarkable success was the top story among financial professionals; she proved her data analytical skills to make complex situations easy. Both of them show that in the uncertain world of finance, the combination of cognitive skills and data-driven strategies can help make professionally informed decisions.

2. Introduction

Accuracy is our north star in this journey, ensuring our insights are grounded in reality. In the current business environment, where prospects, complexity, interconnectivity and unknowns prevail, it has never been more critical to make well-informed decisions. A paradigm shift has occurred from the conventional method, which heavily relied on business knowledge, intuition, experience and limited data, to a contemporary era where data and technology drive decision-making (Brousseau et al., 2006). The discussion below aims to examine the profound effects of data-driven decision-making, elucidating its ability to enable contemporary leaders and organisations to navigate intricate situations effectively. The rapidity of transmission of information is a key factor in underscoring the significant nature of data – the immediate response of financial markets and investment decisions to different events, like geopolitical conditions, environment changes and micro- and macro-economic developments. Financial managers have the potential to gain a competitive edge in situations where high-pressure scenarios can lead to substantial profits or losses by utilising accurate, reliable and timely data.

Data-centric decision-making is not just a buzzword; it is essential for succeeding in the present and future corporate environment, which faces rapid changes and unprecedented challenges. Through the utilisation of data and technology, businesses can gain a competitive advantage, forecast market trends and gain a deeper understanding of consumer behaviour. Nevertheless, it is crucial to acknowledge the inestimable worth of human intuition. The integration of data insights with contextual comprehension guarantees the accuracy and applicability of decisions driven by data. The use of predictive analytics and patient information is significantly transforming resource allocation and treatment plans, even within the healthcare industry (Arjun et al., 2021). Business leaders are unlocking the significance of data in the digital age. The retail industry is also shifting and trying to understand the customers, streamline operations and outperform rivals. Using data analytics to predict customer behaviour allows retailers to tailor products and marketing efforts and identify popular products and promotions to understand customer inclinations (Dekimpe, 2020). The vendors use data analytics for inventory pricing, tracking order levels, reducing waste, accelerating delivery and increasing profitability. Retailers can use data analytics to recommend products based on browsing and buying habits. This can help retailers build customer loyalty (Pereira & Frazzon, 2021).According to Reynolds et al. (2018), financial institutions are capitalising on data-driven insights to evaluate risks and analyse investment opportunities.

The stock market and its insight into trade and investment, fraud detection and prevention and accurate machine learning risk analysis in real-time are only some of these revolutions introduced through big data in the finance industry (Ewen, 2019). Through this, services influence customer satisfaction and sales, expediting traditional procedures in relation to tracking purchases, faster workflow for reliability of system processing, analysis of financial output and monitoring growth. However, some crucial issues concerning big data are present in the finance sector despite such revolutionary service transmissions (Fanning & Grant, 2013). The noticeable issues in extensive data services are privacy and safeguarding of data. The other factors include data quality of data and other regulatory requirements. Other than statistics, data in finance includes a great deal of qualitative information. Contemporary financial managers usually rely on a highly comprehensive data set comprising different elements such as sentiment research, industry trends and customer behaviour patterns. A rigorous picture of forces in the market offers insight into how the data will evolve, thus allowing for better strategic positioning of the organisation's business through the anticipatory approach. Data is critical for risk management, where risks are identified and mitigated before they impact an organisation's operations. It would seem that data management has evolved significantly.

The first phase is recognising that data is a strategic outcome instead of just a byproduct resulting from corporate activities. In a time before data management was commonplace, departments often collected and stored data independently, creating siloes (Abraham et al., 2019). Due to a lack of cohesion, it wasn't easy to have a comprehensive understanding of organisational performance. These silos were broken down when evolution realised that constraint as an integrated approach to data was developed and fostered a united one (Ariyaluran Habeeb et al., 2019). Similarly, the tools used in the processing and storage of data moved forward as technology progressed. However, they have been replaced by more advanced data management technologies that can manage large amounts of structured and unstructured data. The need for real-time analysis alongside the vast quantities of data produced also aided this progress.

One crucial milestone in these successive stages involved adding machine learning (ML) as well as AI into data analytics. They also permitted prediction of future trends and outputs for analysis of the current datasets. Predictive analytics helps financial managers to analyse market patterns, forecast changes in the economy and adjust their investment plans. Another essential element of evolution concerns data governance and securement. This resulted in the creation of frameworks and a straightforward process aimed at safeguarding sensitive data during its transition into a more valuable commodity prone to loss or misuse (Hoffman & Rimo, 2017). The change addressed data quality issues and assured decision-makers of the reliability of the available information.

3. Data-Driven Strategy: A Managerial Perspective

3.1 Data-Driven Decision-Making in Finance

The managers are responsible for strengthening and reinforcing a data-driven decision-making culture within the functional departments. In this regard, the common assumption among financial organisations is that data-driven decision-making is a prerequisite of technological advancement. However, building a data-driven culture within financial teams is not merely a technological transition but a fundamental shift in mindset that empowers individuals to make decisions based on evidence, analysis and collective insights (Yu et al., 2021). What this achieves is an environment that treats data as an asset and empowers the team with skills that can leverage this asset to achieve organisational goals. Education is the cornerstone of this team mindset. Financial teams need to be trained to make them capable of comprehending, interpreting and using data for organisational goals. Key performance indicator interpretation, analytics tools and data literacy training are essential components of training programs. Organisations, to remain competitive, foster a culture of using and interpreting the data within the team members to participate in data-backed decisions. The managers are responsible for creating a business environment where data analysis and strategic decisions are integrated into every functional and operational aspect of the organisation. From sales to human resources and to accounting and financial data, it is used to recognise opportunities, measure performance, boost company growth and improve the recruitment process and employee well-being. The leaders encouraged the employees to be innovative and experiment with the technology. It helps the business be responsive to market changes and persistently improve its performance. The combination of secure, decentralized transactions with data integrity; and the processing capabilities of edge computing can enhance operational efficiency (Wu et al., 2020, 2021). As Nisar et al. (2020) demonstrate in their study, an organisation's overall structure is affected when managers or leaders emphasise data in decision-making procedures and convey the value of data-driven insights; employees perceive data as an essential part of their everyday tasks rather than as an optional add-on thanks to this top-down approach. Kamble and Gunasekaran (2019) find in their thorough review of the effects of data-driven decision-making on organisational processes that it essentially results in increased efficiency for the organisation. This enhancement of efficiency also brings about better communication and increased collaboration – which is another requirement of data-driven decision-making. Chatterjee et al. (2021) further elaborate on this and state that this increased collaboration and enhanced communication results in increased employee satisfaction. These factors related to data-driven decision-making result in overall improved customer service for the organisation. Fig. 7.1 show this process simply and visually.

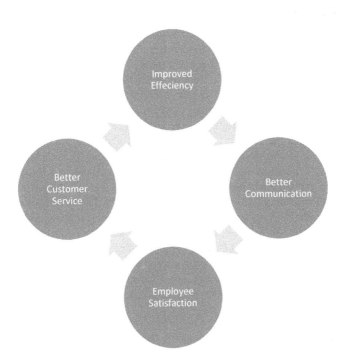

Fig. 7.1.   How Data-Driven Culture Improves Organisational Goals.

3.2 Strategic Planning for Data Management and Analytics

Financial organisations have to plan well in advance to endorse a culture of data management and analytics. It entails using data to propel organisational objectives through a thorough and proactive strategy (Mölder et al., 2021). In addition to guaranteeing efficient data management, this strategic planning links data projects with more general corporate goals. George et al. (2019) researched the effects of strategic planning on organisational performance and found a significant and positive correlation between strategic planning and improved organisational performance. Strategic data management and analytics planning can help organisations enhance their operations and provide an organised path to implement data management techniques. It necessitates an extensive knowledge of the company's objectives as well as an analysis of how data may help those goals. Financial managers must work with key stakeholders to identify significant company procedures, key performance indicators (KPIs) and areas where data might provide valuable insights. The configuration promises that data-based activities are aligned to the measurable, purpose-driven goals of the organisation rather than individual moves (Sarraf, 2023).

Moreover, a strategic working plan creates a steady roadmap for a database management system, averting concerns caused by visionlessness or lack of understanding. This course of action has targeted deadlines, deliverables and resource deployment (Jones et al., 2020). To be effective, a diligently structured line of action must possess the capacity to be modified in response to technological advancements or modifications. In addition, stakeholders are informed of the organisation's technological capabilities through strategic planning. Financial institutions should make sustainable investments in IT infrastructure due to the various advantages it has such as matching ethical standards to investment strategies, green asset infrastructure, including ones on renewable energy power stations, enhancing portfolio's risk-adjusted returns and strengthening economic resilience (Thacker et al., 2019). Several benefits for financial institutions stem from the adoption of sustainable IT infrastructure. It first helps to ensure sustainability and a healthy planet by matching the institution's investment with ethics. Moreover, green infrastructure assets, such as renewable power, also enhance portfolio returns on a risk-adjusted basis, thus contributing to economic robustness (Adriaens et al., 2021). Further, some investors aiming at sustainable impact and future-proofing for their portfolios could take such perspectives (Hebb, 2019). Besides, investments in sustainable infrastructures help financial institutions meet their fiduciary responsibilities as well as long-term growth needs. Strategic planning is a comprehensive, diligent and forward-thinking approach that determines the best solution for the management and analysis of data by evaluating the organisation's needs and capabilities.

3.3 The Role of Managers in Overseeing Data Strategies

Managers' continued commitment and support, effective communication, coordination and the progress of data knowledge and expertise are important factors in implementing data strategies (Tabesh et al., 2019). Additionally, other elements influence decision-making based on data analysis, such as the business environment, competition, managerial commitment, interdepartmental relations and organisational framework (Corea & Corea, 2019). Middle management is helpful in the implementation of effective strategies and is supported by an encouraging work environment and explicit guidance or policy from higher-level executives (Sleep et al., 2019). Organisations must establish guidelines, procedures and processes for data management and transformation with the help of real-time reporting tools like Relational Database Management System (RDBMS), NoSQL, NewSQL and big data (Balakrishnan et al., 2020). Guiding their teams towards a data-driven culture is one of the primary duties of managers (Storm & Borgman, 2020). This entails imparting the knowledge that data is a strategic advantage and the standard modus operandi rather than just a byproduct of some well-thought strategy.

With regard to the environment in financial organisations, managers especially need to create a culture where team members see data as a necessary tool for making decisions and prioritise evidence-based reasoning over their own personal opinions or gut feelings. Additionally, managers operate as a link between the strategic objectives of the company and the day-to-day implementation of data plans. Chatterjee et al. (2021) believe that to ensure that data-driven insights directly contribute to the attainment of key performance metrics and overall success, managers have to integrate data projects with more general business objectives and make sure that employees understand these priorities. A comprehensive knowledge of the organisation's long-term objectives and the data's potential to produce valuable insights are prerequisites. The task of overseeing data initiatives involves the assessment and choice of technological solutions, including analytics tools, data management platforms and similar systems, to ensure that they facilitate prudent technology investment decisions, support scalability and adaptability, and align with the present and future objectives of the organisation (Hupperz et al., 2021). An additional critical component of the duties of a manager overseeing data strategy is risk management. Fraser et al. (2021) recommend that managers maintain a state of constant vigilance concerning potential hazards that can undermine data security, legal compliance or moral and ethical principles. Organisations must take proactive measures to mitigate these risks to strengthen their data infrastructure and avert potential setbacks that could compromise the efficacy of their data-driven endeavours.

Managers promote departmental communication and cooperation, establishing a data-driven decision-making culture throughout the company. It impacts organizational results, including risk minimisation through better communication (Hubbard, 2020). The success of data initiatives depends on the collaboration and feedback provided by organizational teams. Facilitating cross-functional cooperation, maximising data utilization and removing organizational bottlenecks are all responsibilities of managers.

4. Data Collection and Infrastructure

4.1 Standard Practices in Data Collection Techniques

Financial institutions' data collection and infrastructure best practices include addressing data gaps, instituting systems that collect data in a highly disaggregated manner and utilising industry-wide standards for data capture and reporting (Grody, 2018). The practices below in Fig. 7.2 are designed to furnish financial industry regulators with the essential information, grant financial institutions greater flexibility in statistical aggregation for economic policy and streamline reporting obligations (Nejman et al., 2011; Wang et al., 2020). To guarantee confidentiality and equitable access for all market participants, regulation should be applied to the production and dissemination of financial market data, such as trading activity, publicly traded companies and indexes (Carvajal & Elliott, 2007). Through industry-sponsored centralised facilities, collaboration and risk sharing can be extended to the matching and settlement of non-valued data components of financial transactions. This results in decreased operational costs and enhanced transaction failure rates (McLaughlin, 2004). Since financial institutions rely mainly on data transmission and storage, future demands must be addressed about data treatment and management.

Data collection improves and boosts the level of objectivity (Johnson et al., 2020). The formation of specific objectives during data collection is requisite for research activities, strategy planning and decisions in business operations (Chen et al., 2019, 2020). It is a vital corporate issue comprising the administration of legal regulation, data privacy problems and application risks. It provides a comprehensive appreciation of essential factors that help in identifying suitable information regarding data purchase, consumer behaviour, market trends and productivity. Additionally, setting clear objectives helps one have a better understanding and interpretation of the collected data that relates to its purpose.

However, there must be high-quality standards for the acquired data to inform decision-making based on accurate analysis (Cichy & Rass, 2020). Today is an age of technological modernity whereby every business enterprise offering banking facilities should incorporate automation coupled with appropriate

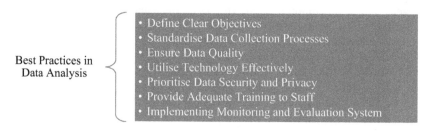

Fig. 7.2.   Data Collection Best Practices. *Source:* Authors' Own Creation.

equipment. According to Kania et al. (2021) the procedure described above is a step in getting an economical way of collecting information based on using sensors, mobile apps, or other digital tools. With automation, all human errors are eliminated, leading to a high level of production that results in vast amounts of data being collected and managed. Technology can also fast-track data collection for the benefit of immediate decision-making within an organisation that never stands still. For instance, Kokina and Blanchette (2019) suggest that financial institutions should use a uniform model for recording data to ensure uniformity and minimise error rates.

In addition, those employees involved in the collection of data should also be appropriately educated and trained. The company should also make sure some errors or mistakes do not follow inadequate preparation, lack of expertise and untrained individuals on the use of the software involved in the project. According to Lin et al. (2021), specially educated personnel reduce mistakes in the procedure of acquiring information, increasing the level of reliability and accuracy of obtained data. Every type of organisation, including financing entities, should adopt the framework that will enable continuous checking of information collectors. Systematic reviews provide an opportunity to identify gaps, data quality concerns or modifications that may be needed due to changes in business imperatives or technology innovations.

4.2 Data Management Platform (DMP)

The data management platform (DPM) acts as the core mechanism through which organisations collect, group and analyse information needed for well-informed decision-making. Managers should go for a platform that caters to their needs (Thanawala et al., 2019). Businesses need their features to integrate into how they work and operate. The areas of concern when looking for data management solutions include flexibility, fit under existing frameworks and safety. A great DMP lies at the heart of any data strategy for any given business since it facilitates storing, manipulating and integrating data (Huang et al., 2020). Examples of widely known systems here include Salesforce, Oracle, IBM, MediaMath and Cloudera. There are numerous ways of assessing those websites. Scalability is also an essential consideration. Besides, a good instrument needs to include the capacity to accommodate the organisation's present data and be effortlessly expandable in case more is needed.

Scalability ensures that the DMP can deal with an increased volume of data and changing business demands while still maintaining the fidelity of the data. You have a lot to uncover concerning the specifics of its design, its ability to handle data, and its connection to other data sources if you want to determine how scalable your platform is. Interoperability is also used for the review process. For the best results, the DMP should work well with the databases, systems and analysis tools that the company already has in place. The compatibility of the platform is the name for this trait. To make a uniform data environment, you may face administrative and operating problems because you need a variety of databases, third-party applications and data formats that can work together (Alzahrani et al., 2022). With seamless integration, you can get a better picture of all of your company's data. The operations run more smoothly by making it easier for data to move between teams and systems.

Safety and compliance issues are evaluated for DMP. The platform needs to follow the regulatory requirements and governing standards in the business for data safety, as well as its legality and permission to use by the governing body. It will be easy for the managers to pick the suitable DMP. Data encryption, control accesses and audit trails are mostly followed for the safety of private information (Udhaya Mugil & Metilda Florence, 2022).

4.3 Implementing a Secure and Scalable Data Storage Strategy

Setting up a data storage strategy that is both safe and scalable is a challenging assignment. Thorough planning, teamwork and a commitment to the highest standards are all needed to do it well. The first step in this process is to look at the criteria that the data management team has set and decide which ones the plan must follow. Managers look at the current amount of data, how it's expected to grow and how much space is needed. Following a clear description of what is needed, the IT or tech team, along with buying and other key stakeholders, starts the difficult task of finding and comparing the best storage options. Cost, flexibility and safety features are some of the things that need to be thought about during this process (Lu et al., 2020). As you make your data store plan, you need to think about a lot of different things. Mazlan et al. (2020) say that these factors might include their ability to grow, their cost, how quickly they can access data, how they secure data while it's being sent and while it's being stored and their security features.

The cybersecurity team's main jobs are to set up security protocols, encrypt data while it's being sent and while it's being stored, enforce strict access controls and do regular security audits (Hoffman & Rimo, 2017). It results in lowering the risk of possible attacks on the storage infrastructure. At the same time, the infrastructure and IT teams carefully plan and carry out expansions, choosing cloud-based platforms that can grow as needed and handle rising data needs efficiently. After that, moving the current data to the new storage system will need ongoing checks to make sure it is correct, cooperation between the IT and data management teams and the creation of a transfer schedule that keeps service as smooth as possible. As the relationship between IT and HR grows, large-scale training programs are put in place to give employees the skills they need to access, store, and safely recover data. At the same time, documentation is created to contain security procedures, troubleshooting guides and best practices. Moving forward, ongoing monitoring and optimisation are put in place, with the IT and data management teams establishing protocols for continuous surveillance of storage performance, security measures and scalability features. Regular reviews are conducted to optimise storage configurations in response to evolving data requirements and technological advancements. The following Table 7.1 simplifies these tasks and identifies which teams may be involved in the tasks.

Table 7.1. Implementing a Secure and Scalable Data Storage Strategy.

Step	Task Description	Teams Involved
1	Needs assessment and planning	IT, Data management
2	Selecting appropriate storage solutions	IT, Procurement
3	Security protocol implementation	Cybersecurity
4	Scalability planning	IT, Infrastructure
5	Data migration and integration	Data management, IT
6	Training and documentation	IT, Human resources
7	Ongoing monitoring and optimisation	IT, Data management

5. Ensuring Data Quality and Governance

5.1 The Framework for Data Quality Assurance

To make sure that the quality of data is upheld, there are several frameworks that managers can use. These frameworks have varying efficiencies in ensuring completeness, accuracy and reliability of data. One of these frameworks is the Total Data Quality Management. This is a general framework that considers data quality throughout the data cycle using an approach that includes profiling and assessing, cleansing and enrichment, monitoring and auditing, and governance and stewardship (Fan & Geerts, 2022). Such a setup ensures the organisation comprehensive data quality management and promotes responsibility among people employed within the setup. The second framework is the Data Quality Dimensions Framework, which is based on age. It provides a structured means of locating and curing problems with quality, where the focus is on some dimensions/aspects of data quality itself.

According to Ramasamy and Chowdhury (2020), quality is measured by a number of dimensions, including accuracy, consistency, timeliness, completeness and reliability. The framework allows organisations to focus on and tailor activities for improving data quality based on the dimensions that have the highest relevance to their goals. It helps outline and tackle select qualities of data based on organisational concerns. One other notable framework is the Six Sigma framework, which consists of six stages of the Define, Measure, Analyze, Design, Improve, and Control & Verify (DMADICV) model. Six Sigma's application of DMADICV incorporates data quality processes in a cyclical and stuctured manner. It relies mainly on statistical analyses and continuous improvement to identify and rectify defects during data processing. DMADICV is an alternative statistical approach to the original process-oriented methodology that relies on constant improvement. It is in this regard that the suitability of a particular framework for an organisation depends on what the need of the organisation requires. Two other broadly applicable frameworks for addressing data quality over the entire data life cycle include the scope and total quality management (TQM) dimensions.

On the other hand, Six Sigma addresses process improvements and not data quality measures. Compared to the other two, the Data Quality Dimension Framework provides a significantly larger degree of operational freedom for managers. It makes it possible to prioritise certain dimensions depending on a manager's particular goal. When creating a culture of data-driven decision-making in the organisation, the TQM of data is more effective. Thus, the needs of the organisation, assessed through a thorough assessment of needs, dictates which framework should be used in that specific environment.

5.2 Regulatory Compliance and Data Governance Models

Regulatory compliance is the single greatest goal of any data governance model and the number one priority of any financial organisation. These regulations safeguard both organisations and the clients they serve. Regulatory compliance refers to the adherence to laws, regulations and industry standards governing the financial sector. The policy of regulatory compliance in companies refers to the overarching adherence of companies' organisations to laws, regulations and industry standards governing the financial sector, ensuring ethical practices, data security and transparency. Data governance models offer additional structures for proper data management that include guidelines, workflows and enforcing systems. Sensitive financial information must be safeguarded. In addition, an orderly environment in which activities in the financial domain are carried out with ease. Thus, the financial institutions, in their complex way of passing the laws like Basel III and General Data Protection Regulation (GDPR) (Haj Khlifa & Zaki, 2021). Basel III emphasises the concept of risk data and information. The GDPR makes use of seven principles to make the data more secure: legitimacy and justifiability, specificity of purpose and time limit for retention, accuracy, integrity and confidentiality, purpose restriction and accountability. It is important to understand in detail for one to be able to come up with efficient data governance. In most cases, these models comprise methods of classification, controlling access and data trails, among others.

Data governance models serve two purposes in the context of regulatory compliance: they offer a flexible platform for preempting and harmonising emerging requirements concerning compliance and aid adherence to existing regulations (Hastig & Sodhi, 2020; Micheli et al., 2020). These approaches typically involve establishing data stewardship positions that ensure the quality, security and compliance of data. These also comprise data lineage and traceability policies whereby firms can demonstrate the source and transformation of data – a must in audit trails. As such, the relationship between regulatory compliance and the data governance model manifests in creating a responsible and accountable corporate culture within financial firms. As regulations continue to evolve and cybersecurity threats become more sophisticated, a robust data governance model, underpinned by effective policies and procedures, becomes a strategic asset. Managers play a pivotal role in ensuring the integrity of data and the adherence to privacy policies within an organisation. As custodians of strategic decision-making and operational excellence, their oversight is crucial to maintaining the trust of clients, stakeholders and regulatory bodies (Liu, 2022). Managing data integrity involves safeguarding the accuracy, consistency and reliability of information throughout its lifecycle. At the same time, privacy policies dictate how sensitive data is collected, stored, processed and shared in compliance with legal and ethical standards.

6. Predictive Analytics and Decision Support

The skill of data storytelling is removing the noise and focussing people's attention on the key insights. – Brent Dykes

6.1 Predictive Analytics in Financial Forecasting

Predictive analytics is a data-driven methodology that leverages statistical algorithms and ML techniques to analyse historical data and make informed predictions about future events or trends (Strielkowski et al., 2023). Moreover, Delen (2020) explains that predictive analytics creates forecasts by finding patterns, correlations and linkages within datasets. This helps businesses foresee outcomes and make proactive decision-making. Predictive analytics, in its simplest form, provides managers with valuable information taken from historical data, allowing them to anticipate future events and reduce associated risks. Predictive analytics is used in financial organisations to improve decision-making, obtain a competitive edge over competitors in the market and reduce risks related to data processes. Numerous factors impact financial markets, making it difficult to forecast market trends, investment possibilities and potential threats.

Predictive analytics helps financial managers analyse historical market data, customer behaviour and economic indicators to forecast future market movements, identify investment opportunities and optimise portfolio strategies. Shakya and Smys (2021) add that predictive analytics also helps with risk management by helping to spot possible fraud, credit problems, and market swings. This enables financial institutions to take preventative action and protect their assets. Managers can optimise the use of predictive analytics in several ways. First and foremost, it is critical to cultivate a data-driven culture within the company. Supervisors have to make sure that groups have the knowledge and tools needed to analyse and apply predictive analytics insights properly. Second, business managers, analysts and data scientists must work together. To ensure that predictive models are in line with business objectives, managers should collaborate closely with analytics teams to establish clear objectives. Third, predictive models must be continuously evaluated and improved. To improve accuracy and relevance, managers should put feedback systems in place and evaluate the predictive analytics models' performance regularly. Thus, predictive analytics play an instrumental role in the analysis of future implications of current indicators – empowering the decision-makers to make an informed and dependable quantitative choice.

6.2 Decision Support Systems in Finance

Decision support systems are those mechanisms through which decision-makers are aided with suitable choices during an event or situation. Algorithmic trading systems, or automated trading systems, are Decision Support Systems used extensively in finance for executing highly specialised forms where trading happens at a high frequency. Computers are programmed to trade on behalf of humans, whereas they manually input the buy and sell orders. Algo trading is currently being used in stock markets to leverage user data, past patterns and a designated set of prespecified instructions to achieve fixed targets.

Buy or sell orders are being executed utilising automated and pre-programmed trading instructions. These systems use sophisticated mathematical models and algorithms to manage portfolios, analyse market movements and carry out trades. Financial institutions can quickly make decisions based on predetermined criteria thanks to algorithmic trading systems, which also enable them to react instantly to market changes and seize opportunities. Algorithmic trading systems use statistical models and quantitative analysis to find trade indications and buy and sell at the best prices. These technologies make it possible for traders to make quick choices by processing vast amounts of market data quickly. By making sure orders are filled swiftly, and trade downtime is kept to a minimum, algorithmic solutions take away the chance of human error and emotion in trading. Putting protection factors into the algorithms reduces the chances of losing money. These items are highly rated such that even some of the prominent investors and hedge funds cannot operate without them.

Financial plans and analytical systems are helpful in decision-making on strategic planning, budgeting, evaluation of performances and forecasting (Rudra Kumar & Kumar Gunjan, 2020). They consist of the same sources of financial information that guide decision-making concerning the best use of resources, investment and maintaining good overall finance. Financial planning, analysis, and advisory (FPA&A) are tools to combine different sources of data for analysis, support strategic decision making process, forecasting, budgeting and financial reporting. FPA&A tools bring together data on finances across business units/departments within the organisation and those sourced outside the organisation to depict the institution's overall financial situation. Complex modelling, incorporating multiple variables and scenarios, is used to forecast financial position under these decision support systems. During "what-if" analyses, financial managers can envision various scenarios, make adjustments and tailor their plans accordingly. On this, Marzuki et al. (2020) elaborate on the advantages of a credit scoring system that enables accurate measurement of people and corporate creditworthiness. Credit score systems use statistical models and machine learning algorithms to understand someone's or an institution's creditworthiness. These include looking into some key financial indicators like payment history, credit history and debt/income ratio (Durairaj & Poornappriya, 2020). The credit scoring system could fast-track and automates financial companies' credit/loan decision-making processes on loan applications. It leads to the efficiency and standardising of the process. Such systems create credit scores that look at multiple financial and non-financial factors. Furthermore, credit scoring systems are crucial to the expansion of financial inclusion because they provide lending decisions on an objective, data-driven basis.

7. Machine Learning: A Managerial Revolution

7.1 Machine Learning Explained for Financial Managers

AI systems assist in the formulation of forecasts, suggestions and decisions by leveraging ML models that possess different levels of autonomy in pursuit of a predetermined set of human-established objectives. AI employs a wide variety of data types, sources and analytical instruments to process massive quantities of information. The techniques of ML are important to analyze the diverse datasets in different domain, including the medicine and biology fields (Zitnik et al., 2019). Data is used to train ML models, which can then learn from their own experiences to become more predictive and perform better on their own without any human intervention or programming. The COVID-19 crisis intensified the megatrend of digitalisation and the use of AI.

The emergence of ML has restructured the financial industry and will continue to evolve in the future. Managers need to understand the ML algorithms and applications and the benefits of the technology to realise while maintaining safeguards of accountability and control as to the ultimate decision-making. ML has a major effect on financial knowledge and has revolutionised every domain of management functions (Levantesi & Zacchia, 2021). The data-controlled decision-making is the combination of unprecedented technological capabilities with managers' human creativity. ML enables unprogrammed computers to acquire knowledge and develop. ML algorithms learn from experience and data as opposed to executing user-defined instructions in the form of code. These data may consist of text, images and videos, in addition to statistical analysis and text (de Prado, 2020). Management assesses market patterns, predicts fluctuations in stock prices and anticipates instability in economic indicators by using deep learning (DL) and ML models. Utilising ML techniques helps in addressing intractable computing problems, assessing risk, detecting fraudulent transactions and formulating policies characterised by low risk, high success chances and significant enhancements in operational efficiency.

Natural language processing algorithms can potentially extract meaning from unstructured data, ML-powered chatbots can address customer questions and RPA powered by ML can enhance administrative tasks, according to Goodell et al. (2021). With the help of ML, financial managers may personalise product suggestions, maximise marketing efforts and boost the quality of service they provide to customers. Financial institutions may enhance their analytical capabilities, fortify their risk management processes, simplify their operations and provide clients with personalised services by utilising ML applications. AI in finance is used in forecasting market cyclical movements, investment strategies and advisory services, risk assessment in credit financing and solutions, incorporating ML for high-frequency trading and technical analysis and is also helpful in detecting anomalies within the transactions (Belhaj & Hachaıchi, 2021). Biju et al. (2023) study the trends of ML and DL standards in financial markets and the need for scholars to develop an extensive approach concerning these disruptive and innovative influences that are reshaping the landscape of finance. Fig. 7.3 below highlights several research agendas emerging further to harness the potential of AI and ML in finance.

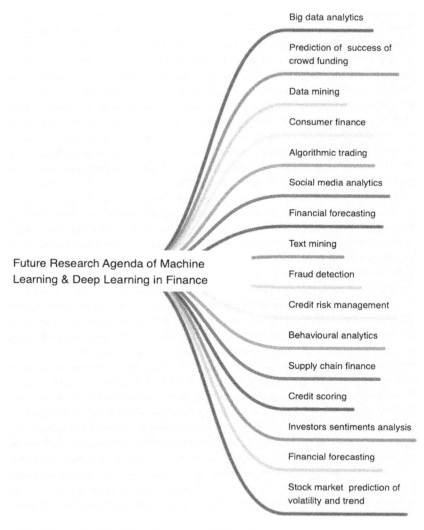

Fig. 7.3.   Artificial Intelligence and Machine Learning Applications in Finance. *Source:* Biju et al. (2023).

7.2 Machine Learning Model Integration

ML gives an edge to financial institutions to achieve more than benchmarks in their portfolios, perform risk assessments, compute credit ratings and identify fraudulent activities (Yuan et al., 2020). The integration process requires forecasting analytics automation for the data driver decisions. The ML and DL tools are not only specific to financial sectors, but they apply to other business domains. ML and DL models are also used for visual reporting and analysis (Spinner et al. 2020). The Integration of ML models can help organisations achieve higher productivity as a whole, gain competitive advantage through automated trading, and efficiently deal with the changing market environment. During ML implementation in conventional financial processes, collaboration between finance practitioners, tech specialists as well as data engineers is critical. It is necessary for compliance with regulatory requirements and cost reduction, and to achieve increased productivity, the better services or goods are provided to consumers. This integration helps banks streamline their decision processes, cut costs and take advantage of a changing financial terrain. Such procedures can involve the supervision of financial issues and free managers from one part of the responsibility. In addition, it is used to improve and simplify existing processes, giving team members enough time to learn about this new technology development.

There are also uses related to algorithmic trading, risk management and customer data management that can serve as a solid foundation for the greater adoption of such technological tools in the future. Thus, the integration of ML into existing processes is the first of many gradual steps that financial organisations should take while allowing managers to adapt to change prudently.

8. Visualisation and Reporting

8.1 Tools for Effective Data Visualisation and Reporting

Data analytics is made possible by the use of some data analytics tools, which may also have visualisation features. Visualisation of data makes it easy for the manager to understand exactly what the data trend is, how it is going to proceed in the future, and, consequently, what decisions need to be made today in light of the data. These tools serve a number of purposes that have much bearing on the managers' role as the lynchpin of team performance. For example, one of the most basic functions of data exploration. Managers use it for interactive dashboards and reports that can be edited. The managers can then explore the data trends to make decisions. In this way, complex information can be plotted on graphs, pictured on pie charts, bar graphs or other ways to simplify the data trend and aid the managers. Another fundamental use of data visualisation tools is the monitoring of employees' KPIs. The real-time dashboards of different software provide business metrics options that managers can track business processes performance and can be monitored to ensure the organization is operating at its best. Such integration of metrices allow the managers to identify the problems with a quick response to the customer's need.

Similarly, reports can be generated on the data using these tools without the need to interpret and create reports manually. One widely used software is Tableau, which is considered a powerful tool because it enables users to create and interact on its shareable dashboard and visualise data using charts, graphs and reports (DigitalYX., n.d.).

The connection of the software to various data sources offers a dependable way to produce visualised data, which includes some features that attract managers working in multinational organisations, such as geographical maps. The user-friendly interface allows the managers to create an interactive dashboard for compelling storytelling. Another tool that is widely used is 'Power BI,' which was developed by Microsoft as a business analytics tool that facilitates data visualisation. The integration of data with Microsoft products and third-party applications is a feature that facilitates a number of business processes. The drag-and-drop is also effective for managerial use (Rare Career, n.d.).

However, the flexibility for customisation and licencing costs for certain advanced features are some of the downsides of using Power BI. There have also been occasional reporting of challenges with handling large datasets. Another data visualisation tool is the Google Data Studio, which is a free, cloud-based data visualisation tool that can be used with the integration of other Google products and real-time monitoring (Google Analytics, 2012).

Its advantages include its free nature and interactive and customisable reports and dashboards. However, there are some disadvantages as well. Its advanced analytics features are limited, and the data visualisation options are not diverse in the free version. There is also a potential limitation for organisations that are heavily reliant on non-Google data sources. Thus, data visualisation tools are used by managers to understand data better and make subsequent decisions.

8.2 Telling Stories With Financial Data

Managers often have to communicate complex information to stakeholders, engage them in discussion and drive decision-making processes (Stackpole, 2020). Telling stories with financial data is a quality of a skilful manager who knows their audience. The story needs to be customised, its details worked out and pieces of evidence from data visualised beforehand according to the needs of the audience (Qin et al., 2020). For example, the data that are presented to employees to drive up performance may not be presented to a meeting with the board of directors. Frequently, managers are responsible for explaining the pattern that data visualisation demonstrates to the audience so that they can make better decisions. This requires a straightforward narrative or storyline for the financial data and the repetition of a clear message or insight that the manager wants to convey. According to Wang et al. (2019), the choice of visual is also important, as some visualisation tools may be more compelling than others. This needs to be done after the creation of a context, which may include any background information or market conditions. Managers also have deep insights into 'why' the visualised data are following a trend – this insight empowers the managers in their role. It needs to be capitalised upon when telling a story using financial data. Whether profits have increased or performance indicators are decreasing, the manager needs to know the reason why the trend is the way it is. An effective narration includes real-life examples and similar case studies and highlights the patterns for future prediction. The managers need to have a clear objective in mind, with what they want to achieve from the storytelling as the paramount concern. The KPIs of the employees can be referred to while explaining the trend in the data. The financial insights in the story can be connected to operational actions, with a focus on how the financial insights can be used in actionable steps. Effective storytelling using financial data can be achieved by following these strategies.

9. Creating a Data-Driven Organizational Culture

9.1 Leadership Strategies for Promoting a Data-Centric Work Environment

The promotion of a data-centric work environment requires strategic leadership so that values of data-driven decision-making are instilled in the work culture of the organisation. Leaders need to incorporate data into their decision-making processes regularly to show that they are dedicated to data-centric practices. Make data-driven decisions visible and explain them. Leaders who give data top priority convey to the whole organisation that data are an essential part of decision-making. Leaders need to emphasise the importance of continuous learning and skill development related to data analysis. Leaders should invest in training programs and resources that enable employees to enhance their data literacy. There also needs to be a clear segregation of responsibilities related to data governance; managers should designate individuals or teams responsible for data quality, accuracy and privacy (Broo & Schooling, 2020). Establishing accountability ensures that there is ownership of data-related processes and that employees understand their role in maintaining the integrity of data. This needs to be done simultaneously with the development and implementation of robust data governance frameworks that include policies, procedures and guidelines for data management. Managers also need to foster collaboration between departments and break down silos that may hinder the sharing of data and insights.

In this regard, there is one aspect of a data-centric work environment that managers need to ensure. This is the training and development of financial teams. The employees should know how to use data for decision-making and what is expected of them. The necessary skills and knowledge must be imparted to the employees to adapt them to the complex financial data. The financial sector is experiencing notable technological advancements with the incorporation of advanced analytics, machine learning and AI; finance teams can use these technologies for improved data analysis, decision-making and work automation if they receive the necessary training (Kumar Dixit et al., 2023). Professionals in finance also need to stay up to date on evolving regulatory environments. Teams that receive training are guaranteed to comprehend and abide by the constantly changing financial legislation, governance standards and reporting obligations.

Additionally, ongoing training enhances financial analysts' proficiency in reporting, data interpretation and analysis. Training sharpens sophisticated financial modelling, data visualisation methods and practical communication skills, enabling finance professionals to provide stakeholders with more informative and persuasive reports. Targeted training programmes and channels for continuous education are highly effective at developing skills and providing knowledge. Managers can utilise them to enhance and empower their staff.

9.2 Measuring the Impact of Data-Driven Culture

The impact of a data-based environment with positive changes and process improvements involves the effectiveness and results of data-governed practices within the organisation. The observable outcomes should have a tangible impact that can be directly associated with the application of a data-centric culture. The effects can be measured with quantitative tools, different metrics, KPIs or economic indicators such as cost vs benefit, improved consumer buying patterns and satisfaction. It is imperative to evaluate both quantitative and qualitative indicators in order to ascertain the impact and efficacy of data-centric practices. The decisions are also based on subjective judgements and non-numerical social or environmental impacts that are somewhat more intangible but affect the potential value of a company. Qualitative methods such as employee questionnaires, research projects and channels for feedback may bring insight into instances of effectiveness when data-driven strategies had favourable results. Qualitative methods offer valuable insights into the perspectives, mindsets and actions of interested parties or coworkers with respect to the utilisation of data in the decision-making process.

Additionally, monitoring the pace of adoption of data tools and technologies and assessing the degree of data literacy among employees provide insights into the shift in organisational culture towards data-driven decision-making (Chatterjee et al., 2021). In essence, the precise assessment of impact is dependent upon the organisation's capacity to utilise data in order to foster innovation, informed decision-making and ongoing enhancement; these factors collectively contribute to the organisation's enduring expansion and competitive edge. Management measures the impact of a data-powered culture through both tangible and qualitative tools. Tangible measurements include data remediation and truncation, data creation and storage facility, data protection and accessibility and effort and resources put into analysing insufficient data (Rashedi, 2022). The setting up of a data-directed culture that drives innovation and decisions based on qualitative assessments results in enhanced business performance and a competitive edge (Orero, 2023). The evaluation of these metrics is conducted by applying business analytics instruments integrated with modern technology, examining marketing metrics and establishing procedures for data regulations and analytics (Chatterjee et al., 2021). The impact of a data-driven culture is also evaluated based on the level of data awareness and engagement within the organisation, as well as the successful implementation of data-related initiatives and the integration of data governance into various business functions (Johnson et al., 2021).

10. Conclusion

Due to the complicated nature of financial data and the problems associated with traditional interpretation, change and framework, organisations must adopt a culture that prioritises data, particularly in the development of financial services. Traditionally, when making decisions, individual experiences and expertise have been preferred over factual information. On the contrary, the implementation of data management tools has empowered managers to comprehend, analyse and communicate intricate data trends more effortlessly, thereby facilitating the implementation of better-informed choices. Supervisors play an integral part in facilitating the adoption of data-focused work cultures by their teams, as they recognise the significance of transitioning from opinion-based to evidence-based decision-making. The increasing complication of financial reporting serves to strengthen the compelling case for incorporating data visualisation tools, which offer managers a clearer perspective while navigating complex financial environments. In essence, the implementation of a data-intensive culture can yield substantial advantages for the administration of any organisation. This transition will facilitate enhanced planning and analysis, more accurate choices and long-lasting competitiveness amidst a dynamic business environment.

References

Abraham, R., Schneider, J., & vom Brocke, J. (2019). Data governance: A conceptual framework, structured review, and research agenda. *International Journal of Information Management*, *49*(2), 424–438. https://doi.org/10.1016/j.ijinfomgt.2019.07.008

Adriaens, P., Tahvanainen, A., & Dixon, M. (2021). Smart infrastructure finance: Investment in data-driven industry ecosystems. In *Green and social economy finance* (pp. 192–225). CRC Press.

Alzahrani, S., Daim, T., & Choo, K.-K. R. (2022). Assessment of the blockchain technology adoption for the management of the electronic health record systems. *IEEE Transactions on Engineering Management*, 1–18. https://doi.org/10.1109/tem.2022.3158185

Ariyaluran Habeeb, R. A., Nasaruddin, F., Gani, A., Targio Hashem, I. A., Ahmed, E., & Imran, M. (2019). Real-time big data processing for anomaly detection: A survey. *International Journal of Information Management*, *45*, 289–307. https://doi.org/10.1016/j.ijinfomgt.2018.08.006

Arjun, A., Srinath, A., & Chandavarkar, B. R. (2021, July). Predictive analytics and data mining in healthcare. In *2021 12th International Conference on Computing Communication and Networking Technologies (ICCCNT)* (pp. 1–7). IEEE.

Balakrishnan, R., Das, S., & Chattopadhyay, M. (2020). Implementing data strategy: Design considerations and reference architecture for data-enabled value creation. *Australasian Journal of Information Systems*, *24*. https://doi.org/10.3127/ajis.v24i0.2541

Belhaj, M., & Hachaichi, Y. (2021, August). *Artificial intelligence, machine learning and big data in finance opportunities, challenges, and implications for policy makers.* https://www.oecd.org/finance/artificial-intelligencemachine-learning-big-data-in-finance.htm

Biju, A. K. V. N., Thomas, A. S., & Thasneem, J. (2023). Examining the research taxonomy of artificial intelligence, deep learning & machine learning in the financial sphere—A bibliometric analysis. *Quality and Quantity*, 1–30.

Broo, D. G., & Schooling, J. (2020). Towards data-centric decision making for smart infrastructure: Data and its challenges. *IFAC-PapersOnLine*, *53*(3), 90–94. https://doi.org/10.1016/j.ifacol.2020.11.014

Brousseau, K. R., Driver, M. J., Hourihan, G., & Larsson, R. (2006). The seasoned executive's decision-making style. *Harvard Business Review*, *84*(2), 110–121.

Carvajal, A., & Elliott, J. (2007). *Strengths and weaknesses in securities market regulation: A global analysis (IMF working Paper No. WP/07/259)*. International Monetary Fund. https://www.imf.org/external/pubs/ft/wp/2007/wp07259.pdf

Chatterjee, S., Chaudhuri, R., & Vrontis, D. (2021). Does data-driven culture impact innovation and performance of a firm? An empirical examination. *Annals of Operations Research*. https://doi.org/10.1007/s10479-020-03887-z

Chen, I.-M. A., Chu, K., Palaniappan, K., Ratner, A., Huang, J., Huntemann, M., Hajek, P., Ritter, S., Varghese, N., Seshadri, R., Roux, S., Woyke, T., Eloe-Fadrosh, E. A., Ivanova, N. N., & Kyrpides, N. (2020). The IMG/M data management and analysis system v.6.0: New tools and advanced capabilities. *Nucleic Acids Research*, *49*(D1), D751–D763. https://doi.org/10.1093/nar/gkaa939

Chen, J., Lv, Z., & Song, H. (2019). Design of personnel big data management system based on blockchain. *Future Generation Computer Systems*, *101*, 1122–1129. https://doi.org/10.1016/j.future.2019.07.037

CichyRass. (2020). An overview of data quality frameworks. *IEEE Journals & Magazine*. https://ieeexplore.ieee.org/abstract/document/8642813/

Corea, F., & Corea, F. (2019). Big data management: How organisations create and implement data strategies. An introduction to data: Everything you need to know about AI. *Big Data and Data Science*, 7–13.

de Prado, M. M. L. (2020). *Machine learning for asset managers*. Cambridge University Press. https://doi.org/10.1017/9781108883658

Dekimpe, M. G. (2020). Retailing and retailing research in the age of big data analytics. *International Journal of Research in Marketing*, *37*(1), 3–14.

Delen. (2020). *Predictive analytics: Data mining, machine learning and data science for practitioners*. FT Press.

DigitalYX. (n.d.). *Marketing analytics with Tableau*. https://www.digitalyx.us/marketing-analytics-with-tableau/

Durairaj, M., & Poornappriya, T. S. (2020). Why feature selection in data mining is prominent? A survey. In *Proceedings of International Conference on Artificial Intelligence, Smart Grid and Smart City Applications: AISGSC 2019* (pp. 949–963). Springer International Publishing.

Ewen, J. (2019). How big data is changing the finance industry. https://www.tamoco.com/blog/big-data-finance-industry-analytics/

Fan, W., & Geerts, F. (2022). *Foundations of data quality management*. Springer Nature.

Fanning, K., & Grant, R. (2013). Big data: Implications for financial managers. *Journal of Corporate Accounting & Finance*. https://doi.org/10.1002/jcaf.21872

Fraser, J. R. S., Quail, R., & Simkins, B. (2021). *Enterprise risk management: Today's leading research and best practices for tomorrow's executives*. John Wiley & Sons.

George, B., Walker, R. M., & Monster, J. (2019). Does strategic planning improve organisational performance? A meta-analysis. *Public Administration Review*, *79*(6), 810–819. https://doi.org/10.1111/puar.13104

Goodell, J. W., Kumar, S., Lim, W. M., & Pattnaik, D. (2021). Artificial intelligence and machine learning in finance: Identifying foundations, themes, and research clusters from bibliometric analysis. *Journal of Behavioral and Experimental Finance, 32*(1), 100577. https://doi.org/10.1016/j.jbef.2021.100577

Google Analytics. (August 2012). http://www.google.com/analytics

Grody, A. D. (2018). Rebuilding financial industry infrastructure. *Journal of Risk Management in Financial Institutions, 11*(1), 34–46.

Haj Khlifa, S., & Zaki, A. (2021). Enhanced prudential standards under basel iii: What consequences for the profitability of banks. *Journal of Optimization in Industrial Engineering, 14*(Special Issue), 9–15. https://doi.org/10.22094/joie.2020.677810

Hastig, G. M., & Sodhi, M. S. (2020). Blockchain for supply chain traceability: Business requirements and critical success factors. *Production and Operations Management, 29*(4), 935–954.

Hebb, T. (2019). Investing in sustainable infrastructure. *Challenges in Managing Sustainable Business: Reporting, Taxation, Ethics and Governance,* 251–273.

Hoffman, D., & Rimo, P. (2017). It takes data to protect data. https://doi.org/10.2139/ssrn.2973280

Huang, S., Wang, G., Yan, Y., & Fang, X. (2020). Blockchain-based data management for digital twin of product. *Journal of Manufacturing Systems, 54*, 361–371. https://doi.org/10.1016/j.jmsy.2020.01.009

Hubbard, D. W. (2020). *The failure of risk management: Why it's broken and how to fix it.* John Wiley & Sons.

Hupperz, M. J., Gür, I., Möller, F., & Otto, B. (2021). What is a data-driven organisation? In *Proceedings of the 27th Annual Americas Conference on Information Systems (AMCIS 2021).* Fraunhofer-Gesellschaft. https://publica.fraunhofer.de/entities/publication/9ef28f35-ecd6-43b6-a3b5-b97ee7a44e77/details

Johnson, J. L., Adkins, D., & Chauvin, S. (2020). A review of the quality indicators of rigor in qualitative research. *American Journal of Pharmaceutical Education, 84*(1), 138–146. https://doi.org/10.5688/ajpe7120

Johnson, D. S., Sihi, D., & Muzellec, L. (2021, September). Implementing big data analytics in marketing departments: Mixing organic and administered approaches to increase data-driven decision making. In *Informatics* (Vol. 8, No. 4, p. 66). MDPI.

Jones, S., Pergl, R., Hooft, R., Miksa, T., Samors, R., Ungvari, J., Davis, R. I., & Lee, T. (2020). Data management planning: How requirements and solutions are beginning to converge. *Data Intelligence, 2*(1–2), 208–219. https://doi.org/10.1162/dint_a_00043

Kamble, S. S., & Gunasekaran, A. (2019). Big data-driven supply chain performance measurement system: A review and framework for implementation. *International Journal of Production Research, 58*(1), 1–22. https://doi.org/10.1080/00207543.2019.1630770

Kania, K., Rymarczyk, T., Mazurek, M., Skrzypek-Ahmed, S., Guzik, M., & Oleszczuk, P. (2021). Optimisation of technological processes by solving inverse problem through block-wise-transform-reduction method using open architecture sensor platform. *Energies, 14*(24), 8295. https://doi.org/10.3390/en14248295

Kokina, J., & Blanchette, S. (2019). Early evidence of digital labor in accounting: Innovation with robotic process automation. *International Journal of Accounting Information Systems, 35*(1), 100431. https://doi.org/10.1016/j.accinf.2019.100431

Kumar Dixit, C., Somani, P., Gupta, S. K., & Pathak, A. (2023). *Data-centric predictive modeling of turnover rate and new hire in workforce management system* (pp. 121–138). CRC Press EBooks. https://doi.org/10.1201/9781003357070-8

Levantesi, S., & Zacchia, G. (2021). Machine learning and financial literacy: An exploration of factors influencing financial knowledge in Italy. *Journal of Risk and Financial Management, 14*(3), 120. https://doi.org/10.3390/jrfm14030120

Lin, S.-S., Shen, S.-L., Zhou, A., & Xu, Y.-S. (2021). Risk assessment and management of excavation system based on fuzzy set theory and machine learning methods. *Automation in Construction, 122*, 103490. https://doi.org/10.1016/j.autcon.2020.103490

Liu, J. (2022). Social data governance: Towards a definition and model. *Big Data & Society, 9*(2). https://doi.org/10.1177/20539517221111352

Lu, Y., Xu, X., & Wang, L. (2020). Smart manufacturing process and system automation–a critical review of the standards and envisioned scenarios. *Journal of Manufacturing Systems, 56*, 312–325.

Marzuki, M., Nik Abdul Majid, W. Z., Azis, N. K., Rosman, R., & Haji Abdulatiff, N. K. (2020). Fraud risk management model: A content analysis approach. *The Journal of Asian Finance, Economics and Business, 7*(10), 717–728. https://doi.org/10.13106/jafeb.2020.vol7.no10.717

Mazlan, A. A., Daud, S. M., Sam, S. M., Abas, H., Rasid, S. Z. A., & Yusof, M. F. (2020). Scalability challenges in healthcare blockchain system—a systematic review. *IEEE Access, 8*, 23663–23673.

McLaughlin, R. (2004). Data in financial institutions. *Journal of Financial Transformation, 11*, 75–80.

Micheli, M., Ponti, M., Craglia, M., & Berti Suman, A. (2020). Emerging models of data governance in the age of datafication. *Big Data & Society, 7*(2). https://doi.org/10.1177/2053951720948087

Mölder, F., Jablonski, K. P., Letcher, B., Hall, M. B., Tomkins-Tinch, C. H., Sochat, V., Forster, J., Lee, S., Twardziok, S. O., Kanitz, A., Wilm, A., Holtgrewe, M., Rahmann, S., Nahnsen, S., & Köster, J. (2021). Sustainable data analysis with Snakemake. *F1000Research, 10*, 33. https://doi.org/10.12688/f1000research.29032.2

Nejman, M., Cejnar, O., & Slovik, P. (2011). Improving the quality and flexibility of data collection from financial institutions. In *Proceedings of the IFC Conference on "Initiatives to Address Data Gaps Revealed by the Financial Crisis", Basel, 25–26 August 2010* (No. 34, pp. 52–59).

Nisar, Q. A., Nasir, N., Jamshed, S., Naz, S., Ali, M., & Ali, S. (2020). Big data management and environmental performance: Role of big data decision-making capabilities and decision-making quality. *Journal of Enterprise Information Management, 34*(4), 1061–1096. https://doi.org/10.1108/jeim-04-2020-0137

Orero, B. M. (2023). *Enhancing big data analytics capabilities: The influence of organisational culture and data-driven orientation.* Doctoral dissertation. Universitat Politècnica de València.

Pereira, M. M., & Frazzon, E. M. (2021). A data-driven approach to adaptive synchronisation of demand and supply in omni-channel retail supply chains. *International Journal of Information Management, 57*, 102165.

Qin, X., Luo, Y., Tang, N., & Li, G. (2020). Making data visualisation more efficient and effective: A survey. *The VLDB Journal, 29*(1), 93–117. https://doi.org/10.1007/s00778-019-00588-3

Ramasamy, A., & Chowdhury, S. (2020). Big data quality dimensions: A systematic literature review. *Journal of Information Systems and Technology Management, 17.* https://doi.org/10.4301/s1807-1775202017003

Rare Career. (n.d.). *How your organization can take Microsoft's Power BI platform to the next level.* https://rarecareer.com/how-your-organization-can-take-microsofts-power-bi-platform-to-the-next-level/

Rashedi, J. (2022). *The data-driven organization: Using data for the success of your company.* Springer Nature.

Reynolds, D., Dcosta, D., Xie, D., & Zhen, S. (2018, October). Deriving client insights in the financial sector. In *Proceedings of the 28th Annual International Conference on Computer Science and Software Engineering* (pp. 394–396). IBM Corp. https://doi.org/10.5555/3291291.3291381

Rudra Kumar, M., & Kumar Gunjan, V. (2020). Review of machine learning models for credit scoring analysis. *Ingeniería Solidaria, 16*(1). https://doi.org/10.16925/2357-6014.2020.01.11

Sarraf, S. (2023). Formulating A strategic plan based on statistical analyses and applications for financial companies through A real-world use case. *arXiv, 2307,* 04778.

Shakya, S., & Smys, S. (2021, September). Big data analytics for improved risk management and customer segregation in banking applications. *Journal of IoT in Social, Mobile, Analytics, and Cloud, 3*(3), 235–249. https://doi.org/10.36548/jismac.2021.3.005.

Sleep, S., Hulland, J., & Gooner, R. A. (2019). The data hierarchy: Factors influencing the adoption and implementation of data-driven decision making. *AMS Review, 9,* 230–248.

Spinner, T., Schlegel, U., Schäfer, H., & El-Assady, M. (2020). ExplaIner: A visual analytics framework for interactive and explainable machine learning. *IEEE Transactions on Visualization and Computer Graphics, 26*(1), 1064–1074. https://doi.org/10.1109/TVCG.2019.2934629

Stackpole, B. (2020, May 20). *The next chapter in analytics: Data storytelling.* MIT Sloan. https://mitsloan.mit.edu/ideas-made-to-matter/next-chapter-analytics-data-storytelling

Storm, M., & Borgman, H. (2020). Understanding challenges and success factors in creating a data-driven culture. http://scholarspace.manoa.hawaii.edu/

Strielkowski, W., Vlasov, A., Selivanov, K., Muraviev, K., & Shakhnov, V. (2023). Prospects and challenges of the machine learning and data-driven methods for the predictive analysis of power systems: A review. *Energies, 16*(10), 4025. https://doi.org/10.3390/en16104025

Tabesh, P., Mousavidin, E., & Hasani, S. (2019). Implementing big data strategies: A managerial perspective. *Business Horizons, 62*(3), 347–358.

Thacker, S., Adshead, D., Fay, M., Hallegatte, S., Harvey, M., Meller, H., O'Regan, N., Rozenberg, J., Watkins, G., & Hall, J. W. (2019). Infrastructure for sustainable development. *Nature Sustainability, 2*(4), 324–331. https://doi.org/10.1038/s41893-019-0256-8

Thanawala, R. M., Jesneck, J. L., & Seymour, N. E. (2019). Education management platform enables delivery and comparison of multiple evaluation types. *Journal of Surgical Education, 76*(6), e209–e216. https://doi.org/10.1016/j.jsurg.2019.08.017

Udhaya Mugil, D., & Metilda Florence, S. (2022, April). Efficient sensitive file encryption strategy with access control and integrity auditing. In *Proceedings of International Conference on Deep Learning, Computing and Intelligence: ICDCI 2021* (pp. 295–304). Springer Nature.

Wang, Z., Dingwall, H., & Bach, B. (2019). Teaching data visualisation and story-telling with data comic workshops. In *Extended Abstracts of the 2019 CHI Conference on Human Factors in Computing Systems.* https://doi.org/10.1145/3290607.3299043

Wang, J., Yang, Y., Wang, T., Sherratt, R. S., & Zhang, J. (2020). Big data service architecture: A survey. *Journal of Internet Technology, 21*(2), 393–405.

Wu, Y., Dai, H.-N., & Wang, H. (2021). Convergence of blockchain and edge computing for secure and scalable IIoT critical infrastructures in industry 4.0. *IEEE Internet of Things Journal, 8*(4), 2300–2317. https://doi.org/10.1109/jiot.2020.3025916

Wu, B., Widanage, W. D., Yang, S., & Liu, X. (2020). Battery digital twins: Perspectives on the fusion of models, data and artificial intelligence for smart battery management systems. *Energy and AI, 1*, 100016. https://doi.org/10.1016/j.egyai.2020.100016

Yu, W., Wong, C. Y., Chavez, R., & Jacobs, M. A. (2021). Integrating big data analytics into supply chain finance: The roles of information processing and data-driven culture. *International Journal of Production Economics, 236*(1), 108135. https://doi.org/10.1016/j.ijpe.2021.108135

Yuan, J., Chen, C., Yang, W., Liu, M., Xia, J., & Liu, S. (2020). A survey of visual analytics techniques for machine learning. *Computational Visual Media, 7*, 3–36. https://doi.org/10.1007/s41095-020-0191-7

Zitnik, M., Nguyen, F., Wang, B., Leskovic, J., Goldenberg, A., & Hoffman, M. M. (2019). Machine learning for integrating data in biology and medicine: Principles, practice, and opportunities. *Information Fusion, 50*, 71–91. https://doi.org/10.1016/j.inffus.2018.09.012

Chapter 8

Regulatory Changes and Compliance Challenges

Wei Xi

UCSI University, Malaysia

Abstract

This chapter delves into the intricate evolution and challenges of regulatory frameworks within the global financial sector, spotlighting the dynamic interplay between technological advancements, globalization and the imperative for stringent regulatory compliance. Initially, it traces the historical lineage of financial regulation from its nascent stages, through pivotal transformations aimed at enhancing market stability and integrity, to contemporary paradigms that balance efficiency with systemic safety. The discourse navigates through various regulatory models – ranging from institutional and functional frameworks to the innovative "Twin Peaks" model – and their respective merits and challenges in aligning with the evolving financial landscape. Furthermore, the paper scrutinizes the multifaceted role of managerial accountability in fostering a culture of compliance, emphasizing proactive risk assessment, regulatory reporting and the integration of ethical considerations into corporate governance. Through an analytical lens, it explores how financial institutions can navigate the complexities of adherence to diverse regulatory mandates, thereby safeguarding financial stability while promoting growth and innovation. The narrative concludes by projecting future trajectories of regulatory frameworks, advocating for a harmonious blend of regulatory rigor and flexibility to accommodate the rapid pace of financial innovation and global interconnectedness.

Keywords: Financial regulation; compliance challenges; regulatory models; managerial accountability; financial stability and innovation

Strategic Financial Management, 119–134

Copyright © 2024 Wei Xi
Published under exclusive licence by Emerald Publishing Limited
doi:10.1108/978-1-83608-106-720241008

1. Introduction

In the rapidly evolving financial sector, characterized by technological advancements and globalization, keeping pace with stringent regulatory frameworks is more critical than ever (Jones & Knaack, 2019). This dynamic landscape demands that financial organizations not only adapt swiftly but also operate within legal boundaries to maintain their credibility and ensure sustained growth. The regulatory frameworks in the financial sector are not merely static rules; they represent a set of dynamic, continually adjusting principles and guidelines aimed at ensuring the stability, integrity and credibility of the global financial system. Their overarching objectives are threefold: to uphold the integrity of financial markets, protect consumer interests and achieve financial stability while emphasizing transparency (Ahern, 2021).

In this paper, we will outline various aspects of the regulatory frameworks in the global financial milieu. We aim to focus on fundamental components such as compliance risk assessment and regulatory reporting, both of which are cornerstones in ensuring an organization's seamless functioning in the intricate financial domain. We provide a comprehensive overview drawn from established theories and real-world applications, which will assist financial managers in skillfully navigating the regulatory terrain (Carlin & Soskice, 2015).

2. The Development of Financial Regulation

2.1 The Embryonic Stage of Financial Supervision

Before the 1930s, the economic policies of Western countries were influenced by classical economic theory. The overall financial system largely relied on the laws of market competition, and most countries had not yet established a meaningful financial regulatory system. In the Middle Ages, due to the interpretations of the Old and New Testaments that deemed "usurious money-making activities as sinful," Western nations implemented regulations prohibiting usury. These policies were primarily influenced by moral considerations rather than financial regulatory objectives. The "Tulip Mania" of the 17th century marked the first recorded financial bubble in human history, and there was no sign of financial regulation during this period (Jones & Knaack, 2019). In June 1720, in response to the "South Sea Bubble," the British government enacted the "Bubble Act," marking a seminal step in the history of global financial regulation. However, this was a targeted regulation of the securities market (Harris, 1994).

From the perspective of Adam Smith, the founder of classical economics and proponent of the "Real Bills Doctrine," "banks should mainly invest in short-term commercial bills that reflect the production of the century. This practice will allow trade to restrict credit supply without leading to inflation or contraction." However, Henry Thornton believed that "the longer the credit chain, the more such bills there will be, and there is a risk of over-issuance that should be centrally regulated." Between 1825 and 1865, the Currency School and Banking School debated the "Real Bills Doctrine." The Currency School, building on Thornton's view, argued that "nothing is more important than regulating the number of banknotes issued in banking activities," while the Banking School supported the Real Bills Doctrine.

In practice, the Currency School's arguments held more sway. The Bank Charter Act of 1844 in the UK was a testament to this, stipulating that pound sterling issuance could "only be collateralized by government bonds up to 15 million pounds, and any additional issuance required gold reserves." Yet, in 1846, due to poor harvests in England and Ireland leading to rising prices and gold outflows, a bank run was triggered. The Bank of England, not playing its role as the "lender of last resort," exacerbated the instability of the banking system. Against this backdrop, some countries began to establish central banking institutions to control currency issuance and stabilize economic development through their role as the lender of last resort. According to Robert Pringle (2009), by 1929, a total of 27 countries had established financial regulatory agencies. However, the regulatory methods and philosophies of this era were nascent and still in their formative stages.

2.2 Emphasis on Safety and Stability Phase

Between 1929 and 1933, a severe economic crisis erupted in the US, quickly spreading worldwide and leading to the Great Depression. The root cause of this crisis stemmed from the inherent contradictions of capitalism, specifically, the tension between private ownership of the means of production and the social nature of production. Directly speaking, the laissez-faire, weakly-regulated economic policies adopted by Western countries resulted in chaos and mounting risks in financial markets. In 1933, Roosevelt introduced sweeping reforms, launching the Glass–Steagall Act (also known as the Banking Act of 1933), separating commercial banking from investment banking to prevent commercial banks from participating in capital market specu-lation. The Federal Deposit Insurance Act was announced, establishing the Federal Deposit Insurance Corporation, and the Securities Act was introduced, forbidding securities institutions from engaging in banking services, and mandating that exec-utives of banks and financial institutions could not hold multiple positions simul-taneously. The onset of the economic crisis also fostered the evolution of economic theories. The once-prevailing belief in the omnipotence of the market was heavily questioned, while Keynesian advocacy for state intervention gained traction, offer-ing theoretical backing for intensified financial regulation during this period. Abba Lerner (1947) posited that any economic activity has its limits and arbitrariness; an unregulated economy is akin to a car without a driver, advocating for heightened state economic oversight. Following this crisis and extending to the 1970s, Western capitalist nations, led by the US, bolstered their financial regulatory efforts, emphasizing the safety and stability of the financial system, restricting cross-industry operations of banks, insurance and securities firms and advocating for segmented regulation. According to Robert Pringle (2009), between 1930 and 1969, 49 countries globally established financial regulatory bodies, and nine established securities and insurance regulatory bodies. In terms of regulatory intensity, nations with financial regulatory agencies amplified their national financial oversight, marking the initial development phase of financial regulation on a global scale (Jones & Knaack, 2019).

2.3 Championing Efficiency and Liberalization Phase

In the 1970s, with the economic resurgence in Europe and the rise of the Japanese economy, Western capitalist nations sequentially faced stagflation challenges. From the perspective of Keynesian economists, it seemed improbable for high inflation and high unemployment rates to coexist. The Keynesian advocacy for government intervention not only failed to address this issue but was instead perceived by Monetarist and supply-side schools of neoliberal economic thought as the root cause of stagflation. Consequently, economic policies favoring government intervention waned, with economic liberalization theories regaining dominance.

According to McKinnon (1973) and Shaw (1973), improper government interference in its financial system via regulatory means can lead to financial repression, subsequently hampering economic growth. Hence, they introduced the concept of financial deepening, advocating for the relaxation of financial regulations and restoring free competition in financial markets. Although their conclusions focused on developing countries, they offered significant insights into financial policy formulation in Western nations (Bhattacharyya & Nanda, 2000). Moreover, with issues like regulatory rent-seeking and regulatory capture emerging in the financial oversight process, Western nations began re-evaluating the limitations of their financial regulation.

Influenced by these factors, from the 1970s to the 1980s, countries like the US and Japan progressively relaxed their financial regulations, prioritizing efficiency and fostering a liberal financial development environment. Through policies such as deregulating interest rates, expanding operational scopes and facilitating foreign capital entry, they stimulated the prosperous growth of financial markets.

2.4 The Phase Emphasizing Both Efficiency and Safety

In the 1990s, the ethos of financial liberalization energized financial markets but also introduced new risk factors. In practice, the road to financial liberalization was not smooth. Latin America, Asia and the US experienced a series of financial crises, primarily due to inappropriate liberalization policies and a lack of adequate financial oversight. In 1982, Mexico faced a severe debt crisis. The subsequent strict financial controls implemented by the Mexican government forced commercial banks to provide funds to the government. Although this relieved the government's debt situation, it also had adverse impacts on market economy development (Kane, 1981). In 1988, Mexico initiated financial liberalization policies, relaxed controls on international capital markets and adopted policies like liberalizing interest rates. Due to a fragile financial system and weak oversight, Mexico saw significant asset price volatility, which culminated in the 1994 Mexican financial crisis.

From the late 1980s to the 1990s, Japan grappled with a bubble economy. Financial liberalization and internationalization altered Japan's financial landscape, reducing the prominence of bank-based indirect financing. Fierce competition prompted financial institutions to take riskier actions. A large influx of funds into real estate and the financial sector led to bubbles in these markets.

Coupled with lagging financial oversight, changing international financial conditions and frequent policy missteps, these factors precipitated the bursting of the bubble. The 2007 financial crisis, originating in the US and rapidly spreading worldwide, was primarily due to excessive financial product innovation and a lax regulatory environment. Former Federal Reserve Chairman Alan Greenspan believed that "less regulation is better regulation." The advancement of information technology in the 21st century facilitated innovation in the subprime mortgage market in the US and the misuse of financial derivatives (Kim et al., 2013). The complexity of financial products reduced transparency, exacerbating information asymmetries in the financial system and intensifying adverse selection and moral hazard issues.

Given this backdrop, economists began to reevaluate the adverse effects of financial liberalization. McKinnon (1989) argued that macroeconomic instability, regulatory lapses and the incorrect sequencing of financial liberalization were the root causes of its failures. This reflection on financial liberalization doesn't mean its outright rejection. It's not about swinging from one extreme (complete liberalization) to the other (heavy regulation). Instead, the challenge is to find a balance between efficiency and safety in financial oversight. The objective is to ensure a financial system that operates both efficiently and stably. This principle will guide future financial regulatory efforts.

3. Financial Regulatory Frameworks

Financial regulatory frameworks refer to the allocation of regulatory powers and responsibilities, the establishment of organizational structures and management philosophies. An apt financial regulatory framework not only ensures a more rational and scientific financial system for a country but also reduces regulatory costs and enhances regulatory efficiency. From an international perspective, using the criteria of regulatory objects, regulatory subjects and regulatory philosophies, financial regulatory frameworks can be broadly categorized into several types. Each of these regulatory modes has its distinct characteristics. By contrasting the advantages and disadvantages of these modes, we can clarify their interrelationships, providing a theoretical basis for optimizing the choice of the best regulatory framework.

3.1 Models Based on Regulatory Objects

Based on regulatory objects, which take the targets of financial regulatory departments as the criterion, the financial regulatory framework can be divided into institutional and functional regulatory models.

3.1.1 Institutional Regulatory Model

The institutional regulatory model represents a more traditional financial regulatory framework, wherein the type of financial institution is the primary focus.

Different regulatory departments are responsible for different types of financial institutions. Under a segmented regulatory framework, institutional regulation is the most typical model. For instance, banking institutions, securities institutions and insurance institutions are regulated by their corresponding banking, securities and insurance regulatory departments, respectively (Greenbaum & Haywood, 1971). The type of financial institutions under institutional regulation needs to be clearly defined by law. The focus of regulation encompasses all financial institutions of the same category, regardless of their business activities, spanning the entire lifecycle from entry, operation, risk control, to exit.

Under a segmented business model, the institutional regulatory model is undoubtedly an excellent choice. Regulatory departments can match the diverse scopes of the financial sector, and specialized and efficient regulation is achievable under clear divisions of labor. This model allows for targeted prudential regulation of financial institutions and avoids overlapping regulations. However, under a mixed business model, where financial institutions operate across markets and industries, the institutional regulatory model may lead to uneven supervision of the same type of financial activity due to their belonging to different financial institutions. This could result in regulatory inequity and foster regulatory arbitrage. With the increasing complexity and diversity of financial products, the boundaries between financial institutions become blurred, potentially leading to regulatory gaps. Additionally, Goodhart (1995) argue that as financial institutions diversify their operations, institutional regulation requires the formulation of regulatory rules for all business activities of financial institutions, leading to redundancy and wastage of regulatory resources.

3.1.2 Functional Regulatory Model

The functional regulation model refers to the regulation of financial businesses and products in the financial system that have the same or similar functions, regardless of which type of financial institution they belong to. The concept of functional regulation was first introduced by American economists Merton & Bodie in the 1990s. They believed that functional regulation had advantages over institutional regulation, emphasizing that while financial institutions evolve, financial functions remain relatively stable. Functional regulation is not constrained by the organizational model of financial institutions. It facilitates cross-product, cross-institution and cross-industry regulation, enabling regulatory authorities to oversee risks beyond specific sectors. Compared to institutional regulation, functional regulation can effectively avoid problems of overlapping or gaps in regulation, thereby improving regulatory efficiency.

The introduction of the financial function perspective in regulatory theory has had a significant impact on the global financial regulatory system. On November 12, 1999, the US formally enacted the "Financial Services Modernization Act" (also known as the Gramm-Leach-Bliley Act or GLBA) to realize financial modernization. This act repealed Section 20 of the 1933 Glass-Steagall Act, which prohibited mixed business operations, legally eliminating the business boundaries of various financial institutions. The enactment of GLBA marked the end of the segmented business model and the arrival of a mixed business model in the US financial sector. Chapter 2 of GLBA, titled "Functional Regulation," introduced a functional regulatory framework for financial institution product brokers and dealers, banking investment companies and other activities. However, Schwarcz (2014) argued that the functional regulatory reforms adopted in the US lack explicit institutional construction and legal support. Instead, they are implemented through coordination, cooperation and competition among institutions, which essentially maintains the institutional regulatory model.

Functional regulation itself has its limitations. By focusing on "functions," it might overlook the risk regulation of "institutions" themselves. Goodhart (1995) believed that pure functional regulation might not provide a clear understanding of the overall management level, risk level and solvency capability of financial institutions. Di Giorgio et al. (2001) and others argued that, due to financial innovation, the number of financial functions has been increasing, leading to higher regulatory costs for financial institutions involved in various business operations. The key to functional regulation lies in defining the responsibilities of "functions." If ambiguities arise, regulatory chaos might ensue. Jackson and Symons (1999) suggested that both regulators and regulated institutions might misuse functional regulation. For example, regulatory authorities might lower regulatory standards to attract more financial institutions under their jurisdiction to appease interest groups or expand their regulatory scope.

Functional regulation is not the opposite of institutional regulation nor can it completely replace it. Yang Jiaohui et al. (2018) believed that institutional regulation still holds significance in a mixed business model. Chen (2015) opined that while functional regulation represents a "horizontal" approach, institutional regulation is "vertical." Both are of paramount importance and should not be isolated from each other. Instead, they should interweave to form a comprehensive "financial regulatory network" (Chen, 2015).

3.2 Classification Based on Regulatory Bodies

When categorized based on regulatory bodies, two typical regulatory models emerge a single regulatory model and a Twin Peaks model.

3.2.1 Single Regulatory Model

As the name suggests, in this model, there's only one regulatory body responsible for supervising all financial institutions, markets and products. This authority oversees both macro- and micro-level aspects of the financial system. This model originated in Nordic countries during the 1980s, like Norway, Denmark and Sweden. The UK's establishment of the Financial Services Authority (FSA) in 1997 popularized this model globally, transforming its previous fragmented regulation approach (Cobham, 2013). The introduction of the Financial Services and Markets Act in 2000 marked the official adoption of this model in the UK, entrusting FSA with the regulation of deposit institutions, insurance, securities investment and financial markets. Many countries followed suit, with at least 46 adjusting their regulatory bodies to some extent based on this model by 2002.

The single regulatory model aims to overcome the overlapping and conflicting jurisdictions seen in multiple regulatory models. It offers several advantages, like avoiding overlaps and maintaining consistency. However, some critics argue that the model may pose risks, especially when the regulatory power gets detached from institutions like the Bank of England, known as the "lender of last resort." Some believe there's no clear evidence suggesting that this model is more efficient than its multi-regulatory counterpart. Due to its concentrated power, it can lead to bureaucratic issues.

3.2.2 Twin Peaks Model

The "Twin Peaks" theory, proposed by the British economist, Taylor in 1995, suggests that financial regulation should address two main goals. First, to ensure the stability of financial institutions and prevent systemic risks. Second, to oversee the conduct of financial institutions, ensuring that the interests of consumers and investors aren't violated. Based on these objectives, two separate regulatory bodies should be established – one for prudential oversight and the other for conduct regulation. Taylor believed that, given the trend toward mixed business operations in the financial sector, the traditional institutional regulatory model might not be the best. This Twin Peaks approach could solve overlaps and contradictions in regulatory goals. Llewellyn (2006) suggests that the Twin Peaks model combines the advantages of a single regulatory system while avoiding its drawbacks.

Australia adopted the Twin Peaks model in 1997 and by 2001, had introduced a series of legislations to reform its financial regulation structure. The Australian Prudential Regulation Authority (APRA) was set up for prudential supervision, while the Australian Securities and Investments Commission (ASIC) was responsible for conduct regulation. Australia's resilience during the 2008 financial crisis showcased the effectiveness of this model. Following the 2008 financial crisis, countries like the UK also reevaluated their regulatory frameworks, and the UK introduced its Twin Peaks approach in the 2012 Financial Services Act.

However, the Twin Peaks model is not without challenges. Some critics argue that the model overly emphasizes the differences between prudential and conduct supervision, even when they are closely related. For countries with inadequate information disclosure systems, the regulatory effectiveness might be compromised. Some also believe that under this model, financial institutions might be regulated by multiple agencies, leading to increased regulatory costs.

3.3 Models Based on Regulatory Philosophy

Both legal rules and legal principles belong to legal norms. The debate on "which norm is superior" remains a classical dialectical logic in legal academia. Similarly, such debates exist in the realm of financial regulation. Using regulatory philosophy as the standard, financial regulatory frameworks can be divided into rules-based and principles-based models.

3.3.1 Rules-Based Regulatory Model

The rules-based regulation (RBR) model is a more traditional form of financial regulation. It's a method where financial regulatory authorities set specific rules to delineate the rights and obligations of entities they oversee to ensure the stable functioning of the financial system. The RBR emphasizes the use of specific rules to govern the operation of the financial system. It demands that regulatory bodies set detailed standards for those they regulate and requires strict adherence. RBR, with its detailed specifications, has the advantage of precision and stability. Its rules are primarily based on past experiences of the regulatory body, aiming to address potential problems in the financial system. Additionally, the consistency of regulatory norms ensures consistent actions by the entities being regulated, mitigates malicious competition and guarantees a robust financial system. This is especially advantageous during the early stages of financial development when financial models are more uniform.

However, with the advancement of technology and frequent financial innovations, traditional RBR models show their limitations, particularly in terms of regulatory lag and restrictions. This lag occurs because even the most comprehensive rules can have oversight gaps. Driven by profit motives, new financial innovations can exploit these gaps, causing delays in regulations, which can lead to hidden financial risks. The purpose of financial regulation is not just to mitigate risks and ensure stability but also to promote financial growth. Overly detailed rules might suppress financial innovation and dampen market vitality.

3.3.2 Principles-Based Regulatory Model

From a jurisprudential perspective, rules and principles are relative concepts; rules tend to be more detailed, while principles usually embody abstract values. The principles-based regulation (PBR) model is one where regulatory bodies primarily use overarching principles to regulate entities. The essence of the PBR model involves: setting broad regulatory goals, emphasizing interaction between regulators and entities to improve compliance, and effectively sanctioning those that breach these overarching principles. The UK's FSA was among the first to adopt the PBR approach. They believed PBR relies more on principles than rules, with a focus on pre-determined outcomes. It doesn't completely abandon RBR but sees both approaches as complementary. PBR was introduced to overcome the drawbacks of RBR, as it is better suited to the complexities of financial innovation and market dynamics. Some post-2008 financial crisis critics mistook PBR as a form of relaxed regulation. However, the FSA believed in its advantages, particularly in enhancing the attractiveness of the UK's financial market. FSA senior official Black (2010) mentioned that companies performed better under PBR during the financial crisis. Theoretically, PBR offers many advantages, but it also faces challenges in practice. For instance, it might lead to "regulatory capture" and unintentional legal breaches by financial institutions due to ambiguous norms.

Looking ahead, Tarbert (2020) envisions a combination of rules and principles in financial regulation, striving for a balance between the two. Liu Ming (2009) believes that while China might not be ready for a full-fledged PBR model, its principles are worth considering by Chinese regulatory authorities.

4. The Challenges of Regulatory Compliance Risk

4.1 Regulatory Risk Assessment

In the intricate milieu of the financial sector, regulatory risk assessment is not just a mandatory process but a critical foundation upon which financial institutions stand. This pillar stands tall, ensuring that organizations not only protect their bottom line but also uphold the trust that stakeholders place in them. Its importance extends beyond mere compliance; it's a compass that points toward risk-mitigated operations and an unblemished reputation.

The regulatory risk assessment process begins with a deep dive into the labyrinth of potential risks and vulnerabilities an organization might face. This encompasses not just the obvious operational hiccups but also delves into subtler aspects like financial discrepancies, changing market dynamics or even shifts in global geopolitics that might influence the regulatory environment.

Central to this process is the risk identification stage. Managers, aided by multidisciplinary teams, sieve through an array of factors, both internal (like IT system vulnerabilities, employee conduct and internal controls) and external (like economic downturns, geopolitical tensions or evolving regulatory stipulations). The aim is to pinpoint anything that could be a potential Achilles' heel in an organization's adherence to regulations.

Following the identification is the risk quantification phase. Here, the identified risks are subjected to rigorous analysis, gauged based on potential impact, likelihood of occurrence and their interplay with other risks. Modern risk assessment often employs sophisticated models, simulation techniques and expert insights to map out worst-case scenarios, ensuring that organizations are not caught off-guard (Ferguson, 2017).

After measurement is the mitigation phase, which is where the rubber meets the road. Here, tailored strategies are devised, not just to respond to risks but to proactively shield the organization. This could mean anything from refining operational procedures, and deploying advanced technology solutions for real-time monitoring, to conducting periodic training sessions for employees, emphasizing the importance of regulatory adherence.

In addition to protocols and controls, an oft-overlooked aspect is fostering a culture of awareness and responsibility. Regular workshops, training sessions and open forums can ensure that employees across hierarchies are not just aware of the regulatory guidelines but are also attuned to the broader implications of non-compliance.

Leading this intricate dance of risk assessment are the managers. With their visionary foresight, they weave a dynamic risk assessment environment that is not static but pulsates, responding adroitly to shifting regulatory landscapes, market dynamics and emerging challenges.

In the grand theater of finance, where the stakes are high and the margins for error are thin, a rigorous regulatory risk assessment becomes more than just a tool. It's the very lifeline that ensures organizations not only navigate the tumultuous waters of the financial market but also emerge as beacons of trust, integrity and resilience.

4.2 Regulatory Reporting and Documentation

In the finely orchestrated symphony of finance, regulatory reporting and documentation play a fundamental role. These rhythmic patterns align the operations of financial institutions with the expectations and requirements of regulatory bodies. It's not just a mandatory routine; it's a pathway that combines transparency with accountability, fostering a culture of trust and reliability within the financial ecosystem (Basel Committee on Banking Supervision, 2016).

Entrusted with this pivotal endeavor, managers shoulder the duty of ensuring that reports are detailed, accurate and timely, effectively echoing the organization's compliance with regulatory norms. This task encompasses comprehensive portrayals of financial health, risk exposures and operational metrics. These portrayals are orchestrated through a meticulous process that merges data integrity with analytical precision. Within these reports lie the tales of an organization's financial exploits, from the nuanced intricacies of balance sheet compositions to the diverse range of instruments capturing market risks, such as derivatives and securitized products.

Beyond mere compliance, astute managers utilize this process as a reflective lens. They scrutinize internal operational methodologies, steering them toward enhanced efficacy, robust governance and evidence-based decision-making. The regulatory reports often act as a mirror, highlighting areas of potential concern, discrepancies in data or opportunities for strategic realignment, thus providing actionable insights for continuous improvement.

Furthermore, the continuous dialog with regulatory entities fosters an adaptive stance, positioning organizations to react with agility and foresight to the dynamic regulatory contours. This adaptive capacity is not just a reactive measure; it is a proactive strategy. By keeping abreast with evolving regulations, managers can anticipate changes, ensuring that institutions remain ahead of the curve and avoid punitive measures or reputational harm.

In laying down this intricate web of reports and documentation, technology emerges as a formidable ally. Integrated systems, sophisticated data analytics tools and automation bring efficiency to the fore, minimizing the margin of error and optimizing report generation processes. The rise of regulatory technology, or

"RegTech," has further revolutionized this domain. Through AI, ML and cloud computing, RegTech solutions simplify complex reporting requirements, ensuring timely submissions and greater accuracy (Li et al., 2023).

In essence, regulatory reporting and documentation stand not merely as a legal obligation but as a testament to an organization's commitment to transparency, governance and trust. They serve as an assurance to stakeholders, signaling the institution's integrity and dedication to upholding the highest standards. In doing so, they chart a roadmap for a reliable, responsive, and resilient financial environment, fortifying the very pillars upon which modern finance rests.

4.3 Managerial Accountability for Compliance

Amidst the turbulent waters of the financial industry, managers bear the weighty responsibility of steering their organizations in adherence to a myriad of regulatory frameworks. This role extends far beyond policy formulation, embodying a 360° approach to compliance, encompassing key functions such as real-time regulatory monitoring, strategy formulation, and coordination of compliance projects in alignment with current and emerging regulatory milieus (Ferguson, 2017). Paramount to this role is nurturing a culture of integrity and adherence to regulatory norms, where compliance isn't seen as a mandate but as a deeply ingrained principle within the organizational fabric. The ripple effects of such a culture permeate throughout the organizational tiers, engendering an ambiance of trust and robust governance (Brennan & Solomon, 2008). Additionally, managers are entrusted with the essential task of proactive compliance management, serving as vigilant custodians shielding their institution from the adverse implications of non-compliance, including hefty fines, reputational damage and potential legal ramifications. To adeptly fulfill this role, managers must be perpetual learners, ensuring they stay abreast with the ever-evolving regulatory dynamics. They also need to foster open channels of communication, encouraging reporting and feedback loops and making responsive and adaptive compliance mechanisms possible. This necessitates honing multifaceted skills, encompassing legal acumen, risk management prowess and a deep understanding of the intricacies of financial sector operations. In conclusion, managers in the financial sector manifest the frontline defense in safeguarding their institutions from regulatory pitfalls. Adopting a comprehensive and proactive approach to compliance management, they aim not just to carve pathways evading regulatory backlash but to nurture organizations anchored in integrity, trust and ethical operations, pivoting toward a landscape of financial stability and sustainable growth.

In the increasingly globalized domain of finance, a manager's role transcends domestic borders, necessitating meticulous approaches to address cross-border regulations. This epitomizes a confluence of challenges and opportunities, as organizations strive to synchronize their operations in regulatory environments that are often divergent and, at times, normative and standardized (Titi, 2015). To effectively navigate this complexity, managers must cultivate a nuanced understanding of the regulatory frameworks pertinent to each jurisdiction their organization operates in.

This demands deep dives into international laws governing cross-border transactions and operations, bilateral agreements and sector-specific directives (Morrison & White, 2009). Additionally, insights into the political and economic backdrops of different jurisdictions become indispensable for devising strategies that are both compliant and advantageous. An integral facet of this role involves establishing robust regulatory compliance systems, equipped with technological platforms capable of real-time monitoring of regulatory shifts across different jurisdictions, promoting proactive regulatory compliance management (Cumming et al., 2017). Such strategies not only help evade regulatory snags but also capitalize on opportunities that regulatory changes might bring forth. Moreover, managers must advocate for collaborations respecting the sovereignty and sanctity of regulations in each jurisdiction, fostering relationships grounded in mutual respect and adherence to legal norms. This involves crafting flexible yet robust agreements, allowing adjustments in the ever-changing regulatory milieu while safeguarding organizational interests. As we elucidate the pivotal role of managers in handling cross-border regulations, it's evident that this role embodies legal astuteness, strategic foresight and a profound respect for international norms and sovereignty. Looking ahead, the managerial lens must continually adapt, weaving a complex yet robust tapestry of compliance, guiding organizations toward successful and ethically sound global operations.

4.4 Compliance Training and Culture

In the contemporary landscape of the financial sector, nurturing a culture deeply rooted in compliance is not only a regulatory requirement but a cornerstone for building a resilient and ethically sound organization. Management steers this effort, guiding the workforce toward a path based on legal adherence and moral righteousness. The key lies in initiating training programs and diligently executing regular training agendas, not just to familiarize employees with regulatory norms but also to cultivate a deeper understanding of the foundational principles governing these rules (Stouten et al., 2012). Through seminars, simulations and case study analyses, employees acquire the necessary practical knowledge and critical thinking skills to effectively navigate the intricate regulatory environment.

Furthermore, the task for managers is to cultivate a culture where compliance transcends mere legal obligation, morphing into a deeply rooted moral duty. This involves promoting open dialogs, allowing employees to voice concerns and seek guidance and fostering a collaborative environment that encourages ethical decision-making. Periodic evaluations of these training initiatives' effectiveness are crucial. Managers must cultivate feedback loops, using analytics to tailor training programs to meet the dynamic needs and preferences of the workforce (Kaptein, 2008). In doing so, they create a symbiotic ecosystem where adherence to compliance not only shields the organization from potential regulatory repercussions but also engenders a working culture of integrity, transparency and mutual respect. Through this lens, compliance emerges as a strategic advantage, driving sustainable growth and consolidating the organization's reputation as a trusted player in the financial domain.

As we articulate the pivotal role of managers in fostering a compliance-centric culture, the effort paints a tapestry interwoven with education, moral integrity and collaborative spirit. Looking ahead, it's a managerial endeavor to nurture a workspace where compliance isn't seen as a chore but as a treasured value, guiding the organization toward a future of success, reverence and ethical fortitude.

5. Conclusion

As we conclude this discourse, it becomes abundantly clear that regulatory frameworks are pivotal for sustaining a stable, ethical and transparent operating environment in the financial sector. These frameworks not only govern the behaviors of financial entities but indeed lay the foundation for trust, reliability and sustainable growth within the industry. At the helm of navigating this complex regulatory web are astute managers, entrusted with the formidable task of steering organizations safely through ever-evolving regulatory waters. Their role surpasses mere rule adherence; they shoulder the profound responsibility of shaping a culture grounded in integrity, ethical resilience, and an unwavering commitment to doing what's right. Given the rapidly shifting financial ecosystem, these leaders bear the onus of instilling a spirit of learning and adaptability, where knowledge pairs with foresight, and vigilance coalesces with innovation. Training, as a component of this process, should be viewed as a dynamic and ongoing endeavor, positioning teams to embrace regulatory shifts not as impediments but catalysts for carving paths of ethical and responsible business practices.

Projecting into the future, we anticipate a complex yet promising domain where the dynamics of regulatory frameworks are bound to evolve, ushering in fresh opportunities and challenges. It will remain the mandate of managerial cadres to navigate these terrains with visionary zeal, rooted in compliance but driven by an aspiration for excellence, not just in financial milestones but in etching an organization's stance on pillars of integrity, trust and unwavering commitment to moral stewardship. Through a culture of regulatory adherence, enriched training and ethical imperatives, financial institutions are primed to tread a path of continual growth and societal trust. This vision, albeit ambitious, is within grasp with diligent managerial leadership at the helm, fostering an ambiance where compliance becomes synonymous not just with legal duty but with ethical business conduct and overall societal benefit.

References

Ahern. (2021). Fintech, racial equity, and an inclusive financial system. *Federal Reserve Bank of San Francisco, Community Development Innovation Review Series, 15*(2), 001–132. https://doi.org/10.24148/cdir2021-02

Basel Committee on Banking Supervision. (2016). *Guidance on the application of the Core Principles for Effective Banking Supervision to the regulation and supervision of institutions relevant to financial inclusion.* https://www.bis.org/bcbs/publ/d383.pdf

Bhattacharyya, S., & Nanda, V. (2000). Client discretion, switching costs, and financial innovation. *Review of Financial Studies, 13*(4), 1101–1127. https://doi.org/10.1093/rfs/13.4.1101

Black, J. (2010). The rise, fall and fate of principles based regulation. *SSRN Electronic Journal.* http://dx.doi.org/10.2139/ssrn.1712862

Brennan, N. M., & Solomon, J. (2008). Corporate governance, accountability and mechanisms of accountability: An overview. *Accounting, Auditing & Accountability Journal, 21*(7), 885–906. https://doi.org/10.1108/09513570810907401

Carlin, W., & Soskice, D. W. (2015). *Macroeconomics: Institutions, instability, and the financial system.* Oxford University Press, Cop.

Chen, J. (2015, January 24). Slowdown brings new risks to banks|Economy|chinadaily. com.cn. Usa.chinadaily.com.cn. https://usa.chinadaily.com.cn/business/2015-01/24/content_19393517.htm. Accessed on July 16, 2024.

Cobham, D. P. U. P. (2013). *The economic record of the 1997–2010 labour government.* Oxford University Press.

Cumming, D., Werth, J. C., & Zhang, Y. (2017). Governance in entrepreneurial ecosystems: Venture capitalists vs. technology parks. *Small Business Economics, 52*(2), 455–484. https://doi.org/10.1007/s11187-017-9955-6

Di Giorgio, G., Di Noia, C., & Piatti, L. (2001). Reshaping financial market regulation and supervision in Italy. *Rivista Italiana Degli Economisti, 1*, 31–60. https://doi.org/10.1427/3688

Ferguson, G. (2017). Marco Arnone and Leonardo S. Borlini. Corruption: Economic analysis and international law. *European Journal of International Law, 28*(1), 343–348. https://doi.org/10.1093/ejil/chx016

Goodhart, E. (1995). *A European Central Bank (1992)* (pp. 303–329). Palgrave Macmillan UK EBooks. https://doi.org/10.1057/9780230379152_15

Greenbaum, S. I., & Haywood, C. F. (1971). Secular change in the financial services industry. *Journal of Money, Credit, and Banking, 3*(2), 571. https://doi.org/10.2307/1991167

Harris, R. (1994). The Bubble Act: Its passage and its effects on business organization. *The Journal of Economic History, 54*(3), 610–627. https://doi.org/10.1017/s0022050700015059

Jackson, H. E., & Symons, E. L. (1999). *Regulation of financial institutions.* West Academic Publishing.

Jones, E., & Knaack, P. (2019). Global financial regulation: Shortcomings and reform options. *Global Policy, 10*(2), 193–206. Wiley. https://doi.org/10.1111/1758-5899.12656

Kane, E. J. (1981). Accelerating inflation, technological innovation, and the decreasing effectiveness of banking regulation. *The Journal of Finance, 36*(2), 355–367. https://doi.org/10.1111/j.1540-6261.1981.tb00449.x

Kaptein, M. (2008). Developing a measure of unethical behavior in the workplace: A stakeholder perspective. *Journal of Management, 34*(5), 978–1008. https://doi.org/10.1177/0149206308318614

Kim, T., Koo, B., & Park, M. (2013). Role of financial regulation and innovation in the financial crisis. *Journal of Financial Stability, 9*(4), 662–672. https://doi.org/10.1016/j.jfs.2012.07.002

Li, J., Maiti, A., & Fei, J. (2023). Features and scope of regulatory technologies: Challenges and opportunities with industrial internet of things. *Future Internet, 15*(8), 256. https://doi.org/10.3390/fi15080256

Lerner, A. P. (1947). *The economics of control: Principles of welfare economics.* Macmillan Company.

Liu, M. (2009). *30 years of reform and opening up in Chinese banking sector (in Chinese).* China Financial Publishing House.

Llewellyn, D. T. (2006). *Institutional structure of financial regulation and supervision: The basic issues.*

McKinnon, R. I. (1973). Money and capital in economic development. *International Journal, 29*(4), 649. https://doi.org/10.2307/40201473

McKinnon, R. I. (1989). Financial liberalization and economic development: A reassessment of interest-rate policies in Asia and Latin America. *Oxford Review of Economic Policy, 5*(4), 29–54. https://doi.org/10.1093/oxrep/5.4.29

Morrison, A. D., & White, L. (2009). Level playing fields in international financial regulation. *The Journal of Finance, 64*(3), 1099–1142. https://doi.org/10.1111/j.1540-6261.2009.01460.x

Pringle, R. (2009). *The dexia central bank directory.* Central Banking Publications Ltd.

Schwarcz, S. L. (2014). The functional regulation of finance. *SSRN Electronic Journal.* https://doi.org/10.2139/ssrn.2437544

Shaw, E. S. (1973). *Financial deepening in economic development.* Oxford University Press.

Tarbert. (2020). ICYMI: Harvard Business Law Review Publishes Chairman Tarbert's Framework for Sound Regulation | CFTC. (n.d.). Www.cftc.gov. https://www.cftc.gov/PressRoom/PressReleases/8183-20

Stouten, J., van Dijke, M., & De Cremer, D. (2012). Ethical leadership. *Journal of Personnel Psychology, 11*(1), 1–6. https://doi.org/10.1027/1866-5888/a000059

Titi, C. (2015). International investment law and the European Union: Towards a new generation of international investment agreements. *European Journal of International Law, 26*(3), 639–661. https://doi.org/10.1093/ejil/chv040

Yang, J.-H., Wang, W., Wang, K.-L., & Yeh, C.-Y. (2018). Capital intensity, natural resources, and institutional risk preferences in Chinese outward foreign direct investment. *International Review of Economics & Finance, 55*, 259–272. https://doi.org/10.1016/j.iref.2017.07.015

Chapter 9

Financial Communication and Stakeholder Relations

Sun Zhuyin[a] and Muhammad Ali[b]

[a]UCSI University, Malaysia
[b]Taylor's University, Malaysia

Abstract

Financial communication refers to the strategies and practices employed by companies to share financial information and engage with investors, stakeholders and the broader financial community. At its core lies investor relations management (IRM), focused on achieving effective two-way communication between the company and these groups for fair valuation of securities. Key financial communication activities include investor meetings, earnings calls, roadshows, annual reports, market analysis and crisis communication. Moreover. stakeholder theory emphasizes identifying and managing relationships with all individuals and entities that can affect or be affected by the company's operations. Stakeholders include shareholders, employees, creditors, suppliers, communities, regulators etc., classified as primary (essential) or secondary (indirectly involved). Proactive stakeholder engagement is crucial for achieving corporate objectives. Additionally, investor relations (IR) specifically deal with managing interactions with shareholders, creditors and potential investors through information dissemination, utilizing finance, marketing and communication techniques. Implementation channels include regulated disclosures, shareholder meetings, media engagement and forums. Other covered aspects include crisis communication strategies, corporate reputation management, internal communication practices, transparency and disclosure guidelines and legal/ethical considerations surrounding corporate communication. Overall, robust financial communication capabilities are vital for corporate success, reputation building and sustainable growth in today's competitive landscape.

Keywords: Financial communication; investor relations; stakeholder engagement; corporate disclosure; reputation management

Strategic Financial Management, 135–154
Copyright © 2024 Sun Zhuyin and Muhammad Ali
Published under exclusive licence by Emerald Publishing Limited
doi:10.1108/978-1-83608-106-720241009

1. Introduction

Financial communications, including market public relations, financing public relations and IR, are a series of strategies, tactics and tools adopted by modern companies to share financial data and advice with investors and other relevant stakeholders (Laskin, 2021). The goal of these activities is to achieve a fair valuation of the company's securities by influencing the company's stock price and cost of capital through effective communication and relationship management (Brennan & Merkl-Davies, 2018).

1.1 Financial Communication

1.1.1 Concept of Financial Communication

IRM or simply IR is the core of this field, which originated in the US in the 1950s (Gupta et al., 2022). IRM is a strategic management responsibility that considers finance, communications, marketing and security law compliance. Its main goal is to achieve the most effective two-way communication between companies, investors, the financial community and other stakeholders to ultimately achieve a fair valuation of company securities (Hoffmann & Binder-Tietz, 2021). IRM activities are usually the responsibility of listed companies, with investors as the main audience, through purposeful and planned dissemination and communication activities, relying on various communication media to maximize the value of relevant stakeholders and strive to gain widespread investors' agreement. It can be understood as financial public relations management (Li et al., 2021).

Activities in this area usually include regular meetings with investors, conference calls, investor roadshows, the release of financial reports, Q&A and explanations, market analysis competitor analysis, etc. (Ahblom & Christner, 2021). Through these activities, the company hopes to build strong relationships and enhance investor trust in the company, thereby affecting the company's stock price performance and financing capabilities. This is important for the long-term success and sustainability of the company.

1.1.2 The Background of Financial Communication

The background of financial communication can be traced back to overseas capital markets, especially mature capital markets, and its origins are mainly rooted in the US (Bell et al., 2012). Financial communications and IRM have experienced a gradual maturation process in the US market (Bell et al., 2012). Before the 1930s, there were irregularities in the US securities market. Insider trading was prevalent, false information was rampant and there was a lack of normal and effective communication between listed companies and investors. In the 1960s and 1970s, financial communication entered an early stage of development and evolution. The term shareholder relations gradually evolved into a synonym for publicity and promotion. The company's annual report became a manual for promoting the company's products, and financial communication personnel played more of a role in producing reports. and technical roles in multimedia presentations.

From the 1980s to the 1990s and the beginning of the 21st century, the status and focus of financial communication in enterprises has gradually changed and matured (Wind & Main, 1998). In 1969, the US established the IR Association, and other countries such as the UK, Canada, Germany, France and Japan also followed suit. In 1990, the International IR Alliance came into being. IRM organizations around the world have successively formulated and improved professional codes of conduct. Although IR is still evolving, practice has proven that the convergence and integration of corporate IR and PR (public relations) is the key and core of financial communication. Relevant scholars have repeatedly emphasized the necessity of integrating the two in corporate communications (Doan & McKie, 2017).

1.1.3 Reasons

One of the reasons for the emergence of financial communication is competition for investment capital (Masulis & Nahata, 2009). In the global capital market, investors have a wide range of choices, with hundreds of thousands of listed companies around the world (Siegel, 2021). In this huge and resource-rich market environment, many listed companies are easily overlooked. A company's business operations, internal management, and financial performance alone are no longer enough to attract investors (Kanakriyah, 2020).

Therefore, the company's management needs to actively disseminate the company's relevant information and development strategies to investors, partners and the financial community and strengthen IRM to improve its competitiveness in the financial capital market and achieve sustained and stable development (Frias-Aceituno et al., 2013). Communication is a key factor. In corporate research, we focus on how companies develop communication strategies, manage relationships with stakeholders and establish social responsibilities. This type of research typically covers theoretical foundations in areas such as public relations and organizational communication (Crane & Glozer, 2016).

In the process of cross-department communication, the financial department should be prepared for preventive communication (Joynt et al., 2010). For some problems that may arise, formulate a relatively reasonable solution in advance and maintain a certain degree of flexibility to improve the efficiency of communication (Dafoe et al., 2020).

In addition, when conducting cross-department communication, you should also be familiar with the main work content and processes of each department, understand their compatibility with the company's strategy and departmental interests and use the minimum communication cost to complete cross-department communication (Luckey, 2021). You can improve the efficiency of communication by preparing preliminary information, including the purpose, feasibility, value and plan to promote implementation, and by "pressuring" the boss or group to make the other party feel the importance of the matter. Preparing for communication in advance plays an irreplaceable role in ensuring the effectiveness of cross-department communication and requires financial managers to pay sufficient attention (Ruuskanen, 2021).

2. Stakeholder Relation

2.1 Definition

The stakeholders of an enterprise include its shareholders, internal employees, creditors, suppliers, retailers, consumers or competitors, etc. (Pirozzi, 2019). They are all stakeholders of the enterprise. The stakeholders of a general enterprise are divided into two parts, including the market part and the nonmarket part. The market part includes shareholders related to the enterprise, including internal employee shareholders and external shareholders, as well as employees, creditors, suppliers, retailers, consumers and competitors; the non-market part includes local governments, social activist groups, media, the general public, pro-business groups, etc. (Isa, 2012). The concept of stakeholders can be traced back to 1780, originally referring to people who have a "stake" in an activity or enterprise (Ferenc et al., 2017).

Freeman, the founder of Stakeholder Theory, gave a classic broad definition: "Stakeholders within an organization are groups or individuals that can affect the realization of the organization's goals or are affected by its realization." Freeman explained: "Stakeholders Investors are those groups that have an interest or claim in a company (Benn et al., 2016). More specifically, I include in this group suppliers, customers, employees, shareholders, the local community and those who represent management." In this definition, Freeman emphasized that the "influence" of a company may be one-way or two-way. This means not only considering individuals and groups who can influence corporate goals as stakeholders but also taking into account those individuals and groups affected by corporate actions in achieving corporate goals, such as local communities, government departments and environmentalists (Cova & Salle, 2006).

Eskerod (2020) believes that the goal of an enterprise is to create wealth and value for all stakeholders (Pererva et al., 2021). An enterprise is a system composed of stakeholders that interact with the larger social system that provides the legal and market basis for enterprise activities (Ufua et al., 2020). According to the way relevant groups bear risks in business activities, stakeholders can be divided into active stakeholders and passive stakeholders. The former are "those people or groups who invest specialized human capital or non-human capital in the enterprise, thereby bearing some form of risk"; the latter is "people or groups who are at risk due to the behavior of the enterprise." Jia et al. (2020) believes that active stakeholders make a key qualification on the definition of narrow stakeholders. The key point of this definition is to distinguish those people or groups with legitimate claims to the enterprise from other stakeholders. , thereby clarifying the scope of narrow stakeholders (DesJardine et al., 2023).

2.2 The Classification of Different Types of Stakeholders

Since the late 1980s, the West has conducted classification research on many stakeholders of enterprises and achieved many remarkable results. The most notable of these are the multidimensional segmentation method and the Mitchell score (Wagner Mainardes et al., 2012).

Clarkson, a representative of the multi-dimensional segmentation method, divides stakeholders into active and passive stakeholders based on the different ways in which relevant groups bear risks in business activities and divides stakeholders according to the degree of interest in the enterprise. Divided into primary and secondary stakeholders. Primary stakeholders refer to those groups that a business cannot operate without, otherwise, the business will not survive, including shareholders, investors, employees, customers and suppliers. Secondary stakeholders refer to those groups that are indirectly affected by corporate operations, such as communities, governments and media (Miles, 2017).

After the mid-1990s, American scholar, Mitchell, studied the development process of stakeholder theory in detail, summarized 27 representative stakeholder definitions and proposed a scoring method (score-based approach) to determine stakeholders (Lu et al., 2017). The Mitchell scoring method believes that stakeholder theory contains two core issues (Miles, 2017): first, determining who are the stakeholders of the enterprise, that is, the identification of stakeholders; second, determining what managers rely on to pay attention to specific groups, that is, stakeholder attributes. He believes that stakeholders must possess at least one of three attributes: legitimacy, influence and urgency. According to the stakeholders' possession of these three attributes, the stakeholders are divided into three categories: determined stakeholders, expected stakeholders and potential stakeholders. Among them, Mitchell's unique feature is that he views stakeholders and their attributes as dynamically changing. During the development stage of the enterprise, individuals or groups can change from one type of stakeholder to another (Freeman et al., 2010).

The Mitchell scoring method has improved the method of identifying stakeholders, promoted the application of stakeholder theory and has gradually become one of the most commonly used stakeholder classification methods. Many scholars use this method to score relevant groups according to the specific circumstances of the enterprise, which provides a strong reference for the enterprise's management decision-making (Jones et al., 2015).

2.3 Summary

Globally, companies need to have strong and proactive financial communication capabilities to successfully promote the development and evolution of the capital markets of the company itself and its industry, thereby achieving good returns and maximizing the company's interests (Hussain & Papastathopoulos, 2022). Financial communication and IRM play a strategically important role in enterprises and have become a trend in many countries, with listed companies attaching great importance to them (Wu & Hąbek, 2021).

However, in the Malaysian financial market, IRM is still in its early stages of development, and there is a large gap compared with IRM in developed capital markets (Noori, 2021). With the globalization of capital markets and the continuous transformation of new media forms, financial communication is facing continuous challenges and developments (Schilirò, 2020). To adapt to this new environment, companies need to continuously improve their financial communication capabilities and actively adopt modern communication tools and strategies to better meet the needs of investors and other stakeholders and ensure the company's success in a highly competitive market (Mărioara et al., 2014).

In short, financial communication and IRM are crucial to the success of a business (Doan & McKie, 2017). They can not only enhance the company's reputation and attractiveness but also provide a solid foundation for the company's sustainable growth and profit maximization. As the market environment continues to evolve, companies should actively adapt to these changes and continuously improve their financial communication strategies to ensure that they stand out in the highly competitive business world (Khuong et al., 2021).

2.4 Corporate Communication Strategy

2.4.1 The Conceptual Definition of Corporate Communication Strategy

Communication is an important part of marketing, and it is also an important step for enterprises to build customer relationship management (CRM) (Cornelissen, 2023). Effective corporate communication strategies are also seen as improving performance. The behavior of specific information exchange in terms of facts, opinions ideas, etc. In the field of marketing, corporate communication emphasizes bidirectional, based on the exchange of information between customers, competitors, channel members and the marketing environment (Brennan & Merkl-Davies, 2018). The objects of communication are different, which include not only communication with enterprises in marketing channels (i.e. channel communication) but also communication with enterprises in marketing channels. Including communication between enterprises and customers, this research mainly focuses on the latter. The content of communication between enterprises and customers content, strategies, methods and effects will have an important impact on customers' emotions, wishes, decisions and behaviors (Brockhaus et al., 2023).

With the development and application of Internet technology, communication between enterprises and customers is not only limited to offline situations but also basically the communication, communication and interaction between enterprises and customers in the online environment are becoming more convenient and in-depth (Volk & Zerfass, 2020). Corporate communication refers to the information connotation conveyed by corporate communication, which includes specific communication strategies in terms of communication content, communication subject, communication object and communication channels (Welch, 2011).

Gao et al. (2023) divided corporate communication strategies into cost reduction based on the difference between cost and value delivered to customers. Employee communication is an important aspect of enterprise (Jiang & Park, 2022). Important forms of communication, and based on the characteristics of corporate employees' communication behaviors, corporate communication strategies are divided into rough mine communication strategy and refined communication strategy. Verk et al. (2021) divide corporate social responsibility communication strategies into reactive corporate social responsibility communication strategies and forward-looking corporate social responsibility communication strategies. According to the value delivered by the company to customers, corporate communication strategies are divided into economic communication strategies and social communication strategies (Jiang & Park, 2022).

According to the different values conveyed by the corporate communication content, corporate communication strategies can be divided into economic communication strategies and social communication strategies. Enterprise economical communication strategy (Ashraf et al., 2022). The impact of economic communication strategies and social communication strategies on customer purchasing behavior. The study found that the impact of corporate economic communication strategies and social communication strategies on customer purchasing behavior changes over time. But on average, the impact of corporate social communication strategies on customer purchasing behavior is stronger than the impact of economic communication strategies on customer purchasing behavior. Packard and Berger (2021) took the communication language in the marketing field as a perspective and explored the impact mechanism of words, sentences and other language factors in corporate communication on consumer reactions.

The results show that the linguistic factors in corporate communication (such as pronunciation, semantics, visual form, rhetoric, sentence structure, segmental narrative and multilingual communication) can influence consumption through processing mechanisms (such as automatic processing and controlled processing). The patient's response (such as attention, memory, attitude, willingness, behavior, etc.) produces differentiated effects (Batra & Keller, 2016).

2.4.2 The Important Role of Communication in Corporate

2.4.2.1 Control Function. In contemporary business management, only by strengthening the communication management of the enterprise can the employees in the enterprise employees clearly understand the current policies and guidelines of the company and understand the current situation faced by the enterprise and then be able to fully understand the decisions of business managers and then have an understanding of the political effective implementation of policies (Posthumusa & Von Solms, 2005).

2.4.2.2 Incentive Effect. The relationship between managers and employees in the enterprise is established sincere and effective communication can make employees fully feel valued and respected by the enterprise and then be able to enough to enhance employees' loyalty to the company and make employees able to actively and proactively engage in work with full enthusiasm work, bringing more benefits to the enterprise. at the same time (Cheng & Coyte, 2014). If managers in an enterprise do not interact with employees, without adequate communication, it is impossible to understand the other party's thoughts and needs, communication can help managers in the enterprise communicate with employees to improve their understanding of each other and master each other's relevant information to solve problems in a timely and effective manner (Seaverson et al., 2009).

2.4.2.3 The Role of Emotional Interaction. In the daily work of the enterprise, whether it is up or down, disagreements can arise between managers and employees cause management is not accurate and in place (Meyer, 1983). When solving problems, adhering to the strong development of the enterprise as the fundamental purpose will be very effective in solving problems, both parties reach a full understanding of each other and produce good sexual and emotional interaction; this is what corporate employees care about feelings (Hardaker & Fill, 2005).

3. Investor Relations and Shareholder Engagement

3.1 Investor Relations

The American IR Association defines IRM as a company's strategic management responsibility, using finance, communication and marketing methods to effectively manage the transfer of information between the company and financial institutions and other investors to achieve corporate relative success (Bushee & Miller, 2012). The Canadian IR Association defines IRM as the company's comprehensive application of finance, marketing and communication methods to introduce the company's operating conditions and future development prospects to existing investors and potential investors so that they can fully understand the information. make investment decisions based on this (Hoffmann et al., 2018). The "Guidelines on Relations between Listed Companies and Investors" issued by the Securities Regulatory Commission defines IRM as follows:

> Investor relations refers to the relationship between a company and its shareholders, creditors or potential investors, and also includes the relationship between the company and its shareholders, creditors or potential investors. The relationship between the company and various capital market intermediaries in the investor communication process. (Hoffmann et al., 2018, pp. 5–6)

It can be seen from these different definitions that the scope of IRM is very broad, including the management of relationships between listed companies and shareholders, creditors and potential investors, as well as the relationship between listed companies and investors in the process of communicating with investors (Chahine et al., 2020). Relationship management between various types of capital market intermediaries. Specifically, IRM mainly includes various channels, such as media, company website, phone calls, interviews, road shows, press conferences, investor forums, etc., based on the company's financial status, business development, strategic planning, etc. Use communication skills to convey company information to existing and potential investors and manage investors' expectations (Rodrigues &

Galdi, 2017). The content of IRM is mainly divided into two aspects, namely management and communication. The management aspect covers the relationship with major shareholders, small- and medium-sized shareholders, financial institutions and regulatory agencies, while the communication aspect includes conveying to investors macroeconomic conditions, corporate development strategies, operating conditions, financial conditions, risk management, major events, information, etc. (Karolyi et al., 2020).

3.2 Implementation Channels of Investor Relations Management

Regular reports are divided into annual reports, interim reports and quarterly reports, all of which are mandatory information disclosures (Guimard, 2013). The annual report discloses the most comprehensive content to investors and contains a large amount of information. ordinary feelings. Under normal circumstances, the annual report is disclosed in a color report, accompanied by the company's board of directors and board of supervisors and management pictures to give investors a sense of the company (Hoffmann et al., 2018).

It is mandatory information disclosure, which mainly includes resolutions of shareholders' meetings, the board of directors, and the board of supervisors and makes announcements on important matters that occur based on the company's operations (Kinanti & Asnawi, 2022). The general meeting of shareholders is the company's highest authority. According to relevant legal provisions. It is held at least once a year, the annual general meeting of shareholders. The company will also be based on major events. Item convened an extraordinary general meeting of shareholders (Yanjie & Bo, 2009). Generally speaking, a company needs to convene a general meeting of shareholders. A certain number of days before (such as necessary for Hong Kong regulatory agencies and domestic companies to list overseas. The terms stipulate 45 days, and the domestic regulatory agency stipulates 30 days) to issue a meeting to investors. Notice of the meeting is provided so that investors can fully understand the content of the meeting. Earnings conferences and road shows are more commonly used to meet face-to-face with investors.

4. Crisis Communication and Reputation Management

4.1 Crisis Communication

4.1.1 Definition

Corporate crisis refers to a situation of high uncertainty in the development process. This situation seriously threatens the overall operation of the company and the rights and interests of relevant stakeholders and requires rapid decision-making and action under tight time constraints and insufficient information. action events. Communication, simply put, is the process of transferring or exchanging understandable information, ideas and emotions between individuals or groups. As an important means of crisis management, crisis communication mainly refers to a series of behaviors and processes to solve and prevent crises through communication (Van der Meer & Verhoeven, 2014). In essence, crisis communication is a defensive communication activity adopted by an organization hit by a crisis. Its purpose is to provide explanations of its behavior in response to public criticism or questioning, thereby maintaining and restoring the organization's reputation and image (Frandsen & Johansen, 2011).

4.1.2 Crisis Communication Strategies

According to Michael Brand's theory, the objects of corporate communication can be roughly divided into four major aspects: the people and organizations affected by the crisis, the units that affect the company's operations, the people or organizations involved in the crisis and the people and organizations that must be informed (Kim et al., 2017). Based on this classification, the main objects involved in corporate crisis communication include consumers, corporate employees, relevant interest groups, media, government and related intermediary organizations. If the company cannot communicate effectively with these objects, it may affect the handling of the crisis and may lead to a more serious crisis (Gunawan et al., 2015). Therefore, in the process of crisis communication, enterprises should determine different communication priorities and strategies based on different objects and combine them with the 3T principles of crisis communication.

4.1.2.1 Company Employees and Relevant Interest Groups. Enterprise employees and related interest groups are important resources of the enterprise and are also part of the company that shares its destiny. When a crisis occurs, companies should promptly inform employees of the situation so that they understand the nature of the current crisis, its impact on the company and changes and reactions to the external environment (Botha, 2015). Effective communication helps prevent misinformation and speculation from spreading internally, keeps employees motivated and reduces the disruption caused by crises. In addition, companies should also inform employees how to respond to the crisis together with the company, give full play to the role of employees, encourage employees to make suggestions, enhance employees' trust in the company's leadership and maintain employee cohesion (Smith, 2023).

4.1.2.2 Relevant Interest Groups. Enterprises should promptly report crisis information to relevant interest groups, such as shareholders, customers, etc., to reduce their distrust and panic, build their confidence in the long-term development of the enterprise and strive for their understanding and support. In crisis communication, it is very important to convey correct information on time and actively respond to the concerns and questions of relevant interest groups, which can effectively reduce the negative impact of the crisis (Stokes, 2020).

4.2 Reputation Management

4.2.1 Definition

Reputation has passed the test of time and is based on comprehensive moral evaluation rather than just simple perceptions and impressions in mass communication (Davies & Miles, 1998). The real close attention of business and management circles to corporate reputation began in 1983 when Fortune magazine launched the Corporate Reputation List (a selection of the most admired American companies). Subsequently, with the rise of the Internet, corporate reputation as an important topic has attracted widespread attention from the business community and management circles (Aula & Mantere, 2020).

The most persuasive definition of corporate reputation is provided by the relational school, which views corporate reputation as the perception of a company that stakeholders form over time based on their direct experience, the company's behavior and comparative information with major competitors (Aula & Mantere, 2020). Comprehensive cognitive, evaluative and affective connections. This comprehensive view of reputation helps to better understand the relationship between a company and its stakeholders, as well as the company's overall image in society and the market.

4.2.1.1 Corporate Image. The external evaluation of a company is the overall impression of the company established by the public by observing various signs of the company, such as product features, marketing strategies, employee style, etc. (Kitchen & Watson, 2010). This impression is other people's cognition, evaluation and emotional connection with the company, including consumers, partners, governments, public welfare organizations and other stakeholders related to the company but not within the company. Studying corporate image helps to understand the overall overview and level of corporate culture, as well as the actual competitiveness of enterprises in market competition (Melewar et al., 2012).

4.2.1.2 Self-Identity. Self-identity, that is, how the company evaluates itself, is also called organizational identity (Mak, 2005). Self-identity involves the cognition, evaluation and emotional connection of the company's internal stakeholders, including shareholders, board of directors, employees, etc. Self-identity answers two basic questions: "Who are we?" and "How do we see ourselves?" Therefore, self-identity is the identification of a company at the organizational level, including not only the evaluation of the company but also the cultural identity of the company. At the same time, self-identity also involves the behavioral aspects of the company, including "How do we do things here?" Therefore, the self-identity of the company is to a large extent related to the cultural identity of the company (López-Romero & Romero, 2011).

4.2.1.3 Expected Recognition. Expected recognition, also called corporate identity, is how the company wants others to view its image (Voswinkel, 2011). It includes visual aspects such as name, logo and symbol, as well as strategic aspects such as vision, mission and values. Desire recognition involves the company communicating its vision and values to external stakeholders to shape external perceptions of the company. Unlike self-identity, expected identification is more related to the company's strategic vision and organizational expectations (Wiedmann & Buxel, 2005).

4.2.2 Difference from Brand

Compared with brand theory, corporate reputation is a richer and more systematic concept and tool (Greyser, 2009). Corporate reputation focuses on the company itself and the cognition, evaluation and emotional connection of various stakeholders to the company as a whole. In short, a brand can be thought of as a good image displayed to the public, while corporate reputation is a comprehensive personal assessment report derived from tracking the opinions of family, colleagues, friends, neighbors and fans over time. Corporate reputation theory requires companies to consider the cognition and evaluation of various stakeholders from a long-term perspective and comprehensively consider corporate image, self-identity and expected recognition so that the company can become a truly respected and sustainable company (Smith et al., 2010).

4.2.3 Strategies

Reputation is an intangible asset of an enterprise, something that is difficult for an enterprise to imitate and irreplaceable core competitiveness, which is the same as material assets, financial capital and human capital together play an important role in the performance of the enterprise. At the same time, corporate reputation is also a reflection of corporate management and an important indicator of control effectiveness. Since corporate reputation is essentially an attitudinal construct, the formation is comprehensive and can only be managed and controlled to a limited extent. Attitudes and behaviors are fundamental factors that determine corporate image and reputation. Therefore, if an enterprise wants to establish a good image and a high reputation, employees' attitudes and behaviors must be effectively managed so that employees can consciously act following the company's values, goals, and requirements (Winn et al., 2008).

5. Internal Communication Best Practices

5.1 Definition

Internal communication within an enterprise, that is, the transmission and exchange of ideas and information among members within an organization, plays a vital role in an enterprise's human resource management. It not only helps drive corporate change but also enhances the cohesion and collaborative spirit of the organization and is a key management tool. However, due to the increasing complexity of modern enterprise organizations, differences in views and opinions between different levels and departments within the organization have gradually emerged. Therefore, how to effectively communicate within the enterprise has become a challenge that has attracted much attention.

5.2 Obstacles to Effective Communication

Only by working hard to eliminate organizational communication barriers and personal communication barriers, we can achieve better communication results. Too large an organization and too many layers are often the main reasons for organizational communication barriers. At the same time, information communication from top to bottom will occur (Meng & Berger, 2012). It also wastes time and affects efficiency. To eliminate this organizational obstacle, the internal organizational structure of the enterprise must be streamlined. Make the company's organizational structure as flat as possible. at the same time. It is also necessary to clarify the responsibilities between various departments and avoid multiple leaders to reduce the psychological pressure on both sides of the communication. Ensure smooth communication (Araújo & Miranda, 2021).

There are many reasons for personal communication barriers: there are barriers caused by personality factors, such as individual character, temperament, attitude and emotions. Differences in opinions will become obstacles to information communication; there are obstacles caused by differences in knowledge and experience levels, as well as obstacles caused by poor individual memory. There are obstacles caused by different attitudes toward information, obstacles caused by mutual distrust, etc. No matter what the reason is for personal communication barriers, managers themselves are required to constantly improve themselves (Smith & Mounter, 2008).

5.3 Solutions

5.3.1 Distinguish Objects

The choice involves two aspects: one is the intention of information transmission and the other is the confidentiality of information transmission. Information has value, but its value varies from person to person. The same information may have different values for different people. Therefore, the targets for information transfer need to be chosen carefully to ensure that the information has practical educational uses. To ensure the quality of information transmission and reduce ineffective work, the relevance of information dissemination needs to be enhanced. At the same time, the scope of use of the information should also be considered. In addition, when improving the pertinence of information delivery, it is also necessary to pay attention to the confidentiality of information to prevent large-scale diffusion of information and flooding of information, which will bring unnecessary psychological burdens to employees and thus affect team morale (Cornelissen, 2023).

5.3.2 Control the Amount of Information Transferred

In management, due to the different roles of hierarchical supervisor Guo Men, each group member considers different issues when transmitting information (Chen et al., 2020). Proper attention should be paid to quantity control. Information that should be made known to subordinates must be passed on as quickly as possible, and information with a limited scope of application must be kept confidential (Ferraris et al., 2020). We should be aware of two tendencies: First, the tendency of information to be too confidential and collaborate with various companies. Employees in various departments maintain confidentiality among themselves and hinder mutual understanding and coordination. Some information materials that should be shared are kept confidential due to artificial reasons (Lo et al., 2010). The result was not communicated to lower-level departments and employees on time, which blocked information, caused unwarranted suspicions and affected the satisfaction of personal social needs. The second is the tendency to diffuse information at will. When transmitting information, the confidentiality of the information is not considered, and the recipient of the information is not selected. Diffuse the collected column information will lead to information confusion.

6. Transparency and Disclosure Guidelines

Transparent information disclosure helps external investors understand the company, enables them to make the best investment decisions and promotes the healthy development of the capital market. Although regulators require listed companies to provide adequate disclosures, companies have a certain degree of discretion regarding the accuracy, timeliness and completeness of mandatory disclosures, as well as voluntary disclosures, resulting in differences in overall information transparency between companies (Fung, 2014).

The key force for the sustainable development of modern enterprises is managers. Their abilities are the most valuable intangible resources of the enterprise and play an important role in promoting the growth of the enterprise (Popa et al., 2009). From the perspective of motivation, managers' ability to identify company economic changes and make corresponding adjustments will affect the company's future performance, and investors' awareness of this ability will affect their expectations for the company's future development. Thereby affecting its assessment of the value of the enterprise. Managers with high capabilities are motivated to make more and more authentic information disclosures, improve corporate information transparency, convey a good corporate image, improve the company's financing environment and enable the company's value to be reasonably evaluated; from the perspective of capabilities, managers The stronger the ability, the more it can improve the company's internal control quality and the more effectively it can identify the company's internal control deficiencies.

7. Legal and Ethical Considerations

Corporate ethics is the reflection and summary of the moral relationships formed in the process of business operation and management and is the sum of the ethical rules that enterprises should abide by when engaging in production and business activities. Corporate ethics is the value standard by which people judge the morality of corporate behavior. It is also the extra-legal norms and norms that companies should abide by when dealing with stakeholders such as consumers, employees, communities and the public (Ikejiaku, 2012).

8. Conclusion

This chapter concludes that organizations are responsible for communicating transparently and effectively with stakeholders using good financial communications. Good relationships with stakeholders and proactive management engagement with investors can increase trust and equitable valuation of their assets. The engagement activities include earning calls, regular meetings with investors and stakeholders and publishing annual reports to distribute information related to market analysis and company financials. Additionally, the corporate aims of managers can be further improved under stakeholder theoretical assumptions. In this regard, crisis communication, an open approach and reputation management can improve effective financial communication between stakeholders and the company. Moreover, ethical and legal principles also play a significant role between both parties. Thus, corporate managers should use a holistic approach to ensure stakeholder and investor relationships with the company, which includes effective marketing, strong financial performance, and aggressive communication strategies to be competitive in a high-growth business environment.

References

Ahblom, P., & Christner, C. H. (2021). Behind closed doors: Exploring the conduct of private meetings between investor and company representatives. *Available at SSRN 4029998.*

Al-Zwyalif, I. M. (2015). The role of internal control in enhancing corporate governance: Evidence from Jordan. *International Journal of Business and Management, 10*(7), 57.

Araújo, M., & Miranda, S. (2021). Multidisciplinarity in internal communication and the challenges ahead. *Corporate Communications: An International Journal, 26*(1), 107–123.

Ashraf, Z., Afshan, G., & Sahibzada, U. F. (2022). Unpacking strategic corporate social responsibility in the time of crisis: A critical review. *Journal of Global Responsibility, 13*(2), 127–156.

Aula, P., & Mantere, S. (2020). *Strategic reputation management: Towards a company of good.* Routledge.

Batra, R., & Keller, K. L. (2016). Integrating marketing communications: New findings, new lessons, and new ideas. *Journal of Marketing, 80*(6), 122–145.

Bell, R. G., Filatotchev, I., & Rasheed, A. A. (2012). The liability of foreignness in capital markets: Sources and remedies. *Journal of International Business Studies, 43*, 107–122.

Benn, S., Abratt, R., & O'Leary, B. (2016). Defining and identifying stakeholders: Views from management and stakeholders. *South African Journal of Business Management, 47*(2), 1–11.

Botha, M. M. (2015). Responsibilities of companies towards employees. *Potchefstroom Electronic Law Journal, 18*(2), 1–67.

Brennan, N. M., & Merkl-Davies, D. M. (2018). Do firms effectively communicate with financial stakeholders? A conceptual model of corporate communication in a capital market context. *Accounting and Business Research, 48*(5), 553–577.

Brockhaus, J., Buhmann, A., & Zerfass, A. (2023). Digitalization in corporate communications: Understanding the emergence and consequences of CommTech and digital infrastructure. *Corporate Communications: An International Journal, 28*(2), 274–292.

Bushee, B. J., & Miller, G. S. (2012). Investor relations, firm visibility, and investor following. *The Accounting Review, 87*(3), 867–897.

Chahine, S., Colak, G., Hasan, I., & Mazboudi, M. (2020). Investor relations and IPO performance. *Review of Accounting Studies, 25*, 474–512.

Chen, H., Yang, D., Zhang, J. H., & Zhou, H. (2020). Internal controls, risk management, and cash holdings. *Journal of Corporate Finance, 64*, 101695.

Cheng, M. M., & Coyte, R. (2014). The effects of incentive subjectivity and strategy communication on knowledge-sharing and extra-role behaviours. *Management Accounting Research, 25*(2), 119–130.

Cornelissen, J. P. (2023). Corporate communication: A guide to theory and practice.

Cova, B., & Salle, R. (2006). *Communications and stakeholders* (pp. 131–146). Blackwell Science.

Crane, A., & Glozer, S. (2016). Researching corporate social responsibility communication: Themes, opportunities and challenges. *Journal of Management Studies, 53*(7), 1223–1252.

Dafoe, A., Hughes, E., Bachrach, Y., Collins, T., McKee, K. R., Leibo, J. Z., Larson, K., & Graepel, T. (2020). Open problems in cooperative ai. *arXiv preprint arXiv: 2012.08630.*

Davies, G., & Miles, L. (1998). Reputation management: Theory versus practice. *Corporate Reputation Review, 2,* 16–27.

DesJardine, M. R., Zhang, M., & Shi, W. (2023). How shareholders impact stakeholder interests: A review and map for future research. *Journal of Management, 49*(1), 400–429.

Doan, M. A., & McKie, D. (2017). Financial investigations: Auditing research accounts of communication in business, investor relations, and public relations (1994–2016). *Public Relations Review, 43*(2), 306–313.

Doorley, J., & Garcia, H. F. (2015). *Reputation management: The key to successful public relations and corporate communication.* Routledge.

Duh, M., & Djokić, D. (2021). Transparency and disclosure regulations—A valuable component of improving corporate governance practice in transition economies. *Social Responsibility and Corporate Governance: Volume 2: Policy and Practice,* 193–228.

Enke, N., & Borchers, N. S. (2021). Social media influencers in strategic communication: A conceptual framework for strategic social media influencer communication. In *Social media influencers in strategic communication* (pp. 7–23). Routledge.

Eskerod, P. (2020). A stakeholder perspective: Origins and core concepts. In *Oxford research encyclopedia of business and management.*

Ferenc, P., Varmus, M., & Vodák, J. (2017). Stakeholders in the various field and relations between them. *Procedia Engineering, 192,* 166–170.

Ferraris, A., Santoro, G., & Scuotto, V. (2020). Dual relational embeddedness and knowledge transfer in European multinational corporations and subsidiaries. *Journal of Knowledge Management, 24*(3), 519–533.

Frandsen, F., & Johansen, W. (2011). The study of internal crisis communication: Towards an integrative framework. *Corporate Communications: An International Journal, 16*(4), 347–361.

Freeman, R. E., Harrison, J. S., Wicks, A. C., Parmar, B. L., & De Colle, S. (2010). Stakeholder theory: The state of the art.

Frias-Aceituno, J. V., Rodriguez-Ariza, L., & Garcia-Sanchez, I. M. (2013). The role of the board in the dissemination of integrated corporate social reporting. *Corporate Social Responsibility and Environmental Management, 20*(4), 219–233.

Fung, B. (2014). The demand and need for transparency and disclosure in corporate governance. *Universal Journal of Management, 2*(2), 72–80.

Gao, S., Meng, F., Wang, W., & Chen, W. (2023). Does ESG always improve corporate performance? Evidence from firm life cycle perspective. *Frontiers in Environmental Science, 11*, 1105077.

García-Sánchez, I. M., & García-Sánchez, A. (2020). Corporate social responsibility during COVID-19 pandemic. *Journal of Open Innovation: Technology, Market, and Complexity, 6*(4), 126.

Greyser, S. A. (2009). Corporate brand reputation and brand crisis management. *Management Decision, 47*(4), 590–602.

Guimard, A. (2013). Implementing Best Practices in Investor Relations. In *Investor Relations: Principles and International Best Practices in Financial Communications* (pp. 92–187). London: Palgrave Macmillan UK.

Gunawan, S., Shieh, C. J., & Pei, Y. (2015). Effects of crisis communication strategies and media report on corporate image in Catering Industry. *Acta Oeconomica, 65*(s2), 399–411.

Gupta, P., He, D., Ma, Y., & Yur-Austin, J. (2022). Do investors listen? Exploring the effect of investor relationship management on firm-specific stock return variation. *Research in International Business and Finance, 60*, 101598.

Hardaker, S., & Fill, C. (2005). Corporate services brands: The intellectual and emotional engagement of employees. *Corporate Reputation Review, 7*, 365–376.

Heide, M., & Simonsson, C. (2014). Developing internal crisis communication: New roles and practices of communication professionals. *Corporate Communications: An International Journal, 19*(2), 128–146.

Hoffmann, C. P., & Binder-Tietz, S. (2021). Strategic investor relations management: Insights on planning and evaluation practices among German Prime Standard corporations. *Journal of Communication Management, 25*(2), 142–159.

Hoffmann, C. P., Tietz, S., & Hammann, K. (2018). Investor relations – A systematic literature review. *Corporate Communications: An International Journal, 23*(3), 294–311.

Huang, Y. H. (2008). Trust and relational commitment in corporate crises: The effects of crisis communicative strategy and form of crisis response. *Journal of Public Relations Research, 20*(3), 297–327.

Hussain, M., & Papastathopoulos, A. (2022). Organizational readiness for digital financial innovation and financial resilience. *International Journal of Production Economics, 243*, 108326.

Ikejiaku, B. V. (2012). Consideration of ethical and legal aspects of corporate social responsibility: The issue of multi-national corporations and sustainable development. *NJCL*, iii.

Isa, S. M. (2012). Corporate social responsibility: What can we learn from the stakeholders? *Procedia-Social and Behavioral Sciences, 65*, 327–337.

Jensen, M. C. (2009). Corporate control and the politics of finance. In *US Corporate Governance* (pp. 243–279). Columbia University Press.

Jia, L., Qian, Q. K., Meijer, F., & Visscher, H. (2020). Stakeholders' risk perception: A perspective for proactive risk management in residential building energy retrofits in China. *Sustainability, 12*(7), 2832.

Jiang, Y. N., & Park, H. (2022). Mapping networks in corporate social responsibility communication on social media: A new approach to exploring the influence of communication tactics on public responses. *Public Relations Review, 48*(1), 102143.

Jones, K. G., Mitchell, K. R., Ploubidis, G. B., Wellings, K., Datta, J., Johnson, A. M., & Mercer, C. H. (2015). The Natsal-SF measure of sexual function: Comparison of three scoring methods. *The Journal of Sex Research, 52*(6), 640–646.

Joynt, G. M., Loo, S., Taylor, B. L., Margalit, G., Christian, M. D., Sandrock, C., Danis, M., Leoniv, Y., & Sprung, C. L. (2010). Chapter 3. Coordination and collaboration with interface units. *Intensive Care Medicine, 36*, 21–31.

Kanakriyah, R. (2020). Dividend policy and companies' financial performance. *The Journal of Asian Finance, Economics and Business, 7*(10), 531–541.

Karolyi, G. A., Kim, D., & Liao, R. (2020). The theory and practice of investor relations: A global perspective. *Management Science, 66*(10), 4746–4771.

Khuong, M. N., Truong An, N. K., & Thanh Hang, T. T. (2021). Stakeholders and Corporate Social Responsibility (CSR) programme as key sustainable development strategies to promote corporate reputation—Evidence from Vietnam. *Cogent Business & Management, 8*(1), 1917333.

Kiambi, D. M., & Shafer, A. (2016). Corporate crisis communication: Examining the interplay of reputation and crisis response strategies. *Mass Communication and Society, 19*(2), 127–148.

Kim, S., Marina Choi, S., & Atkinson, L. (2017). Congruence effects of corporate associations and crisis issue on crisis communication strategies. *Social Behavior and Personality: An International Journal, 45*(7), 1085-1098.

Kinanti, Z. P., & Asnawi, S. K. (2022). The role of investor relations in the Indonesian stock exchange: An important communication bridge. *Jurnal Komunikasi Dan Bisnis, 10*(1), 24–35.

Kitchen, P. J., & Watson, T. (2010). Reputation management: Corporate image and communication.

Laskin, A. V. (2011). How investor relations contributes to the corporate bottom line. *Journal of Public Relations Research, 23*(3), 302–324.

Laskin, A. V. (2021). *Investor relations and financial communication: Creating value through trust and understanding.* John Wiley & Sons.

Li, Z., Wang, P., & Wu, T. (2021). Do foreign institutional investors drive corporate social responsibility? Evidence from listed firms in China. *Journal of Business Finance & Accounting, 48*(1–2), 338–373.

Lo, A. W., Wong, R. M., & Firth, M. (2010). Can corporate governance deter management from manipulating earnings? Evidence from related-party sales transactions in China. *Journal of Corporate Finance, 16*(2), 225–235.

López-Romero, L., & Romero, E. (2011). Reputation management of adolescents in relation to antisocial behavior. *The Journal of Genetic Psychology, 172*(4), 440–446.

Lu, C., Liu, H. C., Tao, J., Rong, K., & Hsieh, Y. C. (2017). A key stakeholder-based financial subsidy stimulation for Chinese EV industrialization: A system dynamics simulation. *Technological Forecasting and Social Change, 118*, 1–14.

Luckey, B. J. (2021). *Exploring the value of technology within cross-departmental communications.* Doctoral dissertation. Walden University.

Mak, A. K. (2005). Identity-centered model of reputation management: A case study of Iowa tourism office and its industry partners. *The Impact of PR in Creating a More Ethical World: Why Can't We All Get Along?* 270.

Mărioara, B. B., Dorina, P., Oana, C. C. A., & Camelia, A. B. (2014). Financial communication and intellectual capital reporting practices. *Annals of the University of Oradea, Economic Science Series, 23*(1).

Masulis, R. W., & Nahata, R. (2009). Financial contracting with strategic investors: Evidence from corporate venture capital backed IPOs. *Journal of Financial Intermediation, 18*(4), 599–631.

Melewar, T. C., Sarstedt, M., & Hallier, C. (2012). Corporate identity, image and reputation management: A further analysis. *Corporate Communications: An International Journal, 17*(1).

Meng, J., & Berger, B. K. (2012). Measuring return on investment (ROI) of organizations' internal communication efforts. *Journal of Communication Management, 16*(4), 332–354.

Miles, S. (2017). Stakeholder theory classification: A theoretical and empirical evaluation of definitions. *Journal of Business Ethics, 142*, 437–459.

Mishra, K., Boynton, L., & Mishra, A. (2014). Driving employee engagement: The expanded role of internal communications. *International Journal of Business Communication, 51*(2), 183–202.

Noori, N. (2021). *The Effects of Financial Risks Management on Financial Performance of Commercial Banks in Malaysia.* Limkokwing University, for the award of the degree of Master of Business Administration in Finance and Banking.

Packard, G., & Berger, J. (2021). How concrete language shapes customer satisfaction. *Journal of Consumer Research, 47*(5), 787–806.

Pererva, P., Kobielieva, T., Tkachov, M., & Diachenko, T. (2021). Management of relations with enterprise stakeholders based on value approach. *Problems and Perspectives in Management, 19*(1), 24.

Pirozzi, M. (2019). Stakeholders, who are they. *PM World Journal, 8*(9), 1–10.

Popa, A., Blidisel, R., & Bogdan, V. (2009, November). Transparency and disclosure between theory and practice. A case study of Romania. In *Proceedings of FIKUSZ'09 Symposium for Young Researchers* (pp. 173–183).

Posthumusa, S., & Von Solms, R. (2005). IT oversight: An important function of corporate governance. *Computer Fraud & Security, 2005*(6), 11–17.

Rim, H., & Ferguson, M. A. T. (2020). Proactive versus reactive CSR in a crisis: An impression management perspective. *International Journal of Business Communication, 57*(4), 545–568.

Rodrigues, S. D. S., & Galdi, F. C. (2017). Investor relations and information asymmetry. *Revista Contabilidade & Finanças, 28*(74), 297–312.

Ruuskanen, M. (2021). *The role of effective supplier relationship management in value creation.*

Schilirò, D. (2020). Towards digital globalization and the covid-19 challenge.

Seaverson, E. L., Grossmeier, J., Miller, T. M., & Anderson, D. R. (2009). The role of incentive design, incentive value, communications strategy, and worksite culture on health risk assessment participation. *American Journal of Health Promotion, 23*(5), 343–352.

Siegel, J. J. (2021). *Stocks for the long run: The definitive guide to financial market returns & long-term investment strategies.* McGraw-Hill Education.

Smith, K. T., Smith, M., & Wang, K. (2010). Does brand management of corporate reputation translate into higher market value? *Journal of Strategic Marketing, 18*(3), 201–221.

Smith, L., & Mounter, P. (2008). *Effective internal communication.* Kogan Page Publishers.

Smith, V. (2023). *Managing in the corporate interest: Control and resistance in an American bank.* Univ of California Press.

Stokes, L. C. (2020). *Short circuiting policy: Interest groups and the battle over clean energy and climate policy in the American States.* Oxford University Press.

Tennie, C., Frith, U., & Frith, C. D. (2010). Reputation management in the age of the world-wide web. *Trends in Cognitive Sciences, 14*(11), 482–488.

Timothy Coombs, W., Frandsen, F., Holladay, S. J., & Johansen, W. (2010). Why a concern for apologia and crisis communication?. *Corporate Communications: An International Journal, 15*(4), 337–349.

Ufua, D. E., Olujobi, O. J., Ogbari, M. E., Dada, J. A., & Edafe, O. D. (2020). Operations of small and medium enterprises and the legal system in Nigeria. *Humanities and Social Sciences Communications, 7*(1), 1–7.

Van der Meer, T. G., & Verhoeven, J. W. (2014). Emotional crisis communication. *Public Relations Review, 40*(3), 526–536.

Van Riel, C. B., & Fombrun, C. J. (2007). *Essentials of corporate communication: Implementing practices for effective reputation management.* Routledge.

Verghese, A. K. (2017). Internal Communication: Practices and Implications. *SCMS Journal of Indian Management, 14*(3).

Verk, N., Golob, U., & Podnar, K. (2021). A dynamic review of the emergence of corporate social responsibility communication. *Journal of Business Ethics, 168,* 491–515.

Volk, S. C., & Zerfass, A. (2020). Alignment: Explicating a key concept in strategic communication. *Future Directions of Strategic Communication,* 105–123.

Voswinkel, S. (2011). Reputation: A sociological view. In *Reputation Management* (pp. 31–45). Springer.

Wagner Mainardes, E., Alves, H., & Raposo, M. (2012). A model for stakeholder classification and stakeholder relationships. *Management Decision, 50*(10), 1861–1879.

Welch, M. (2011). The evolution of the employee engagement concept: Communication implications. *Corporate Communications: An International Journal, 16*(4), 328–346.

Wiedmann, K. P., & Buxel, H. (2005). Corporate reputation management in Germany: Results of an empirical study. *Corporate Reputation Review, 8,* 145–163.

Wind, Y., & Main, J. (1998). *Driving change: How the best companies are preparing for the 21st century.* Simon and Schuster.

Winn, M. I., MacDonald, P., & Zietsma, C. (2008). Managing industry reputation: The dynamic tension between collective and competitive reputation management strategies. *Corporate Reputation Review, 11,* 35–55.

Wu, X., & Hąbek, P. (2021). Trends in corporate social responsibility reporting. The case of Chinese listed companies. *Sustainability, 13*(15), 8640.

Yanjie, F., & Bo, X. (2009, August). Strategic management framework of investor relations. In *2009 ISECS International Colloquium on Computing, Communication, Control, and Management* (Vol. 2, pp. 72–75). IEEE.

Chapter 10

Financial Decision-Making in Uncertain Markets

Liu Zihang[a] *and Muhammad Ali*[b]

[a]UCSI University, Malaysia
[b]Taylor's University, Malaysia

Abstract

The purpose of this study is to explore the financial decision-making process under the uncertain market environment. Through in-depth analysis of market volatility and its driving factors, behavioral finance considerations, investment decision-making framework, risk and return trade-off, management investment strategy and emergency plan in uncertain period, this study puts forward a series of management suggestions for different fields. It is pointed out that understanding macroeconomic information and nonlinear effects is very important for better forecasting market fluctuations. In addition, through the understanding of investors' bias, the decision-making process of investors can be improved, thus reducing investment mistakes. In investment decision-making, the understanding of institutional conflict and the alignment of management objectives and shareholders' interests through governance structure are emphasized. The balance between risk and reward reveals the challenges faced by management in decision-making, while the investment strategy of management discusses the advantages and disadvantages of active and passive management strategies. Finally, the formulation of emergency plan is a key strategy to fight against uncertainty, which requires managers to conduct careful environmental analysis and build an effective communication and cooperation network. The purpose of this study is to provide a comprehensive framework to help understand and deal with the challenges of financial decision-making in uncertain markets.

Keywords: Market volatility; behavioral finance; investment decision-making framework; risk and return; emergency plan

Strategic Financial Management, 155–167
doi:10.1108/978-1-83608-106-720241010

1. Introduction

1.1 Market Volatility and Its Drivers

Commodity price volatility is a key element in risk management, hedging and valuing commodity-dependent claims. Additionally, it influences how much the option embedded in inventory is worth, which has an impact on production choices. Therefore, investors, producers and policymakers must comprehend the causes of its changes (Prokopczuk et al., 2019). Similarly, when forecasting risk indicators, such as Value-at-Risk (VaR) or expected shortfall, which are frequently employed in risk assessment, the creation of risk-mitigation techniques, and for compliance reasons, accurate volatility projections for asset values are essential (Mittnik et al., 2015).

One challenge that managers go through when they try to estimate market volatility is that various variables need to be put into consideration when calculating market volatility. Moreover, different finance scholars have used different methods to calculate market volatility and these methods produce varying results and different types of market volatility. Additionally, a large number of research findings on forecasting financial market risk have solely used past return records as conditional information. Only a small number of research have examined how much information found in other macroeconomic or financial variables aids in improving volatility forecasts.

Schwert (1989), for example, used autoregressive models to investigate the connection between stock volatility and macroeconomic factors such as GDP fluctuations, company activity and financial leverage. To project the volatility of US stock returns, Engle et al. (2013) integrated industrial production and inflation using a mixed-frequency generalized autoregressive conditional heteroscedasticity (GARCH) model. They demonstrate that macroeconomic fundamentals are important even at short horizons and that including economic fundamentals in volatility models benefits long-horizon forecasting. Real macroeconomic variables' effects on total equity returns were examined by Flannery and Proto-papadakis in 2002, while Engle and Rangel discovered that macroeconomic data could be used to predict the low-frequency component of volatility in 2008.

Larger sets of macroeconomic parameters and a wider variety of asset classes are taken into account by Paye (2012) and, in particular, Christiansen et al. (2012). Both incorporate lagged volatility, financial and macroeconomic variables as predictors and log-transformed realized volatility into their linear models. The prediction of volatility for various markets is often examined by Christoffersen and Diebold (2000). Depending on the asset class, they conclude that volatility is unpredictable when the interest horizon is longer than 10 or 20 days. Implied volatility is the topic of a further fascinating field of research (Canina & Figlewski, 1993; Christensen & Prabhala, 1998; Jiang & Tian, 2005; Prokopczuk & Simen, 2014).

Prokopczuk et al. (2019). demonstrate that the volatility of the commodity markets is correlated with financial and economic unpredictability and that this correlation is substantially more pronounced during economic downturns. To investigate how well a group of theoretically driven economic variables can forecast the volatility of the commodities market, Prokopczuk et al. (2019) estimate predictive regressions. As Prokopczuk et al. (2019) conclude their study, they discovered fresh indicators of volatility in the commodity market that are linked to credit risk, funding liquidity risk, unpredictability in the equities and bond markets and variation in actual economic conditions.

2. Behavioral Finance Considerations

The goal of behavioral finance, the study of how psychology affects investor behavior, is to identify why and how investors tend to be their own worst enemies. Behavioral finance emphasizes how investors frequently act irrationally (i.e. make decisions based on reasoning), are heavily influenced by personal biases and occasionally exhibit an inability to manage their emotions, all of which lead to poor investment decisions (Brickman, n.d.).

The effects of the "average investor" and their decisions to purchase, sell and switch into and out of investments throughout a range of periods have been tracked by Dalbar, Inc. ("Dalbar") since 1994. The net aggregate sales, redemptions and swaps of mutual funds are used by Dalbar as a gauge of investor activity each month (Brickman, n.d.). Dalbar estimates that during the 20 years ending December 31, 2018, the "average investor" gained 1.9% annually, compared to gains of 5.6% for the S&P 500 Index and 4.5% for the Barclays Aggregate Bond Index during that same period. The "average investor" underperformed significantly over 20 years compared to aggressive, 100% domestic equity and conservative, 100% taxable bond portfolios, regardless of the investor's risk tolerance, demonstrating the enormous influence investor decision-making has on long-term performance (Brickman, n.d.).

There are primarily two theories explaining the behavioral elements of investors: Expected utility theory or standard finance and prospect theory or behavioral finance. Markowitz developed the descriptive theory of standard finance in 1952, and the theory assumes that markets are effective and are quite conservative and analytical (Antony, 2020). The theory also emphasizes maximizing wealth. The notion of predicted utility maximization has a mathematical counterpart called prospect theory. A picture of genuinely rational conduct under certainty is provided by the utility theory. The expected utility theory argues that investors are risk-averse (Antony, 2020). The declining marginal utility of wealth is similar to risk aversion. Each extra unit of wealth is worth less than the last gain in wealth of equal value. Despite the expected utility theory's evident appeal, it consistently fails to predict how people act, at least under certain conditions.

When managing investors, managers are at times caught in between losses caused by the poor decisions made by investors due to investor biases. Several investor biases have been discovered via behavioral finance. When working with clients and potential clients and these biases include

- *Representativeness.* Investors categorize investments as good or bad depending on how they have performed recently due to representativeness. As a result, people purchase equities once the price has increased. Anticipating those growth rates to persist and disregard stock prices when they are below what they are truly worth, investors should test and iterate on a clearly defined analytical process.

- *Loss (regret) aversion.* The sense of regret felt after making a decision that ends up being an inferior decision is referred to as regret aversion. Investors who expect to regret their decisions are incentivized to take less risk since the likelihood of unfavorable outcomes is reduced. Investor reluctance to sell "losing" investments can be attributed to regret aversion because doing so signals to them that they have made poor decisions (Baker & Ricciardi, 2014). Overcoming the unwillingness to accept losses is a prerequisite for disciplined investing.
- *Disposition impact.* The disposition effect – the propensity to sell well-performing stocks too soon and hold onto underperforming equities for an excessively long period is closely related to the desire to steer clear of regret. As it may boost capital gains taxes paid by investors and can lower profits even before taxes, the disposition effect is unfavorable for investors (Baker & Ricciardi, 2014).
- *Familiarity bias.* This bias shows up when investors favor tried-and-true investments despite the apparent benefits of diversification. In addition to portfolios that are skewed toward domestic securities, investors also show a preference for local assets that they are better familiar with (Baker & Ricciardi, 2014). Investors may have poor portfolios as a result of familiarity bias.

Investors who are subject to self-attribution bias sometimes blame external sources for adverse results while attributing favorable outcomes to their actions. This bias is frequently displayed by them as a kind of self-preservation or self-improvement. Self-attribution bias can make investors overconfident, which can lead to trading excessively and unfavorable outcomes.

Investors tend to follow the herd when making decisions. Investors who follow the crowd tend to be more affected by instinct and emotion than by independent thinking (Brickman, n.d.). Studies have shown that being a contrarian investor or going against the grain can make some people feel physically and mentally uncomfortable. When an investor purchases a stock because it is "hot" or because they received a stock tip from a friend without conducting any research to determine the investment's underlying merits, this is an example of herd mentality in action.

Hindsight bias is the belief that results are clear in retrospect. In hindsight, the dotcom collapse of the late 1990s, which was brought on by speculative investments in unsuccessful internet-based enterprises, and the real estate crash of the late 2000s, which was caused by thousands of Americans buying homes they could not realistically afford, were horrible times to invest (Brickman, n.d.). But if we look at history, those investing experts who pointed out these now obvious problems were either ridiculed or completely disregarded at the time.

Loss aversion is the propensity to place a greater emphasis on preventing or minimizing a loss than on realizing investment profits. According to research, investors experience the delight of generating a profit more than twice as strongly as they experience the anguish of a loss (Brickman, n.d.). A person who invests in low-return, guaranteed assets while having the financial means and ability to do so is an example of loss-averse behavior.

3. Investment Decision Frameworks

Certain conflicts of interest occur between executives, staff members, shareholders and debtors when a firm resolves to invest. A similar thing happens when an organization chooses how to spend its resources. On the contrary, the company's investment decisions are extremely important in making sure its viability and expanding its market. Making the right investments is important since it determines how profitable the company will be. Karuna (2007), Akdoğu and MacKay (2012), and Laksmana and Yang (2015), who assert that investment decisions can raise the value of the company, all support this.

In addition, investment would limit the ability of the rival company to grow, but it has a short-term impact (Gilbert & Lieberman, 1987). Most researchers state that there is a relationship between agency theory and investment decisions. This is a product of the agency theory's core seven predefined assumptions, which include information as a good or service, information asymmetry, limited thinking, goal disagreements, personal interests and operational excellence (Eisenhardt, 1989).

Agency conflicts between controlling shareholders and minority investors, as well as the issue of information asymmetry between the government and financial institutions and between leadership and shareholders, are thought to have a significant impact on company investment decisions according to studies by Myers and Majluf (1984), Jensen (1986) and Fazzari et al. (1988). However, Aivazian (2005) suggests that agency issues arise primarily from the relationships among debtors, shareholders, and the leadership team.

To safeguard shareholder interests, reduce agency costs and maintain aligned interests, the agency theory has several methods (Davis et al., 1997). Jesen (1983) proposes two types of agency theories that have both been developed: principal-agent and positivist. To uncover agency concerns and governance methods that highlight agency problems, positivist researchers have placed a strong emphasis on governance processes, particularly in large businesses. As per Eisenhardt (1989), positivist academics have solely concentrated on unique principal-agent relationships between landlords and managers of public enterprises.

Ross (1973) was the first to look at the agency issue, but Meckling and Jensen (1976) were the first to offer a thorough theoretical examination of agency theory, contending that the manager of a business is the "agent" and the principal is the "shareholder." The agency connection in agency theory, according to Jensen and Meckling (1976), is a point of contact between the manager, who supervises property use and the principal, who is the landlord of the financial assets.

According to Messier et al. (2006), this agency relationship causes two obstacles: (a) information asymmetry, in that the leadership frequently knows more about the owner's actual economic standing and position regarding the firm's operation; (b) the emergence of a conflict of interest brought on by an imbalance in the goals of the parties involved, when managers fail to behave in the owner's best interests. The agency problem must be avoided or minimized by providing agency expenses that will be paid for by both the principal and the agent.

4. Risk-Return Trade-offs

Following Sharpe's (1964) and Lintner's (1969) conditional formulations of the Capital Asset Pricing Model (CAPM), there should be a favorable risk-return trade-off, or a positive correlation between the stock market's yields (conditional) and its (conditional) anticipated gain (Barroso & Maio, 2023). Even though theory implies unequivocally that the conditional market risk premium and conditional variance have a positive relationship, several research studies conducted by Campbell (1987) and Glosten et al. (1993) suggest that the risk-return trade-off is probably negligible or negative.

The returns are usually negative because of the following risks that managers encounter as they make their decisions. Credit risk relates to a company's or business's credit worthiness. If a company's finances are in good shape, it will be able to fulfill its present and future obligations and make timely debt repayments. This will result in a favorable credit rating. Credit risk is a result of the company's declining financial condition. Liquidity risk arises from the company's inability to generate sufficient revenue to cover its debts and keep a high level of working capital. Interest rates risk refers to the ability of a business to borrow money that can be impacted by changes in interest rates in an economy. Inflation causes the value of investments and future cash flows to decline. Market risk, also known as systemic risk, can result from a variety of market-related variables, such as interest rate and currency changes, political and economic unrest, and other issues. They significantly affect investors. Specific risks generally concern the business itself. Through monitoring and diversification, they may be contained.

Some of the risk management challenges that managers encounter as they try to manage risk to maximize return include banks and other financial institutions must constantly innovate and advance their operational and technical procedures, which is expensive and time-consuming. It is also true that in the contemporary setting, credit risk management has become more important (Feridun, 2006). The banking sector is moving more and more toward a quantitative assessment of the risk in its loan portfolios. Before recently, credit risk management has steadily surpassed market concerns as the primary concern for quantitative risk management. Quantitative risk management has presented staff with both opportunities and several obstacles. These difficulties include modeling problems that are quantitative as well as concerns with change management.

The difficulties that financial organizations have in controlling liquidity risk have become increasingly obvious both during and after the economic downturn (Bank of Japan, 2010). The organizations must first assess the financing and operational procedures as well as their liquidity risk characteristics. Furthermore, these firms must set up an organization-specific risk management framework.

Priority must be accorded to this, especially for universities without reliable funding. In a liquidity stress phase, institutions must also increase their adaptability or resilience. Third, there are international financial institutions that have a unique difficulty when it comes to managing risks both locally and globally.

5. Managerial Portfolio Strategies

A portfolio is an assortment of assets that belong to an individual or institution, including stocks, bonds, real estate and even cryptocurrencies (O'Connell, 2022). There are two portfolio management strategies, and they include active portfolio management and passive portfolio management. Active portfolio management refers to the use of available information and the manager's skills to make stock-by-stock forecasts of pure active returns by information that has not been affected by the price (Siegel & Waring, 2009). One challenge that active managers face is that they need to be very good at forecasting or they will make losses for the investor (Siegel & Waring, 2009). To overcome this challenge, active managers should ensure that they sharpen their forecasting skills to become superior forecasters.

Making the argument for active portfolio management in the financial markets can be challenging. While many people choose to invest in index funds, some people trust their money to active managers who are looking for positive alphas and cheap equities. The question is whether investing in an actively managed stock fund has any financial benefit (Greenhill, 2014). Although active managers claim to be able to provide superior returns, the fees associated with investing frequently prevent their funds from being as appealing or lucrative. These active managers frequently fall short of their benchmarks due to management costs and high turnover rates. On the other hand, passive (Index) funds are far less expensive because they attempt to replicate an index and trade much less frequently.

However, there are always some difficulties that are frequently unsolvable, regardless of the technique employed. Even with the best portfolio management strategy, an investor's investments are still subject to unpredicted market volatility and changes. Even the best management plan could cause significant losses. Despite being important to portfolio management, diversification can be challenging to attain. The best mix of asset classes and investment products to balance risk and return requires a deep understanding of the market and each investor's tolerance for risk (Hayes, 2023). Additionally, it could be expensive to buy a range of securities to attain the required diversification.

6. Contingency Planning in Uncertain Times

A contingency plan enables a company to choose how to respond to conceivable future events. Organizations typically develop contingency plans that address what to do if a worker leaves their position or when they encounter a financial crisis. Although firms need contingency plans, managers frequently run into difficulties while attempting to create one. Among the difficulties is that managers typically lack support from top executives, stockholders and employees because most individuals do not have an understanding of situations when the business might fail or may be impacted by a negative occurrence. The complexity and ambiguity of the internal and external environments are additional obstacles that managers frequently encounter. For instance, the COVID-19 pandemic was not adequately anticipated by the majority of enterprises, which ultimately led to a significant number of them collapsing. The absence of resources, such as time, money, employees or equipment, poses a third problem for contingency planning. Planning for contingencies may be a difficult and drawn-out process that calls for committed and knowledgeable staff, sufficient resources and the right tools. Some companies, however, could experience resource limitations, conflicting priorities or budget cuts that restrict their capacity to plan successfully.

The lack of coordination across different divisions, units or roles within your business is a fourth obstacle to contingency planning. High levels of cooperation and communication are needed for contingency planning both within the company and with external partners like suppliers, clients or regulators. However, silos, conflicts or gaps may exist inside some companies, impeding collaboration and integration. The lack of testing and evaluation of the plans is the fifth obstacle to contingency planning. The process of contingency planning is a never-ending cycle of development and learning. It is essential to test and evaluate the plans often using simulations, drills or audits to ensure that they are dependable, viable and valid. However, some businesses may ignore or postpone this stage owing to indifference, overconfidence or a lack of resources.

7. Recommendations

To be able to predict market volatility and its drivers in a better way, managers need to use both macroeconomic information and the presence of nonlinear effects (Mittnik, Robinzonov & Spindler). This approach is appealing because it is simple, and it allows for the incorporation of external risk drivers. When the external factors enter the model linearly, short-term projections also benefit. Nevertheless, they increase accuracy in the medium and long run by permitting volatility to react asymmetrically and with leaps. These results support the conclusions of Engle et al. (2013), who claim that the addition of macroeconomic variables enhances the long-term predictability of US stock return. Additionally, they are consistent with those of Christoffersen and West and Cho (1995) and Diebold and Kilian (2000), who employed data sets devoid of macroeconomic factors, discovering that the accuracy of volatility predictions rapidly deteriorates as the prediction horizon expands.

Aligning managers' objectives with shareholders' interests and requiring them to act in a way that maximizes shareholder wealth are two ways to address the shareholders-managers agency problem. To shape them, regulate them through governance structures or impose limitations on them through leverage, managers are compensated in the form of incentives. Agency costs make up the cost of putting the solutions into action. Agency costs fall into three main categories:

opportunity costs, which appear when shareholders wait for agreement before allowing executives to act, costs related to putting strategies in place to monitor managers' actions, such as paying independent auditors' fees and costs related to structuring the business' organizational structure to prevent managers from working against shareholders' interests.

Keeping a record of one's failures and accomplishments, as well as creating accountability systems like asking for others' helpful criticism, may assist investors in becoming more aware of self-attribution bias (Baker & Ricciardi, 2014). Investors must cast a broader net and expand their portfolio allocation selections to get wider diversification and risk reduction to overcome this bias. Investments abroad help mitigate familiarity bias (Baker & Ricciardi, 2014).

For active managers to outlive passive funds, they should be able to bring in enough revenue to cover the costs associated with trading and maintaining the fund (Greenhill, 2014). Selecting assets, identifying positive alphas and producing returns are the responsibilities of an active portfolio manager. Although it seems straightforward, adding value in a highly competitive market is challenging. Due to their lower costs, improved tax efficiency and capacity to avoid spending an increasing amount of time investigating companies, passive funds are currently quite alluring (Carosa, 2005). Many fund managers think they can beat the market, but according to Jarrow, "the existence and persistence of positive alphas is more a fantasy than a fact (Guofu, 2008)." Thus, another solution for active managers is to shift to passive portfolio management.

To overcome the challenges that present themselves due to contingency planning, managers must undertake a thorough and methodical examination of the environment, using a variety of tools and techniques, such as SWOT, PESTLE or scenario planning, to get beyond this obstacle. Prioritize the most important and likely hazards as well as define flexible and unambiguous criteria and triggers for plan activation. Managers must show the value and advantages of contingency planning, such as cost savings, improved performance or increased resilience, to get past this obstacle. Additionally, they must include the pertinent parties in the planning process, get their input and address any issues they may have. Additionally, managers should create a transparent governance structure and procedure for contingency planning, together with clearly defined roles, responsibilities and accountabilities, to get beyond this obstacle. Managers also need to employ efficient technologies and channels for communication and information exchange and cultivate a culture of transparency, trust and teamwork.

To effectively manage lack of resources, managers must budget and justify the resources required for contingency planning using a cost-benefit analysis. Additionally, they must make the best use of already available resources, enlist outside assistance and, if necessary, outsource some duties. High levels of cooperation and communication are needed for contingency planning both within the company and with external partners like suppliers, clients or regulators. However, silos, conflicts or gaps may exist inside some companies, impeding collaboration and integration. To get beyond the obstacle of lack of testing and evaluation of plans, managers must organize and carry out routine testing and evaluation of the plans using pertinent and realistic scenarios and standards. Additionally, you must gather, examine and update data and feedback as necessary.

8. Conclusion

In the current uncertain market environment, financial decision-making is facing unprecedented challenges. Through in-depth analysis of market volatility and its driving factors, the influence of behavioral finance, investment decision-making framework, the balance between risk and return, management investment strategy and emergency plan in uncertain period, this study provides a series of targeted management suggestions to help investors, decision-makers and policymakers better cope with these challenges.

The in-depth analysis of market volatility reveals the internal relationship between macroeconomic factors and financial markets and emphasizes the importance of comprehensively considering macroeconomic information and nonlinear effects when forecasting market volatility. Behavioral finance reveals irrational factors in investors' decision-making, such as personal prejudice and improper emotional management, and how these factors affect the investment results.

The discussion of investment decision-making framework and management's investment strategy emphasizes the importance of considering agency problems and conflicting interests in investment decision-making and puts forward some suggestions on aligning the interests of management and shareholders through governance structure adjustment and incentive mechanism. In addition, the trade-off analysis of risk and return points out the necessity of identifying and managing different risk types in the decision-making process.

The formulation of emergency plan is the key to deal with uncertainty. This study points out the difficulties in formulating effective emergency plan and puts forward strategies to overcome these difficulties, such as careful environmental analysis, establishing transparent governance structure and using efficient technology and communication channels.

Generally speaking, this study not only provides a theoretical framework for understanding and coping with the challenges of financial decision-making in uncertain markets but also provides practical suggestions for decision-making in practice. By comprehensively considering macroeconomic factors, investors' behavior, agency problems and risk management, managers and investors can make more wise decisions in the changing market environment, thus realizing long-term return on investment and enterprise value-added.

References

Aivazian, S. (2005). Synthetic indicators of quality of life: Construction and utilization for social-economic management and comparative analysis. *Austrian Journal of Statistics, 34*(2), 69–77.

Akdoğu, E., & MacKay, P. (2012). Product markets and corporate investment: Theory and evidence. *Journal of Banking & Finance, 36*(2), 439–453.

Antony, A. (2020). Behavioral finance and portfolio management: Review of theory and literature. *Journal of Public Affairs, 20*(2), e1996.

Baker, H. K., & Ricciardi, V. (2014). *How biases affect investor behaviour.* Financial Planning Association Chapters | FPA. https://chapters.onefpa.org/greaterindiana/wp-content/uploads/sites/17/2019/11/Nov-2019-Qrtly-Paper-4-How-Biases-Affect-Investor.pdf

Bank of Japan. (2010). *Liquidity risk management in financial institutions following the global financial crisis* (pp. 1–25). https://www.boj.or.jp/en/finsys/fs_policy/data/fss1007a.pdf

Barroso, P., & Maio, P. F. (2023). The risk-return tradeoff among equity factors. https://doi.org/10.2139/ssrn.2909085

Brickman, D. (n.d.). *Financial boot camp series: Behavioral investing challenges.* Schneider Downs Tax Services | Audit Services | Business Consulting Services. https://www.schneiderdowns.com/our-thoughts-on/behavioral-investing-challenges

Campbell, J. Y. (1987). Stock returns and the term structure. *Journal of Financial Economics, 18*(2), 373–399.

Canina, L., & Figlewski, S. (1993). The informational content of implied volatility. *Review of Financial Studies, 6*(3), 659–681.

Carosa, C. (2005). Passive investing: The emperor exposed? *Journal of Financial Planning, 18*(10).

Christensen, B. J., & Prabhala, N. R. (1998). The relation between implied and realized volatility. *Journal of Financial Economics, 50*(2), 125–150.

Christiansen, C., Schmeling, M., & Schrimpf, A. (2012). A comprehensive look at financial volatility prediction by economic variables. *Journal of Applied Econometrics, 27*(6), 956–977.

Christoffersen, P. F., & Diebold, F. X. (2000). How relevant is volatility forecasting for financial risk management? *The Review of Economics and Statistics, 82*(1), 12–22.

Davis, J. H., Schoorman, F. D., & Donaldson, L. (1997). Toward a stewardship theory of management. *Academy of Management Review, 22*(1), 20–47.

Diebold, F. X., & Kilian, L. (2000). Unit-root tests are useful for selecting forecasting models. *Journal of Business & Economic Statistics, 18*(3), 265–273.

Eisenhardt, K. M. (1989). Building theories from case study research. *Academy of Management Review, 14*(4), 532–550.

Engle, R. F., Ghysels, E., & Sohn, B. (2013). Stock market volatility and macroeconomic fundamentals. *The Review of Economics and Statistics, 95*(3), 776–797.

Fazzari, S., Hubbard, R. G., & Petersen, B. (1988). Investment, financing decisions, and tax policy. *The American Economic Review, 78*(2), 200–205.

Feridun, M. (2006). Risk management in banks and other financial institutions: Lessons from the crash of long-term capital management (LTCM). *Banks and Bank Systems, 1*(3), 132–141.

Flannery, M. J., & Protopapadakis, A. A. (2002). Macroeconomic factors do influence aggregate stock returns. *Review of Financial Studies, 15*(3), 751–782.

Gilbert, R. J., & Lieberman, M. (1987). Investment and coordination in oligopolistic industries. *The RAND Journal of Economics*, 17–33.

Glosten, L. R., Jagannathan, R., & Runkle, D. E. (1993). On the relation between the expected value and the volatility of the nominal excess return on stocks. *The Journal of Finance, 48*(5), 1779–1801.

Greenhill, T. (2014). *Active vs. Passive portfolio management.* https://digitalcommons. bryant.edu/cgi/viewcontent.cgi?article=1016&context=honors_mathematics

Guofu, Z. (2008). On the fundamental law of active portfolio management: How to make conditional investments unconditionally optimal. *Journal of Portfolio Management, 35*(1), 12.

Hayes, A. (2023, November 25). *Portfolio management: Definition, types, and strategies.* Investopedia. https://www.investopedia.com/terms/p/portfoliomanagement. asp

Jensen, M. C. (1986). Agency costs of free cash flow, corporate finance, and takeovers. *The American Economic Review, 76*(2), 323–329.

Jesen, G. E. (1983). Windthorst: A political biography. By Margaret Lavinia Aaderson. Oxford University Press, 1981. xi+ 522 pp. $69.00. *Church History, 52*(2), 227–228.

Jiang, G. J., & Tian, Y. S. (2005). The model-free implied volatility and its information content. *Review of Financial Studies, 18*(4), 1305–1342.

Karuna, C. (2007). Industry product market competition and managerial incentives. *Journal of Accounting and Economics, 43*(2–3), 275–297.

Laksmana, I., & Yang, Y. W. (2015). Product market competition and earnings management: Evidence from discretionary accruals and real activity manipulation. *Advances in Accounting, 30*(2), 263–275.

Lintner, J. (1969). The valuation of risk assets and the selection of risky investments in stock portfolios and capital budgets: A reply. *The Review of Economics and Statistics,* 222–224.

Meckling, W. H., & Jensen, M. C. (1976). Theory of the firm: Managerial behavior, agency costs and ownership structure. *Journal of Financial Economics, 3*(4), 305–360.

Mittnik, S., Robinzonov, N., & Spindler, M. (2015). Stock market volatility: Identifying major drivers and the nature of their impact. *Journal of Banking & Finance, 58,* 1–28.

Myers, S. C., & Majluf, N. S. (1984). Corporate financing and investment decisions when firms have information that investors do not have. *Journal of Financial Economics, 13*(2), 187–221.

O'Connell, B. (2022, November 28). What is a portfolio? *Forbes Advisor.* https://www. forbes.com/advisor/investing/portfolio/

Paye, B. S. (2012). 'Déjà vol': Predictive regressions for aggregate stock market volatility using macroeconomic variables. *Journal of Financial Economics, 106*(3), 527–546.

Prokopczuk, M., & Simen, C. W. (2014). The importance of the volatility risk premium for volatility forecasting. *Journal of Banking & Finance, 40,* 303–320.

Prokopczuk, M., Stancu, A., & Symeonidis, L. (2019). The economic drivers of commodity market volatility. *Journal of International Money and Finance, 98,* 1–33.

Ross, S. A (1973). The economic theory of agency: The principal's problem. *The American Economic Review, 63*(2), 134–139.

Schwert, G. W. (1989). Why does stock market volatility change over time? *The Journal of Finance, 44*(5), 1115–1153.

Sharpe, W. F. (1964). Capital asset prices: A theory of market equilibrium under conditions of risk. *The Journal of Finance, 19*(3), 425–442.

Siegel, L., & Waring, B. (2009). Understanding active portfolio management. In *Investment management: A modern guide to security analysis and stock selection* (pp. 539–565). Springer.

West, K. D., & Cho, D. (1995). The predictive ability of several models of exchange rate volatility. *Journal of Econometrics, 69*(2), 367–391.

Chapter 11

Corporate Governance Benefits for Small- and Medium-Sized Enterprises (SMEs): An Effective Policy Management

Muhammad Faisal Sultan[a], Israr Ahmed Jatoi[a] and Kashif Riaz[b]

[a]KASB Institute of Technology, Pakistan
[b]Shaheed Zulfiqar Ali Bhutto University of Law, Pakistan

Abstract

This study is one of the premier ones that is written to highlight the significance of corporate governance for small and medium-sized enterprises (SMEs). The purpose of writing this chapter is to increase knowledge and understanding of SMEs and their management. Thus, the scope of this study is much broader as compared to the previous studies. Other than scope, this chapter also bridges the research gaps and tries to relate literature with shortcomings and relatively unexplored areas associated with SMEs and their governance. For these reasons elements, claims, reasons and pieces of evidence were collected from diverse literature and presented in a scholarly way to address readers' interest and provide scope for further studies and research. Overall, this chapter is a form of descriptive study which his purposively conducted to induce more research work on corporate governance practices and their significance for SMEs.

Keywords: SMEs; corporate governance; benefits of corporate governance; board of directors; listed SMEs and non-listed SMEs

1. Background

Corporate Governance is perceived as the most significant term of the last decade. Multiple studies explored the characteristics as well as effects of corporate governance on the performance of the firm (Gul et al., 2017). Corporate governance can easily be defined as the set of rules, procedures and policies that are used for adequately managing the firm. Every company has a board of directors are element

Strategic Financial Management, 169–176
doi:10.1108/978-1-83608-106-720241011

that shapes the structure of corporate governance for the specific firm (Rustam & Narsa, 2021). The purpose of corporate governance is to protect shareholders by separating ownership from the management of the company (Clarke & Klettner, 2009). However, implementing corporate governance must not be the only objective, and the company must try to ensure good practices of corporate governance. Thus, it essential is to ensure sound financial reporting, auditing and control. Ensuring these activities will not only reduce any form of financial crimes and fraud but also provide adequate mechanisms to the firm which acts as the backbone of the mechanism of corporate governance (Rustam & Narsa, 2021).

1.1 Introduction

Characteristics of SMEs are different from large-sized firms. Hence, there is a need to understand how SMEs are responding to the regime of corporate governance, and what are the differences in the implementation and implications of corporate governance between SMEs and large-sized firms? Overall, the academic research associated with these issues is still in its infancy (Clarke & Klettner, 2009). Therefore, there might be differences in the mechanism of corporate governance as well as the level of performance for large firms and SMEs. The major reason behind the difference is an ownership structure that differentiated SMEs from large-sized corporates. In fact, in SMEs, there is a minimal probability of agency problems as the control of management is with majority shareholders (Afrifa & Tauringana, 2015).

However, qualitative attributes of non-executive directors like knowledge, personal motivation and background are the major reasons for SMEs to move toward corporate governance practices (Clarke & Klettner, 2009). Regardless of these points, facts and figures SMEs are profoundly in neglecting the practices of corporate governance. These issues are dominant is Asia where SMEs have failed to adopt corporate governance. Major reasons for ignorance are a lack of awareness of the benefits that CG may provide to SMEs and the cost of implementation of corporate governance (Mahzan & Yan, 2014).

1.2 Gray Area and Statement of Problem

SMEs are becoming quite interesting for researchers. Hence, we are evidencing more research and empirical investigation. However, the major focus of research on SMEs is on the understanding of the process of business planning and management systems (Crossan & Henschel, 2012). Analyzing the corporate governance mechanism of family-owned firms, it has been observed that the practices and structure of family-owned firms are significantly different as compared to the non-family-owned firms. However, there is a need of more transparent practices of corporate governance for familial businesses as compared to the non-familial business. In fact in developed countries, shareholders as well as investors prefer to have more transparency of business processes as well as professionalism in the operating practices of the firm (Bartholomeusz & Tanewski, 2006).

On the other side, family-owned businesses tend to prefer family relations; therefore regardless of qualities like faster decision-making, better future planning, control and less monitoring cost, etc., severe issues are hindering the way of glory for corporate governance (Alim & Khan, 2016). However, most of the studies on the topic of corporate governance gauged the concept either concerning larger firms or listed firms (Gul et al., 2017). Similar is the case even in 2023 when most of the empirical studies on corporate governance mechanisms of SMEs are concerning European Companies. Therefore, more qualitative research work is required to assess the nature of governance mechanisms for SMEs along with their interrelated concepts (Teixeira & Carvalho, 2023).

2. Theoretical Underpinning

Afrifa and Tauringana (2015) highlighted that multiple theories are associated with the use of corporate governance for SMEs. The purpose of all of these theories is to identify and relate variables with the practices of corporate governance to provide a better structure of governance (Hakimah et al., 2019). However, most of the time researchers use agency theory to reflect the benefits of corporate governance and its scope. However, the smaller firms most of the time rely on stewardship rather than following agency theory. Hence for managing smaller firms, it is recommended to use stewardship theory rather than any other theoretical assumption related to corporate governance (Christensen et al., 2015). Studies, e.g., Afrifa and Tauringana (2015) also mentioned resource-based view (RBV) as one of the prime theories for corporate governance. RBV is also used to highlight the importance and significance of the board of directors on the performance of SMEs (Hillman et al., 2009).

RBV theory postulated that board is mainly providing two major benefits that are classified as (a) obtaining of essential resources and (b) securing essential resources of the firm through expertise and experience of the board members. The theory also highlighted the linkage between the compensation of directors and the firm's performance by highlighting the need to hire directors with high competencies to enhance the firm's performance. Hence, the ability of the firm to extract, use and capitalize on internal as well as external resources hinges upon the abilities and skills of directors (Afrifa & Tauringana, 2015).

2.1 Literature Review

Corporate Governance also has its implications and benefits for SMEs. Studies also claim that the implementation of corporate governance in SMEs may produce considerable improvement in business performance. Major impacts are associated with accountability, transparency and equity (Asiimwe, 2017). Therefore, SMEs must not be afraid of the cost of implementation of corporate governance as the evolution of mid-term and short-term benefits of corporate governance tends to overcome the cost of implementation (Mahzan & Yan, 2014). In fact, according to Rustam and Narsa (2021), the implementation of corporate governance in SMEs may result in numerous benefits, e.g., better managerial practices, better mechanisms for internal auditing and control, mass opportunities for growth and development and a modern outlook due to the presence of non-executive directors. Hence legitimate to declare that the implementation of codes of corporate governance may also provide significant benefit to SMEs. Some of these possible benefits are as under.

2.1.1 Access to Resources

Several studies highlighted challenges for SMEs. Most of these challenges are associated with a lack of resources. Hence, it is recommended that SMEs must incorporate strategies and mechanisms that lure SMEs with abundant resources (Mahzan & Yan, 2014). The implementation of a code of corporate governance is perceived as the optimal choice for making firm use and access to resources effectively and efficiently. Therefore, this advantage is not only limited to internal resources as use of corporate governance will extend firms access to resources that are outside the control of any independent firm like funding, etc (Rustam & Narsa, 2021). Similar indications have also indicated other studies that highlighted access to external resources is the major benefit of independent directors. The statement is true as independent directors will also bring multiple stakeholders to the firm which ultimately increases the firm's access to external resources like funds, etc (Shapiro et al., 2015).

2.1.2 Creativity in Decision-Making

The inclusion of diverse members will provide a range of choices to the board during the process of decision-making. Hence, decisions will become more creative which tends to flourish the firm's growth (Rustam & Narsa, 2021). Previous studies also mentioned that concentrated ownership or large shareholding of any one member of the family will negatively affect innovation. Similar has been shown in the studies that were conducted with the reference of Chinese SMEs. The main reason behind this behavior is the risk aversion nature of major shareholders. Other than this, applying corporate governance will also make firms inclined toward effective long-term planning which results in radical changes in work processes. Thus, SMEs may prefer patents rather than sales (Shapiro et al., 2015).

2.1.3 Better Monitoring

The Implementation of corporate governance provides the room for inclusion of outside directors that are not directly associated with the family who owns business. The inclusion of these directors resulted in the formulation of more rigorous and sound practices for managing the firm and obtaining profitability (Rustam & Narsa, 2021). Obviously, non-executive directors have the ability to observe and monitor suboptimal decisions, frauds and any other activity that actually harms the firms' operation (Christensen et al., 2015). Hence, legitimate to declare that the inclusion of non-executive directors is beneficial in supplementing the firm with the adequate and modern inventory of skills required for the firm's growth as managers and members from one family may not have the required skills inventory (Rustam & Narsa, 2021). This was also evident which highlighted that there is a high significance of the inclusion of non-executive directors over the return on investment (Mahzan & Yan, 2014).

2.1.4 Prepared for Initial Public Offering (IPO)

One of the other major benefits of corporate governance for SMEs that is associated with long-term growth is making firms prepared for initial public offering (IPO) (Abor & Adjasi, 2007). The postulate is valid as for approaching IPO firms may have effective financial reports (Shezi, 2013). Similar are the indications of Okabe and Suez-Sales (2021) that legitimized the scope of corporate governance for preparing effectively for IPO through validating and refining key processes. Hence, optimal to write that incorporation of a code of corporate governance will not only add skills and competencies to the firm but will also provide a strong position to the firm in the eyes of investors, governing bodies and other stakeholders. These behaviors are the key for the firm in getting prepared for IPO (Rustam & Narsa, 2021). Similar is also reflected by one of the latest studies by Teti and Montefusco (2022), corporate governance in companies is negatively associated with underpricing at the time of IPO.

2.1.5 The Formulation of Effective Strategies

The Implementation of a code of corporate governance will also enable firms to develop effective strategies that are required to obtain external funding. The presence of effective board is positively associated with the obtaining of the required level of external funds and substantiation of the firm's growth (Rustam & Narsa, 2021). Good strategies improve the credit rating of SMEs and hence may also enable SMEs to gain funding from the government (Singh & Pillai, 2022). However, the use of CG practices works better for public sector SMEs in comparison to the non-public (Günay & Apak, 2014).

2.1.6 Improves Financial Outcomes

Implementation of corporate governance causes diversity in the board of directors. Diversity improves decision-making and adds creativity as well as choices for decision-makers. Hence, ultimately increasing return on assets and profitability (Hakimah et al., 2019). However, one of the latest studies by Singh and Rastogi (2023) reflected that SMEs are found to be unable to attain desired benefits through the implementation of SMEs. In evidence study uses a negative association between CG in listed SMEs of India and financial performance. Contrary to the previous postulated indication of Kisswani and Bakri (2023) and Musah et al (2023) highlighted otherwise and out a positive association between the implementation of CG and the financial performance and sustainability of the firm.

3. Methodology

This study is specifically developed to address the advantages that SMEs may earn through applying corporate governance mechanisms. Therefore the development of this study is supplemented with Alim and Khan (2016); Asiimwe (2017); Bartholomeusz and Tanewski (2006); Hillman et al. (2009); Mahzan and Yan (2014) and Rustam and Narsa (2021), etc. Hence, the study has a higher level of rigor and generalizability which makes researchers select epistemology as the philosophy of research. Epistemology is reflected as the philosophy of research by Saunders et al. (2007) and supported by Pritchard (2013), as epistemology is the philosophy of knowledge. Therefore, suited most as compared to other philosophies as the major purpose of this chapter is to foster knowledge. The philosophical stance used for content generation as well as association with each other is constructivism, which has been highlighted by Syed and McLean (2021) and reflected as one of the leading philosophical stances for developing literature through secondary data. The research approach is deductive and the research strategy is archival which addresses the selection of epistemology and constructivism as the philosophical stance by Syed and McLean (2021). The methodological choice is mono-method qualitative and the time horizon is cross-sectional as indicated by Saunders et al. (2015).

4. Conclusion

This study indicated the use of corporate governance for SMEs. There are multiple advantages of corporate governance for SMEs, but previous research on corporate governance does not focus on SMEs. Especially the SME sector of developing worlds like Pakistan, India Sri Lanka, etc., remains unexplored for the mechanism and advantages of corporate governance. Hence, by considering the significance of corporate governance for SMEs, it is possible to implement the structure of corporate governance for SMEs of the developing world. These implications and adaptability not only refine the corporate governance practices in the SME sector but will also make SMEs work more effectively to resolve issues and problems related to their performance.

4.1 Discussion and Study Significance

The study is used to make readers, academicians, and researchers understand the benefits and scope of corporate governance for SMEs. The chapter highlights the benefits for listed and not-listed SMEs. Hence, the scope is broader and significance is higher than other studies. The postulate is true as the chapter not only addresses the relevant literature but also indicates research gaps and points out relevant theories and concepts that redress the use of corporate governance in SMEs.

Hence, it is one of the pervasive studies that underline relevant theoretical frameworks, research gaps and variables of interest and compile all these in a unique blend. This unique blend is used to make readers interested in this study and also foster further research work in the area of corporate governance practices by SMEs. However, the negative association between the implementation of CG and the financial performance of listed SMEs in India (Singh & Rastogi, 2023) makes a serious question mark over the benefits of CG for SMEs operating in emerging Asian markets. However, there are some other studies from emerging Asian markets that also which are indicating multiple benefits along with the betterment of financial measures, e.g. Kisswani and Bakri (2023) and Musah et al. (2022).

4.2 Policy Implications

This study has a broader scope which has also been reflected through the above sections. Hence through using parameters and literature of this study, better policy making might be induced in familial and non-familial SMEs that are listed or considering to be listed through IPO. The elaboration of benefits that SMEs may seek through the implantation of corporate governance may increase the inclination of SMEs toward corporate governance. This is valid for public as well as non-public SMEs as effective strategies, improvement and credit rating and access to scarce resources are beneficial for all forms of SME (Günay & Apak, 2014).

References

Abor, J., & Adjasi, C. K. (2007). Corporate governance and the small and medium enterprises sector: Theory and implications. *Corporate Governance: The international journal of business in society*, 7(2), 111–122.

Afrifa, G. A., & Tauringana, V. (2015). Corporate governance and performance of UK listed small and medium enterprises. *Corporate Governance*, 15(5), 719–733.

Alim, W., & Khan, S. U. (2016). Corporate governance and cash holdings: Evidence from family controlled and non-family business in Pakistan. *Pakistan Journal of Applied Economics*, 26, (Special Issue)

Asiimwe, F. (2017). Corporate governance and performance of SMEs in Uganda. *International Journal of Technology Management*, 2(1), 14.

Bartholomeusz, S., & Tanewski, G. A. (2006). The relationship between family firms and corporate governance. *Journal of Small Business Management*, 44(2), 245–267.

Christensen, J., Kent, P., Routledge, J., & Stewart, J. (2015). Do corporate governance recommendations improve the performance and accountability of small listed companies? *Accounting and Finance*, 55(1), 133–164.

Clarke, T., & Klettner, A. (2009). Governance issues for SMEs. *Journal of Law and Governance*, 4(4), 23–40.

Crossan, K., & Henschel, T. (2012). Corporate governance: an holistic model for SMEs. *Journal of Management and Financial Sciences*, 5(8), 54–75.

Gul, S., Muhammad, F., & Rashid, A. (2017). Corporate governance and corporate social responsibility: The case of small, medium, and large firms. *Pakistan Journal of Commerce and Social Sciences (PJCSS)*, 11(1), 1–34.

Günay, G. Y., & Apak, S. (2014). Comparison of public and non-public SMEs' corporate governance strategies in Turkey. *Procedia-Social and Behavioral Sciences*, 150, 162–171.

Hakimah, Y., Pratama, I., Fitri, H., Ganatri, M., & Sulbahrie, R. A. (2019). Impact of intrinsic corporate governance on financial performance of Indonesian SMEs. *International Journal of Innovation, Creativity and Change, 7*(1), 32–51.

Hillman, A. J., Withers, M. C., & Collins, B. J. (2009). Resource dependence theory: A review. *Journal of Management, 35*(6), 1404–1427.

Kisswani, N. M., & Bakri, A. A. A. (2023). The role of corporate governance in the sustainability of small and medium enterprises in the United Arab Emirates using'limited liability company as a model. *International Journal of Private Law, 11*(1), 29–51.

Mahzan, N., & Yan, C. M. (2014). Harnessing the benefits of corporate governance and internal audit: Advice to SME. *Procedia-Social and Behavioral Sciences, 115,* 156–165.

Musah, A., Padi, A., Okyere, B., E. Adenutsi, D., & Ayariga, C. (2022). Does corporate governance moderate the relationship between internal control system effectiveness and SMEs financial performance in Ghana? *Cogent Business & Management, 9*(1), 2152159.

Okabe, K., & Suez-Sales, M. G. (2021). The use of the statement of cash flows by Japanese SMEs. *Eurasian Journal of Business and Management, 9*(4), 268–282.

Pritchard, D. (2013). *What is this thing called knowledge?* Routledge.

Rustam, A. R., & Narsa, I. M. (2021). Good corporate governance: A case study of family business in Indonesia. *The Journal of Asian Finance, Economics and Business, 8*(5), 69–79.

Saunders, M., Lewis, P., & Thornhill, A. (2007). Research methods. In *Business students* (4th ed., Vol. 6, No. 3, pp. 1–268). Pearson Education Limited.

Saunders, M. N., Lewis, P., Thornhill, A., & Bristow, A. (2015). *Understanding research philosophy and approaches to theory development.* Pearson Education.

Shapiro, D., Tang, Y., Wang, M., & Zhang, W. (2015). The effects of corporate governance and ownership on the innovation performance of Chinese SMEs. *Journal of Chinese Economics and Business Studies, 13*(4), 311–335.

Shezi, M. (2013). *SMEs' corporate governance systems: Status and effect on continuity.* University of Pretoria (South Africa).

Singh, K., & Pillai, D. (2022). Corporate governance in small and medium enterprises: A review. *Corporate Governance: The International Journal of Business in Society, 22*(1), 23–41.

Singh, K., & Rastogi, S. (2023). Corporate governance and financial performance: Evidence from listed SMEs in India. *Benchmarking: An International Journal, 30*(4), 1400–1423.

Syed, M., & McLean, K. C. (2021). Disentangling paradigm and method can help bring qualitative research to post-positivist psychology and address the generalizability crisis. *Behavioral and Brain Sciences, 45,* 58–60.

Teixeira, J. F., & Carvalho, A. O. (2023). Corporate governance in SMEs: A systematic literature review and future research. *Corporate Governance: The International Journal of Business in Society.* https://doi.org/10.1108/CG-04-2023-0135

Teti, E., & Montefusco, I. (2022). Corporate governance and IPO underpricing: Evidence from the Italian market. *Journal of Management & Governance, 26*(3), 851–889.

Chapter 12

Cost, Issues and Hindrances for Implementing Corporate Governance in SMEs

Muhammad Faisal Sultan[a], *Muhammad Asim*[b] *and Kashif Mehmood*[a]

[a]KASB Institute of Technology, Pakistan
[b]University of Karachi, Pakistan

Abstract

Academic research is now moving toward understanding best practices that may be coped up by small and medium-sized enterprises (SMEs) to increase their performance. However, the implementation of CG is not free from cost and other prevalent issues that create hindrances in the implementation of CG practices in SMEs. However, there is a lack of literature related to these issues and costs that may hinder in implementation of effective CG practices. There is also a need to incorporate new theory with the literature of corporate governance to define cost, issues and hindrances in the process of corporate governance of SMEs. Hence, this chapter is written purposively to describe these limiting factors concerning SMEs to increase research and improve policymaking. Therefore, the significance of this study has several folds, and with epistemology as the base of the study, this work is a rare study that tends to improve academia, research and policy-making.

Keywords: SMEs; corporate governance; issues; hurdles; cost and challenges to corporate governance

1. Introduction

Small and medium-sized enterprises (SMEs) have high significance for the developing world. Governments of developing countries are also trying to devise policies and procedures that may assist the growth and development of SMEs. The

Strategic Financial Management, 177–183
doi:10.1108/978-1-83608-106-720241012

major reason behind all these points is the contribution of the SME sector to the GDP as well as to the employment ratio of developing countries (Umrani et al., 2015). Therefore, in recent times SMEs are also found inclined toward the implementation of CG practices for attracting investors as well as the base for sustainability, growth and competitive edge over rivals. In fact, in developing countries like India use of CG practices may not only increase sustainability, growth and development of the country but also the entire country (Dhondge, 2023). However, there are some obstacles, hurdles and issues associated with leadership and corporate governance that are reducing the growth and success of SMEs (Lekhanya, 2015). Therefore, the debate in academia has shifted from the need for corporate governance in SMEs to an effective corporate governance mechanism for SMEs (Meressa, 2017).

1.1 The Significance of Study

Effective corporate governance is perceived as one of the prime areas of global socioeconomic development. However, research associated with corporate governance mostly focused on large-sized organizations rather than SMEs (Lekhanya, 2015). On the other side, the use of quantitative modeling to assess the impact of corporate governance practices might also look difficult due to the absence of authentic accounting data (Ciampi, 2015). However, SMEs may take significant advantage through applying corporate governance. The use of corporate governance may provide significant growth and competitiveness to the firm without increasing its size (Asiimwe, 2017). Thus, legitimate to declare that the use of effective corporate governance practices will lead to an increase in the performance of SMEs (Meressa, 2017). However, the implementation of corporate governance may also have some drawbacks (Günay & Apak, 2014) as well as challenges (Umrani et al., 2015).

1.2 The Purpose of Study

The major purpose of this study is to highlight various limiting factors and drawbacks that may create hindrances in the implementation of CG in SMEs. These forms of issues are highlighted either as the cost to implement CG or elements that create effective corporate governance practices. However, these forms of studies are rare, and this study has been conducted purposively to accumulate all these elements and costs in the single script for enhancing the knowledge and understanding of readers. Hence, it is a form of pervasive studies that assist academicians, researchers, scholars and policymakers in conducting further research for optimizing policies, processes and practices for better practices of CG.

2. Theoretical Framework

Most of the time stewardship theory has been used for discussing the role of managers in optimizing corporate governance mechanisms in SMEs. Managers are required to improve the firm's performance to protect the concerns of the majority of the stakeholders (Ijeoma & Ezejiofor, 2013). However, this study is based on cost, issues and hindrances that are faced by SMEs in implementing the effective code of corporate governance. Therefore, it is legitimate to use resource scarcity theory formulated by Cairns (1990) to discuss hurdles in the implementation of CG by SMEs. The theory was also been used in various studies associated with the scarcity of resources in SMEs, e.g. Woschke et al. (2017).

Previously corporate governance was mostly associated with different theories like agency theory and resource dependency theory as most of the time research is associated with the board of directors and their role in the company as indicated by Madhani (2017). However, this study is very different as compared to the rest of the studies conducted to explore, discuss and elaborate the corporate governance. Therefore, the use of resource scarcity theory is effective as it discusses, defines and deals with the scarce resources that are causing issues in the implementation of effective CG practices in SMEs.

Another theory that may be associated with this form of study is the stakeholders' theory which can also be associated with the corporate governance mechanism of SMEs. Theory entails that it is necessary for the board that they are to protect the interests of all the stakeholders instead of any specific form of stakeholders (Magaisa et al., 2013). Hence, the upcoming literature represents the costs, hurdles and challenges that are required to be understood by the boards of SMEs.

3. Literature Review

CG is found to be beneficial for large-sized firms as well as SMEs. However, large-sized firms are also found to be struggling in the implementation of the appropriate mechanisms of corporate governance. Hence, it is also difficult for SMEs to implement CG easily. Thus, a distinctive set of measures is required to overcome issues and challenges that are present in the way of implementing corporate governance practices (Dhondge, 2023). There are some studies e.g. Günay and Apak (2014) and Umrani et al. (2015) that discussed the issues, challenges and hurdles that may be encountered by SMEs. This section is specifically developed to discuss these issues, hurdles and challenges in detail that SMEs may face while implementing CG practices.

3.1 Cost

It is much more difficult to identify the cost of corporate governance in terms of dollars. However, the implementation of corporate governance is found to be costly for SMEs. The cost is divided into monetary cost, time cost and energy cost (Clarke & Klettner, 2009).

3.2 Monetary Cost

Monetary cost may not be the major form of the cost for SMEs while implementing corporate governance. However, it is composed of the cost incurred as the salaries of nonexecutive directors as well as the cost incurred for training and development and construction of web pages, etc (Clarke & Klettner, 2009).

Although in OECD countries, the advantages of implementation of corporate governance may overshadow the cost-related issues. However, the rule of one size fits all may produce a negative impact on the SMEs. Similar is the case of SMEs from Canada (Briozzo et al., 2019).

3.3 Energy Cost

This form of cost is based upon the efforts that SMEs are required to put into changing the structure of their board as well as understanding the requirements and methods to implement CG in SMEs (Clarke & Klettner, 2009).

3.4 Time Cost

Time cost is one of the major forms of cost that SMEs have to bear for implementing corporate governance as rules, procedures and practices developed for implementing CG may vary concerning size. Hence, one particular type of procedure, policy and document does not fit all forms of companies (Clarke & Klettner, 2009).

3.5 Concentrated Ownership

SMEs are mostly operated by closely bound families. Hence, the companies have a concentrated ownership structure. Therefore, the induction of family members and offspring resulted in the violation of the rights of minority shareholders (Umrani et al., 2015). The point was indicated initially by Storey (1994) that most small firms do not have adequate resources as well as competencies. Other than those, nonexecutive directors also aid SMEs with a better understanding of the market and competitors and hence aids in strategic decision-making and assessing better opportunities. However, in developing countries, most of the SMEs are still operated either by owners or by their offspring (Yap & Ng, 2015). Similar indications have also been proved by the study of Van Gils (2005) that most of the SMEs in the Netherlands are either working on the directives of the CEO and companies are working without the support of any board etc.

3.6 Illegal Investment and Frauds

It has also been found that owners of SMEs are also found to be involved in illegal activities as well as fraudulent investments. Hence, companies are unable to follow instructions from governing bodies. Therefore, the collapse of SMEs is common. Similar has been found in Malaysia where the failure rate of SMEs is touching 60% (Umrani et al., 2015). Similar is the findings of the study from the Netherlands where most of the CEOs do not use adequate governance mechanisms for reporting, transparency and maintenance of standards. CEOs were not using governance mechanisms on a volunteer basis (Van Gils, 2005).

3.7 The Lack of Skills Inventory in CEO and Top Management

The lack of skills and abilities of the CEO and the top management of SMEs is also termed as one of the major obstacles to the sustainability and growth of companies. This lack may also cause the failure of SMEs. Studies in this vein also pointed out leadership as the major skill that is required by the CEO and top management of the firm to survive and grow. Leadership is especially required to make employees follow the vision of top management to pursue business goals and objectives effectively. However, the lack of leadership capabilities is also perceived as the major reason behind the failure of SMEs (Umrani et al., 2015).

3.8 The Unavailability of Appropriate Code of Corporate Governance

There is no code of cooperate governance for SMEs. That may cause difficulty in protecting the rights of the minority shareholders (Umrani et al., 2015). This issue may become more serious as SMEs are regulated by different bodies (Ijeoma & Ezejiofor, 2013). The CEOs of SMEs are not fully aware of the implications of corporate governance. Therefore, effective measures to implement corporate governance are also missing from the managerial practices (Van Gils, 2005).

4. Methodology

This study is based on epistemology as the purpose is to increase knowledge about the area of corporate governance that is rarely been discussed. Hence, it is connected with the research onion given by Saunders et al. (2007). The philosophical stance that is used to connect research philosophy with research approach and research technique is constructivism developed by Syed and McLean (2021). The research approach is deductive, the methodological choice is mono-method (qualitative), the research strategy is archival and time horizon is cross-sectional (Saunders et al., 2015). Hence, it is a descriptive study that has been developed through minimal researcher interference (Sekaran & Bougie, 2016).

5. Conclusion

SMEs are developed and developing parts of the world are trying to implement corporate governance. However, cost and ownership concentration are traced out to be the main hurdles in the implementation of effective corporate governance practices for SMEs. Hence in line with Briozzo et al. (2019), it is required that different governance mechanisms are required for SMEs of different sizes as well as from different countries to increase transparency in auditing and managing of SMEs.

References

Asiimwe, F. (2017). Corporate governance and performance of SMEs in Uganda. *International Journal of Technology Management, 2*(1), 14.

Briozzo, A., Cardone-Riportella, C., & García-Olalla, M. (2019). Corporate governance attributes and listed SMES'debt maturity. *Corporate Governance: The International Journal of Business in Society, 19*(4), 735–750.

Cairns, R. D. (1990). A contribution to the theory of deplete able resource scarcity and its measures. *Economic Inquiry, 28*(4), 744–755.

Ciampi, F. (2015). Corporate governance characteristics and default prediction modeling for small enterprises. An empirical analysis of Italian firms. *Journal of Business Research, 68*(5), 1012–1025.

Clarke, T., & Klettner, A. (2009). Governance issues for SMEs. *Journal of Law and Governance, 4*(4), 23–40.

Dhondge, N. N. (2023). Application of corporate governance measures in Indian small and medium enterprises: A way forward. *Indian Journal of Commerce & Management Studies, 14*(2), 14–21.

Günay, G. Y., & Apak, S. (2014). Comparison of public and non-public SMEs' corporate governance strategies in Turkey. *Procedia-Social and Behavioral Sciences, 150*, 162–171.

Ijeoma, N., & Ezejiofor, R. A. (2013). An Appraisal of corporate governance issues in enhancing transparency and accountability in small and medium enterprises (SME). *International Journal of Academic Research in Business and Social Sciences, 3*(8), 162.

Lekhanya, L. M. (2015). Leadership and corporate governance of small and medium enterprises (SMEs) in South Africa: Public perceptions. *Corporate Ownership and Control, 12*(3), 215–222.

Madhani, P. M. (2017). Diverse roles of corporate board: Review of various corporate governance theories. *The IUP Journal of Corporate Governance, 16*(2), 7–28.

Magaisa, G. M., Duggal, S., & Muhwandavaka, R. (2013). Corporate governance perspectives for Zimbabwean SMEs. *International Journal of Economy, Management and Social Sciences, 2*(8), 616–619.

Meressa, H. A. (2017). Application of corporate governance principles for the sustainability and competitiveness of small and medium scale enterprises: A literature review. *European Journal of Business and Management, 9*(10), 31–37.

Saunders, M., Lewis, P., & Thornhill, A. (2007). Research methods. In *Business students* (4th ed., Vol. 6, No. 3, pp. 1–268). Pearson Education Limited.

Saunders, M. N., Lewis, P., Thornhill, A., & Bristow, A. (2015). *Understanding research philosophy and approaches to theory development*. Pearson Education.

Sekaran, U., & Bougie, R. (2016). *Research methods for business: A skill building approach*. John Wiley & Son.

Syed, M., & McLean, K. C. (2021). Disentangling paradigm and method can help bring qualitative research to post-positivist psychology and address the generalizability crisis. *Behavioral and Brain Sciences, 45*, 58–60.

Umrani, A. I., Johl, S. K., & Ibrahim, M. Y. (2015). Corporate governance practices and problems faced by SMEs in Malaysia. *Global Business & Management Research, 7*(2).

Van Gils, A. (2005). Management and governance in Dutch SMEs. *European Management Journal, 23*(5), 583–589.

Woschke, T., Haase, H., & Kratzer, J. (2017). Resource scarcity in SMEs: Effects on incremental and radical innovations. *Management Research Review, 40*(2), 195–217.

Yap, A. K. H., & Ng, Y. L. (2015). Corporate governance mechanisms: Evidence from small-and medium-sized enterprises (SMEs). *Modern Accounting and Auditing, 11*(7), 353–362.

Printed in the USA
CPSIA information can be obtained
at www.ICGtesting.com
JSHW011800031224
74704JS00004B/120